LONDON'S BUSES 1979–1994

THE CAPITAL'S BUS NETWORK IN TRANSITION

Front cover: The first of the three Alexander R bodied Volvo-Ailsas participating in the Alternative Vehicle Evaluation, V1 (A101 SUU), exits Trafalgar Square en route to the terminus of the 170 in Aldwych during July 1985.

LONDON'S BUSES 1979–1994

THE CAPITAL'S BUS NETWORK IN TRANSITION

ANDREW BARTLETT

First published in Great Britain in 2021 by
Pen and Sword Transport
An imprint of
Pen & Sword Books Ltd
Yorkshire - Philadelphia

Copyright © Andrew Bartlett, 2021

ISBN 978 1 52675 546 9

The right of Andrew Bartlett to be identified as Author of this work has been asserted by him in accordance with the Copyright, Designs and Patents Act 1988.

A CIP catalogue record for this book is available from the British Library.

All rights reserved. No part of this book may be reproduced or transmitted in any form or by any means, electronic or mechanical including photocopying, recording or by any information storage and retrieval system, without permission from the Publisher in writing.

Maps and copyright supplied by Maproom at Thames Media Projects Ltd.

Typeset by SJmagic DESIGN SERVICES, India.

Printed and bound by Printworks Global Ltd, London/Hong Kong.

Pen & Sword Books Ltd incorporates the Imprints of Pen & Sword Books Archaeology, Atlas, Aviation, Battleground, Discovery, Family History, History, Maritime, Military, Naval, Politics, Railways, Select, Transport, True Crime, Fiction, Frontline Books, Leo Cooper, Praetorian Press, Seaforth Publishing, Wharncliffe and White Owl.

For a complete list of Pen & Sword titles please contact

PEN & SWORD BOOKS LIMITED
47 Church Street, Barnsley, South Yorkshire, S70 2AS, England
E-mail: enquiries@pen-and-sword.co.uk
Website: www.pen-and-sword.co.uk

or

PEN AND SWORD BOOKS
1950 Lawrence Rd, Havertown, PA 19083, USA
E-mail: Uspen-and-sword@casematepublishers.com
Website: www.penandswordbooks.com

CONTENTS

Glossary *7*

Maps:

    1. Greater London *8*

    2. North West London, showing LT garages at 1979 and 1994 ....*10*

    3. North East London, showing LT garages at 1979 and 1994 ....*11*

    4. South West London, showing LT garages at 1979 and 1994 ....*12*

    5. South East London, showing LT garages at 1979 and 1994 ....*13*

Introduction *14*

Annual reviews, 1979–1994:

    1979 ....*17*

    1980 ....*29*

    1981 ....*39*

    1982 ....*50*

    1983 ....*61*

    1984 ....*72*

    1985 ....*80*

    1986 ....*90*

    1987 ....*101*

    1988 ....*115*

    1989 ....*129*

    1990 ....*140*

1991 ....*154*

1992 ....*168*

1993 ....*181*

1994 ....*192*

Appendices:

London Buses Fleet List 1979–1994 ....*206*

LRT Tendering Results 1985–1994 ....*216*

900 Series Mobility Routes *248*

London Transport Garages 1979–1994 ....*250*

GLOSSARY

BEL	Bus Engineering Ltd
DiPTAC	Disabled Persons' Advisory Committee
DLR	Docklands Light Railway
ECW	Eastern Coach Works (bus bodybuilders)
GLC	Greater London Council
GRT	Grampian Regional Transport (based in Aberdeen)
LBL	London Buses Ltd
LOTS	London Omnibus Transport Society
LRT	London Regional Transport
LT	London Transport
LTB	London Transport Buses (from 1994)
MD	Managing Director
NBC	National Bus Company
OLST	Original London Sightseeing Tour (from 1992)
OLTST	Official London Transport Sightseeing Tour (until 1992)
OPO	One-person operated
PTE	Passenger Transport Executive (as in West Midlands PTE, Tyne & Wear PTE)
RLST	Round London Sightseeing Tour
RM	AEC Routemaster

VEHICLE BODY CODES

Where quoted, standard vehicle body codes are used. First, the type of bus is identified:

B	Single deck bus
C	Coach
H	Double decker bus
O	Open-top bus

This is then followed by seating capacity; for double deckers, the upper deck is shown first. For one-person operated single deckers, the number of standing passengers allowed is shown at the end of the code, after a plus sign.

Finally the entrance position(s):

F	Front entrance with platform doors
R	Rear entrance with no doors
RD	Rear entrance with doors
D	Dual (front entrance and centre exit doors)

So for example:
A Routemaster (RM) would be shown as H36/28R
A Metrobus (M) would be shown as H43/28D
A Red Arrow Leyland National 2 (LS) would be shown as B24D+46

MAPS

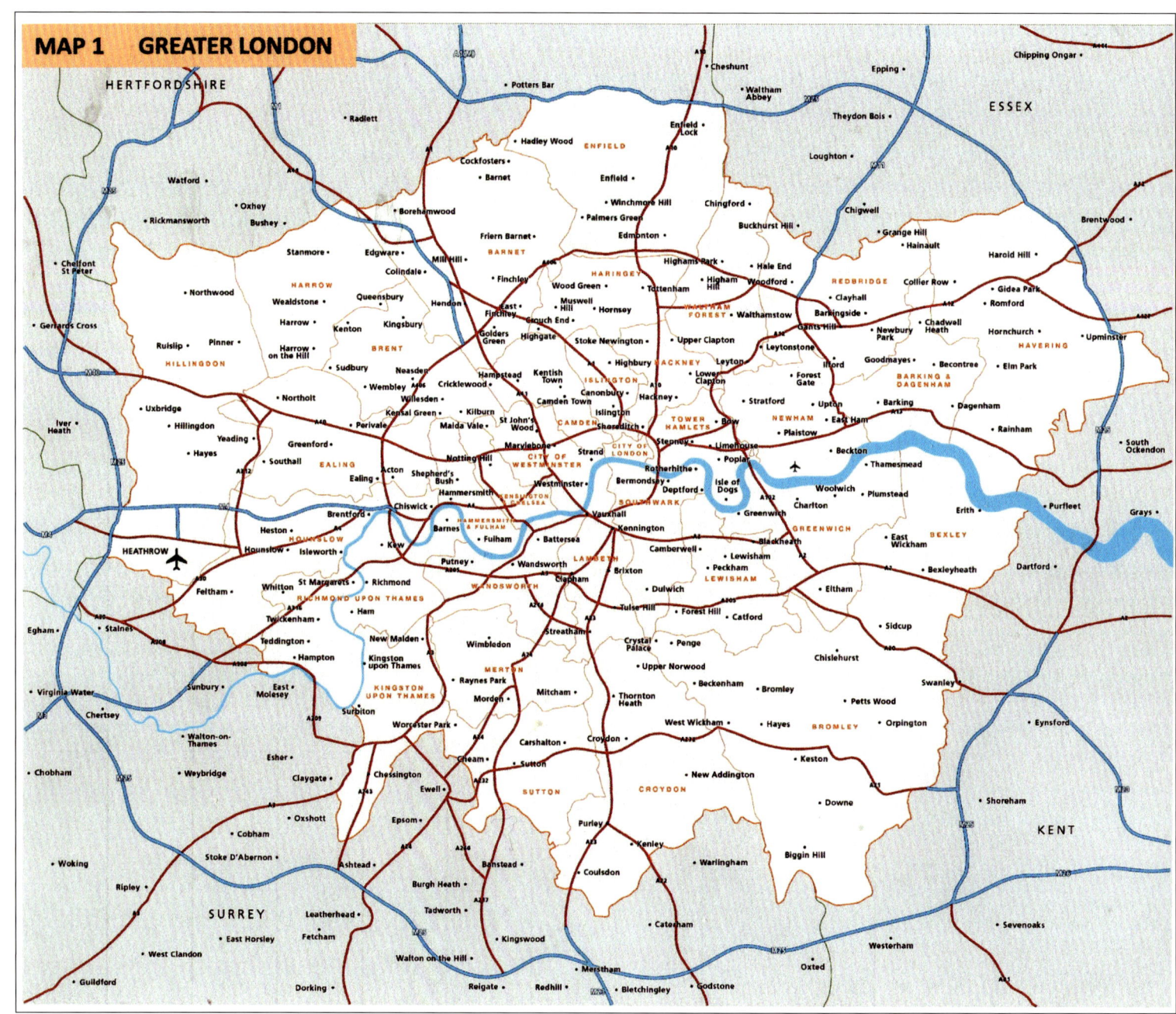

MAP 1   GREATER LONDON

NOTES

The following four maps show the approximate locations of all London Transport bus garages and outstations during the period 1979-1994. Each is colour-coded as follows:

   Open throughout the period

   Opened after January 1979

   Open at January 1979, closed before December 1994

   Opened after January 1979, closed before December 1994

Acton, Clapham, Stamford Brook and Walworth were older garages re-opened during the period under review.

Peckham, Plumstead and Uxbridge garages moved to new premises during the period under review but without loss of continuity.

Bexleyheath, Clapton, Kingston and Norwood were closed for a time during the period under review but have been treated as though they were continually in service.

Harlesden was a garage acquired on takeover by one of the London Buses subsidiary companies.

10 • LONDON'S BUSES, 1979–1994

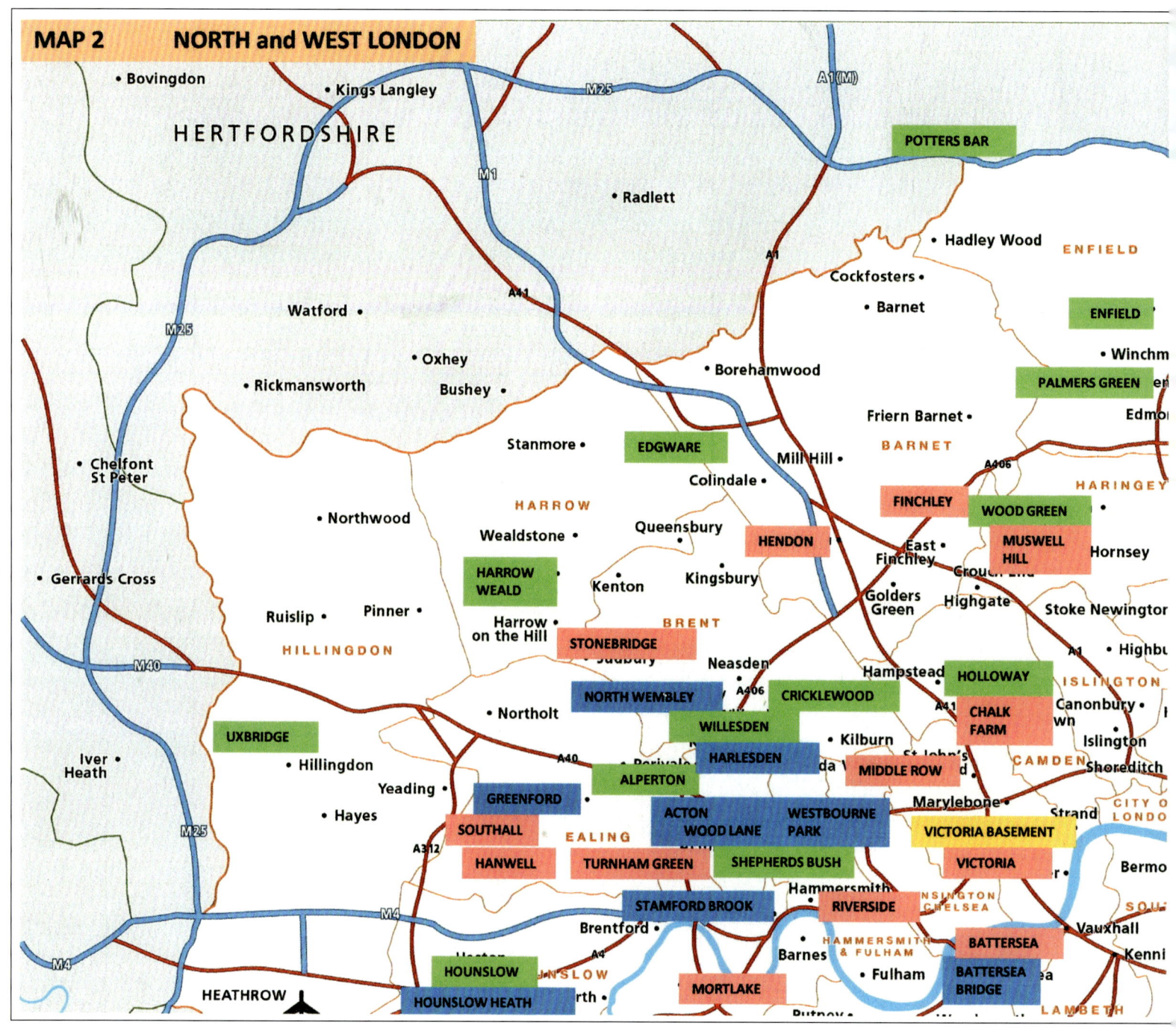

MAP 2 — NORTH and WEST LONDON

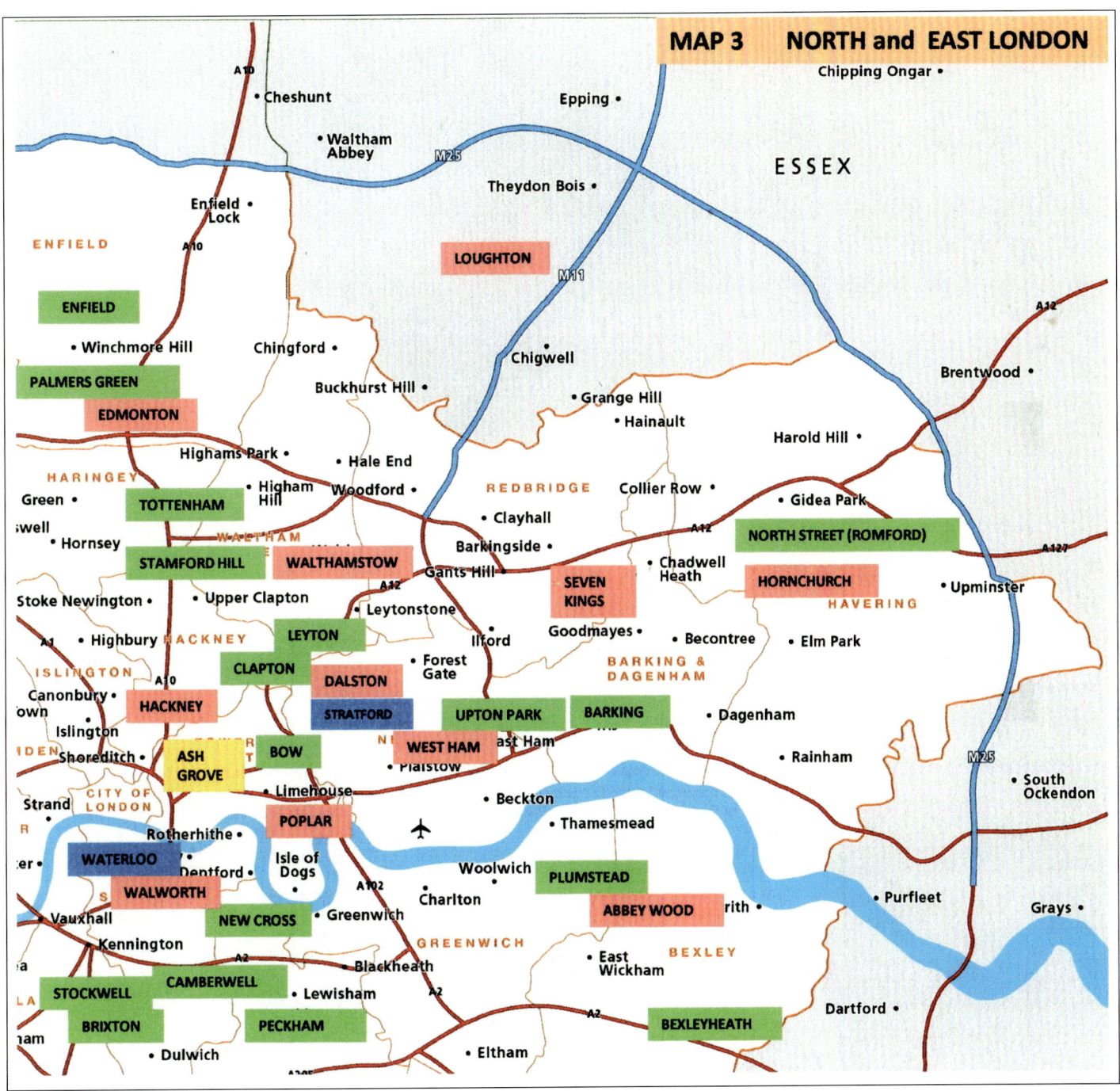

12 • LONDON'S BUSES, 1979–1994

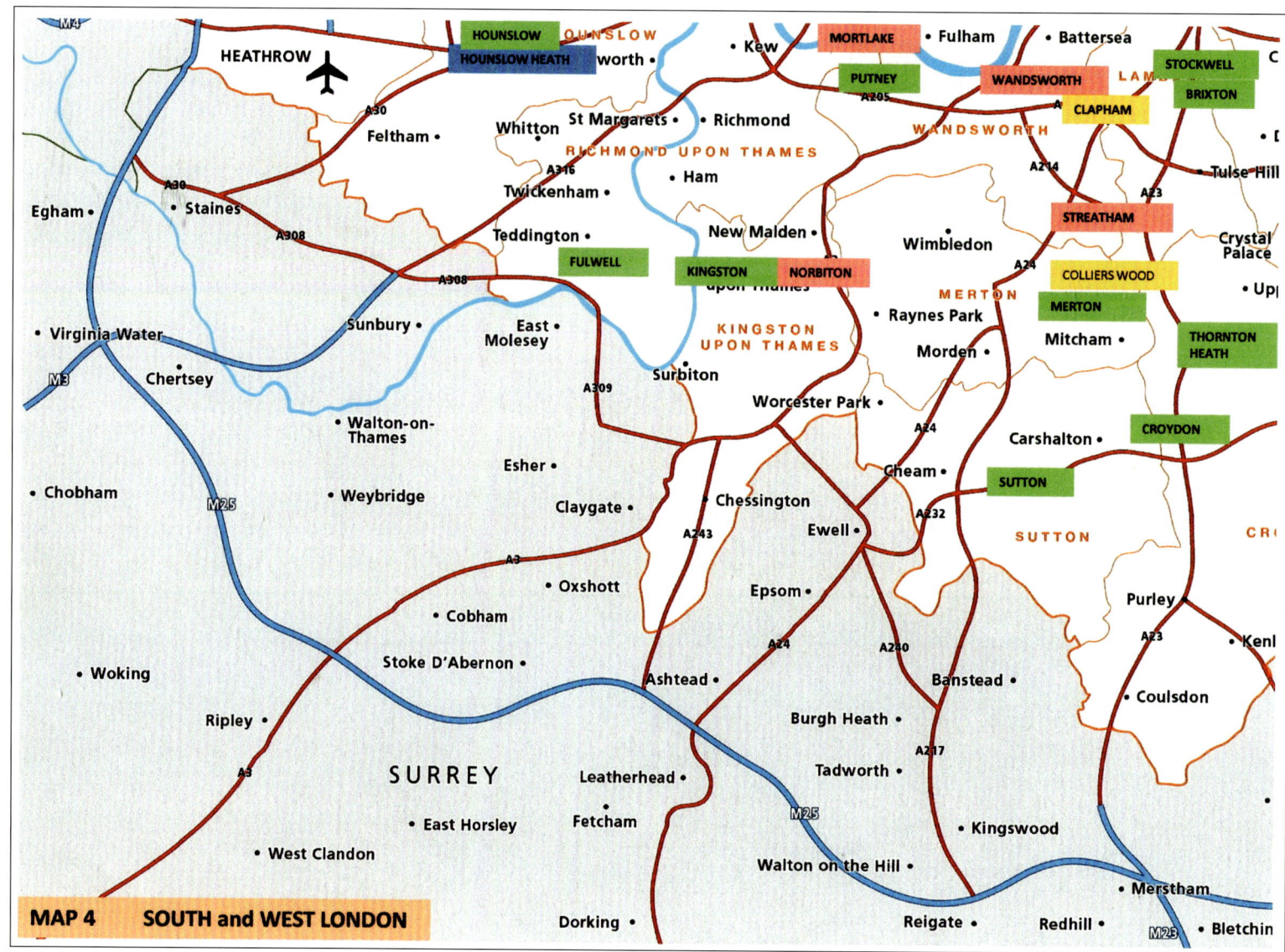

MAP 4 SOUTH and WEST LONDON

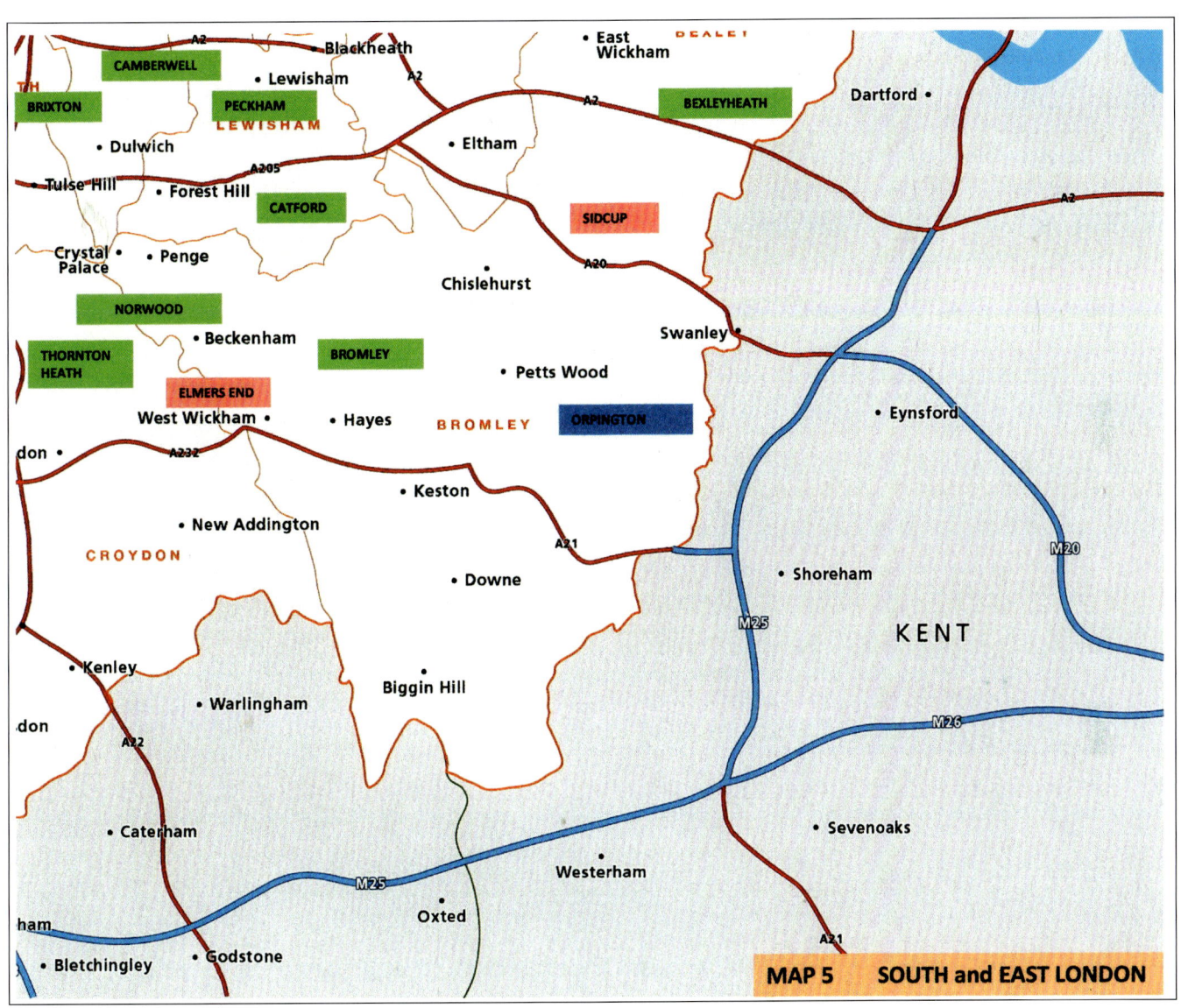

INTRODUCTION

Herbert Stanley Morrison, as Minister of Transport during Ramsay MacDonald's National Government (1929-31), was responsible for the 1930 Transport Act. This was a far-reaching piece of legislation that, inter alia, introduced a raft of measures pertaining to the bus industry, including the licensing of vehicles, drivers, conductors, and above all, services, to be overseen by newly appointed Traffic Commissioners. Congestion issues apart, Morrison's measures successfully restored order to the streets after the free-for-all that had become progressively worse during the 1920s. His reforms were to last for almost fifty years.

But the voters of Hackney South withdrew their support and he lost that seat in the 1931 election. He had, however, been elected to the London County Council several years earlier, and in 1933 became leader of the Labour group. Having already committed his views to paper in his book *Socialisation and Transport: the Organisation of Socialised Industries with Particular Reference to the London Passenger Transport Bill*, he put them into practice in the capital by the setting up of the London Passenger Transport Board, which unified bus, tram, trolleybus and underground services under the one umbrella. This organisation would go on to serve Londoners well for close on fifty years.

So what was the catalyst responsible for disturbing the status quo? In a nutshell, Thatcherism. Coming to power in 1979, Margaret Thatcher's Conservative party sought to reduce great swathes of state control by means of deregulation and privatisation. Insofar as the reforms affected the bus industry generally, successive Transport Acts loosened the ties that bound coach operators (1980) and the National Bus Company/Scottish Bus Group (1985). Unsurprisingly, however, London was initially regarded as something of a special case, and had the Tories not ceded power to Labour in the Greater London Council (GLC) election in 1981, it is possible that there could have been a different outcome. But within 24 hours of taking over at County Hall, the new administration had elected a new leader, Ken Livingstone, from the left wing of the party, and by immediately enacting his 'Fares Fair' manifesto pledge, he set himself and Labour on a collision course with Westminster.

As we now know, but could perhaps have guessed at the time, there could only be one winner in the ideological policy stakes. It took a few years before it happened, but eventually the GLC was disbanded and responsibility for reforming London Transport fell to the Department of Transport. This is where the fun started, for having achieved the twin goals of deregulation of services and privatisation of the National Bus Company (NBC) in England, Scotland and Wales, it was the Conservative plan that London should follow suit. Every year noises were made about how this would benefit bus users in the capital; every year it seemed that there were other imperatives that took precedence. Three years into John Major's premiership, and after another, unexpected, general election win, a definite timescale for the privatisation of the ten London Buses subsidiary companies was finally announced in late 1993 and achieved a year later when South London was the last to be sold. Deregulation was put on the back burner and has never reappeared.

Therefore it can safely be said that the sixteen-year period between 1979 and 1994 witnessed the greatest and most far-reaching changes to the capital's bus services since the days of Herbert Morrison, and that is the period upon which this history concentrates. The effective starting point in 1979 is 1 October, when a new system of management based on eight (later reduced to six, and later still, five) districts was put in place. The fallout from the successful legal challenge to 'Fares Fair', the introduction of a zonal fare structure, the 1984 London Regional Transport Act, which removed control from the GLC and paved the way for a system of tendering that allowed other operators to bid for London Transport services, the reorganisation into semi-autonomous companies in 1988, and the privatisations of 1992 (London Coaches) and 1994 (the other companies) can all be found here. The fleet is also examined on a year-by-year basis. Who might have imagined in 1979 that less than two decades later, minibuses, which had seen only minimal use in London prior to the mid-1980s, and their larger counterparts such as the Dennis Dart, would arrive in ever-increasing numbers until by 1994 they would account for around 25 per cent of the total fleet?

A regular visitor to London between 1979 and 1984, I moved there for work between 1985 and 1992, based in offices on High Holborn, Kingsway and Lancaster Place. Plenty of opportunity therefore to sample all the different routes that conveyed me

London Northern RM1218 (218 CLT) crosses from Park Road into Baker Street on 4 August 1992, leaving no doubt of its attachment to the 139. This was a new route, begun just five months earlier, between West Hampstead and Trafalgar Square, replacing that part of the 159.

away from (and back to) King's Cross during that time, and planning forays for lunchtimes and late afternoons helped while away many a commute. Then after one of the Government's periodic attempts to move civil servants out of London, for the final two years covered by the book I was based in Nottingham, but ironically, most of the work I undertook during that time brought me back to London again! So one way or another, my camera and I could still witness the transition from London Buses Ltd to the privatised companies at first hand.

So each yearly chapter comprises an analysis of the major points of interest, particularly those driven by the Government and politicians of the day, the changes to the LT/LBL fleet in terms of new vehicles in and older ones out, the more important service news, and any other items that were worthy of comment. There are photographs relating to events of each year, as well as what might be called galleries, where vehicles are grouped by subject rather than year. In addition, I have endeavoured to compile a schedule of all vehicles in LT/LBL stock at 1 January 1979 and acquired in each of the following years up to 31 December 1994. It seemed to me however that a complete list of all London routes during the period would have been excessive; I have opted instead to detail tenders from 1985 onwards and the operators that took over the contracts. Finally, a record of the garages, complete with openings and (more usually) closures, is also included. Any errors or omissions, particularly in a work as list-heavy as this, are almost certainly my responsibility. It was not my intention to get too heavily involved in the minutiae; that has been, and continues to be, the province of the London Omnibus Transport Society (LOTS) and the PSV Circle, both of which organisations are highly recommended.

There are many people I have to mention who have helped me bring the book to fruition. My wife Debbie, for putting up with the hours I spend poring over a laptop; my friend and long-time resident of London W4, Howard Potter, whose advice on design issues in the early stages has been much appreciated; my friend and proof-reader Alan Carter, and the photographers who have graciously allowed me to use their work, in particular Martin Baulf, Stewart J. Brown, Mark Davis, Geoff Gould, Hugh Jones, Stuart Robbs and Les Simpson. I must mention LOTS once again, whose *London Bus* magazines and Fleet Books are essential, detailed guides to the London bus scene; Ian Armstrong, whose website contains a vast amount of information about London bus routes since October 1934, Ian Smith, whose website 'Ian's Bus Stop' is an ever-growing history of so many of the types that have operated for LT and its successors , and Mike Harris, publisher of excellent current and historic London bus maps, for his advice. My thanks to them all.

Andrew Bartlett

1979

In what proved to be a watershed year for LT (and indeed for the wider bus industry too), the first tentative steps towards a system based on a form of regional autonomy were taken. The events that unfolded had their genesis in the GLC elections that had taken place two years earlier. With control passing from Labour to the Conservatives, it soon became apparent that a different policy towards LT was being pursued in the areas of organisation and provision of revenue support.

Early January found LT still in the middle of implementing 'Busplan '78', a network-wide review which began prior to the 1977 elections and sought, inter alia, to improve off-peak coverage and to standardise frequencies. The first two sets of changes had been introduced in April and October 1978; the third and final tranche was implemented on 31 March 1979. However, driver shortages at several garages were a continuing cause for concern and had an impact on the roll-out.

Proposals were also put forward in 1978 to reorganise LT into eight districts. The plan was that each one should be run by a general manager with control over all the resources required to run the operations in his area, including maintenance, planning and liaison. Hopes that implementation would take place early in 1979 never came to fruition; it took until 1 October for the ambition to be realised. At the same time, London Buses was announced as the new trading name for LT's bus work.

The new districts, and the garages allocated to them, were as follows:

ABBEY – AF - Putney, B - Battersea, CF - Chalk Farm, GM - Victoria, HT - Holloway, R - Riverside, S - Shepherds Bush, SW - Stockwell, WD - Wandsworth, X - Middle Row

CARDINAL – AV - Hounslow, FW - Fulwell, HL - Hanwell, HW - Southall, K - Kingston, M - Mortlake, NB - Norbiton, UX - Uxbridge, V - Stamford Brook

FOREST – AP - Seven Kings, BK - Barking, L - Loughton, NS - North Street, RD - Hornchurch, T - Leyton, U - Upton Park, WW - Walthamstow

LEASIDE – AD - Palmers Green, AR - Tottenham, E - Enfield, EM - Edmonton, FY - Finchley, MH - Muswell Hill, PB - Potters Bar, SF - Stamford Hill, WN - Wood Green

SELKENT – AM - Plumstead, AW - Abbey Wood, BX - Bexleyheath, NX - New Cross, PM - Peckham, SP - Sidcup, TB - Bromley, TL - Catford

TOWER – BW - Bow, CT - Clapton, D - Dalston, H - Hackney, PR - Poplar, Q - Camberwell, WH - West Ham, WL - Walworth

RF504 (MXX 481) entered service in March 1953 at Sidcup, and moved from Uxbridge to Kingston in 1976. Seen here in Portsmouth Road on its way to Staines with a 218 working in March 1979, it appears to be in reasonably good condition, but withdrawal came that same month, and after a period with a private owner, it was used as a source of spares for preserved RF444.

WANDLE – A - Sutton, AK - Streatham, AL - Merton, BN - Brixton, ED - Elmers End, N - Norwood, TC - Croydon, TH - Thornton Heath

WATLING – AC - Willesden, AE - Hendon, EW - Edgware, HD - Harrow Weald, ON - Alperton, SE - Stonebridge, W – Cricklewood

Vehicle news – single deck fleet

It was time to say farewell to the most venerable saloon in the fleet, the RF. Now over twenty-five years since their introduction, the 218/219 (Kingston – Staines/Weybridge) became their final haunt, and RF507 performed the last rites on Friday 30 March, Leyland Nationals taking over thereafter. Only one RF was left in LT ownership by 31 December.

So far as the AEC Swifts were concerned, there was little or no major change to numbers of either the MB or SM classes scheduled for service, at around 245, though the stock of SMs dropped by approximately 130 during the year. But on the plus side, over 150 Leyland Nationals (LS) were delivered in 1979, bringing the total to 435. Finally, five new Ford Transits with Dormobile sixteen-seat bodywork, FS22-26, arrived in October and November and entered service at Hampstead Garden Suburb, for the H2, and Potters Bar, on the PB1.

Vehicle news – double deck fleet

The other old stager, a stalwart of the fleet for almost forty years, was the RT, which by the beginning of 1979 was only found regularly on the 62 (Creekmouth/Barking-Barkingside). The type was finally withdrawn on 7 April, RT624 having the distinction of being the last one in service before taking part in a parade headed by the restored and preserved RT1. They could still be seen on London's streets, as over 100 were retained as staff buses and trainers, but they too were gone by the year end.

Daimler Fleetlines were being delivered right up until August 1978, but the type was neither totally reliable or especially popular, and the decision was taken to concentrate resources on the better Park Royal examples. Once those in poor condition – a number had suffered fire damage – had gone, Metro-Cammell bodied withdrawals began in April, although they immediately started appearing elsewhere in the country, most notably in Oxford and for the West Midlands PTE. Away from London, they would in the main give several more years' service for their new operators. Out of a total of 2,646

The 62 had for just over twenty years been the province of the RT, the type taking over from the RTL in November 1958. It turned out to be the final RT-operated route, and Saturday 7 April 1979 marked the end, with RMs taking over progressively during the day. RT624 was the last to go, but Weymann bodied RT3016 (NLE 906), pictured in High Street, Barkingside, was one of the twelve reported as still active up to that point, although it was then immediately withdrawn.

With the distinctive white upper deck window surrounds, DM2626 (THX 626S) prepares to leave Victoria bus station for Brent Cross on a 16A working in October 1979.

built, less than 2,300 remained by the year end, and of those, only around 1,850 were scheduled for service.

Even the future of some more recent stock was looking precarious. The Scania BR111DH or Metropolitan, of which 164 were acquired in the period 1975-77, was prone to corrosion and was of questionable reliability. Seven accident victims were scrapped during 1979, and it was planned to withdraw the type as their certificates of fitness expired.

Routemaster news principally concerned the return to LT of former London Country vehicles, RMCs, RCLs and RMLs, a process that had begun two years earlier. Most were put into store until they could be prepared for service. LT also acquired nine ex Northern General Routemasters, numbering them RMF2761-69. Finally, with the ending on 31 March 1979 of the British Airways service populated by the RMA class, LT acquired thirty-eight of the type and many were soon utilised as staff buses or trainers.

Metro-Cammell had only supplied the bodywork for the Metropolitan, but decided subsequently to take over the entire process. The result, the MCW Metrobus, was trialled in London at the end of 1977 using vehicle TOJ 592S, and the first five production models came in 1978, though only three were used in service before the year end, with their classification revised from MT1-3 to M1-3. Further orders were placed, and by the end of 1979, deliveries had reached M205, with 300 more due in 1980.

While the Metropolitan was still entering service, LT engineers worked alongside British Leyland in the development of a new double decker, code-named B15. Prototypes NHG 732P (1976) and BCK 706R (1977) were tested, and the first seven production models, now known as the Titan, entered service in 1978. Once again the original class letters, in this case TN, were amended to a simple T, before they arrived. A further 119 appeared in 1979, and the original order for 250 was eventually fulfilled the following year. However, Leyland announced during 1979 that production of the Titan at Park Royal would cease with the closure of the plant there.

Service news

Perhaps the most unusual event was the collapse of the carriageway in Petersham Road in January, affecting the 65 (Ealing-Chessington) and 71 (Richmond-Leatherhead). Until it was filled in, buses terminated on either side of the obstruction. However, a later and more serious crater opened up, leading on 5 May to the curtailment of the 71 at Petersham, while the 65 ran in two sections, Ealing-Petersham (River Lane) and Petersham (Fox & Duck)-Chessington. By this time the 71 had been withdrawn from the Surbiton-Leatherhead section, which was now the preserve of a new OPO route 265. Normal service was not resumed until September 1980. As already mentioned, the LS took over from the RF on the 218/219 from 31 March. But as the LS was too large for Kingston, the vehicles and the routes were reallocated to Norbiton. On this date also the service from the West London Air Terminal to Heathrow operated for British Airways ended.

'Shop Linker' was a new initiative launched on 7 April which involved sixteen Routemasters in an eye-catching yellow and red livery. Operating approximately every ten minutes between 0900 and 1700 (and at twenty-four minute intervals on

Stewart J Brown's photo shows RM2188 (CUV 188C) in Shop Linker livery at work on the final day. The 'Good Buy' destination was a nice touch, while the notice attached to the radiator grille proclaimed that this was the final service. Considering it had not been well patronised since April, RM2188 carries a healthy passenger load; one wonders how many actually were shoppers, and how many were there simply for the last chance of a ride.

Above: All eyes on the top deck appear to be trained on the photographer and not the local scenery. DMO1 (CRU 182C) has the wider white band between decks to accommodate the artist's depictions of the landmarks to be found en route; the name *Stockwell Princess* can be seen below the fleet number. All seven were withdrawn in 1981, although DMO3 did see some further work in 1983 before it was finally sold.

Left: There were two editions of the London-wide bus map during 1979. Both featured the '1829-1979 Omnibus' symbol, while the second one showed the new bus districts.

Thursdays until 2030) and with a flat 30p fare, it ran from Marble Arch in clockwise and anti-clockwise loops to Notting Hill Gate, Kensington, Knightsbridge, Piccadilly, Regent Street and Oxford Street. RMs 59, 2139/46/51/54/59/62/63/67/71/72/74/87-89, 2207 were involved, and sponsors, including Selfridges, Liberty's and HMV, were found, but the route was not successful and it was withdrawn on 28 September.

An increase in vehicles allocated to the Round London Sightseeing Tour was met by DMs from Stockwell garage. The seven Bournemouth DMO class convertible open-top Fleetlines which entered service in 1978 were re-roofed for the winter season but emerged, topless once more, in May. Three were named; DMO1 became *Stockwell Princess*, DMO2 *Southern Queen* and DMO3 *Britannia*.

The newly opened Ealing Hospital was served by extensions to the 83 (from Hanwell) and 92 (from Southall garage).

Route conversions to take account of the new vehicle intake took place throughout the year. Broadly speaking, the chief casualty was the DMS, and a shortage of the type later in the year led to LSs, and even SMSs, appearing in their place.

Other events

The 150th anniversary of George Shillibeer's original horse-drawn omnibus, which began operations between Paddington and Bank in 1829, was commemorated in fine style. Twelve Routemasters and a solitary Fleetline were chosen to carry a special livery, a close approximation of the green and cream carried in Shillibeer's day. Lucky recipients were DM2646 and RMs 2130/42/53/55/58/60/84/86/91/93, 2204/08. RCL2221 was also similarly treated, and was decked out for use as a mobile exhibition and cinema. All except the RCL were sponsored; their advertisements were carried between decks and either side of the route and destination equipment. The celebrations were launched at the Guildhall on 2 March; there was a parade at Battersea Park on 15 April, and a special run that traced (so far as possible) Shillibeer's original route, on 8 July. Contracts ran until 30 November (though in practice they went into 1980), and the thirteen service buses served at three different garages on a variety of routes during the year.

In addition, a real horse bus service was introduced! Operated on LT's behalf, it began on 9 July, operating between Baker Street station and London Zoo, and four different replica vehicles were used during the few weeks of operations.

RM2184 (CUV 184C) looks a treat in George Shillibeer 150th anniversary livery, sponsored by the Scottish Tourist Board. It was allocated to Walworth for the 12, moving to Tottenham for the 73, and ending up at Riverside for the 9, although on this occasion, it was waiting at Cricklewood garage before embarking on a Sunday working of the 266.

A new bus station was officially opened at Euston in October, though it had been in part-use for some months already. Finally, the last of the many Routemasters to carry advertising livery during the 1970s, RM1237, appeared in November 1979 with a scheme for Wisdom Toothbrushes, which it retained until January 1981.

LT introduced fare increases twice during the year, on 17 June and 9 September. Approximately 165 million bus miles were operated, while passenger journeys totalled 1,234 million, an annual decrease of 4.1 per cent and 5 per cent respectively. There was free travel on Christmas Day, and again on New Year's Eve after 22:30, which on this occasion was sponsored by Fiat.

FAREWELL TO THE RT

As this history begins, it was the end of an era for several types operated by LT, not least the AEC Regent III RTs, which were originally introduced almost forty years earlier. They had been replaced on no fewer than fourteen routes during 1978, one of the last of which was the 94 (Lewisham-Petts Wood-Orpington). This lovely photo of RT1790 (KYY 628) in August 1978 was quite probably taken to mark their passing on the 94, as from 28 August RMs were the order of the day.

RT4454 (OLD 674) on a 62 working to Barkingside, photographed at the junction of Newham Way and Ripple Road in Dagenham towards the end of its career. It was withdrawn in 1978, Wombwell Diesels becoming its final resting place. The pub in the background, The Volunteer, lasted until 1999, when it was demolished as part of an A13 widening scheme.

After a number of false starts during the course of the 1970s, the RTs last days were played out at Barking garage, largely upon the 62 (Barkingside-Barking-Gascoigne Estate), although there was still a limited presence on the 87, also worked by Barking. In October 1978, from left to right, RTs 1782 (KYY 620), 449 (HLX 266), 2061 (LUC 324) and 2797 (LYR 967) were lined up at the garage; RT449 would go on to undertake training duties for a while, but the others had turned their last wheel in LT service.

A NOTABLE ANNIVERSARY

To celebrate the 150th anniversary of George Shillibeer's first horse bus, twelve RMs and one DM were given special liveries, and were allocated to different garages over the course of the year. Sponsorship played its part, as can be seen on RM2160 (CUV 160C), which advertised Esso. Allocations changed twice during the year; RM2160 spent Stage 1 at Palmers Green for the 29, moving to Walworth for the 12 between June and August (Stage 2), finishing at Tottenham from September (Stage 3) on the 76. Meanwhile, DM2646 (THX 646S), seen at London Bridge, had been at Cricklewood for the 16 during Stage 1, and had now moved to Muswell Hill where, in addition to the 43 (Friern Barnet), it would also see service on the 134 (Tottenham Court Road-Potters Bar). It was the last B20 Fleetline delivered to LT, in August 1978, just as the Metrobuses and Titans were beginning to come on stream. Sponsored by British Leyland, it has advertisements for the Titan on either side of the route and destination boxes.

THE END IS NIGH

AEC Regal IV/Metro-Cammell RF481 (MXX 458) entered service in February 1953 at Muswell Hill garage. After almost twenty-four, years it was withdrawn from Uxbridge and stored for a short time until the opportunity to end its days on the 218/219 came. It was in a pretty poor state when seen in March 1979, on its way to Kingston-upon-Thames on the 219 from Weybridge. It was withdrawn in the same month and stored until December, when it was scrapped.

After a six-month trial of the Scania CR111MH in 1970, LT eventually placed an order for six. These had Metro-Cammell bodywork and arrived in mid-1973. They were given a revised livery which incorporated a white roof, and were put to work from August on the S2 (Clapton-Bromley-by-Bow). Their stay was short-lived, however; MS1 was stored in January 1975, and the remainder followed in June 1976, when they were replaced by SMSs. MS1/3-6 were sold to Newport Corporation in late 1978, but MS2 (PGC 202L) was retained and moved to Chiswick Works, where it assumed experimental status. This photo was taken there in the summer of 1980, a few months before it was sold for spares, though there are reports that it was eventually secured for preservation.

MBA609 (AML 609H) makes its way along Park Lane towards Oxford Street on 4 May 1980. Originally part of an MBS sub-class, conversion for Red Arrow work took place not long after acquisition and henceforth it could accommodate twenty-five seated and forty-eight standing passengers. Two months after the photograph was taken, it was put into store, and final withdrawal came in May 1981.

1980

There was no news this year that would dominate the headlines, but various improvements made to services were to some degree overshadowed by adverse publicity created by a report LT had itself commissioned. The Conservative administration began to make its presence felt in the area of both budgets and costs. Leslie Chapman, a former regional director at the Ministry of Public Building and Works, published *Your Disobedient Servant* in 1978, a hard-hitting treatise on waste in the Civil Service. He was invited to join the London Transport Executive in 1979 and produced a report that pointed to 'disgraceful' waste and potential savings of up to £50 million. LT chairman Ralph Bennett did not agree with the findings, but the GLC sought two further independent reviews in 1980. The first, by Deloittes, appeared in February and considered there had been insufficient time to complete a thorough investigation but that LT management exhibited what they called 'moderate competence'. The second, by PA Consulting, reported that this same top management was 'weak in the skills required to run a large business' although, like Deloittes before, it found no fault at lower levels. Bennett resigned, and Chapman, who continued to rail against continuing extravagance, was dismissed early in 1981.

Concurrently, and perhaps coincidentally in the light of Chapman's findings, the Government issued an edict to the GLC, requiring a cut of £50 million to LT's budget in the 1980/81 financial year. This inevitably affected a number of improvement plans in the pipeline. There could be no clearer sign that politics would be playing a far greater role than previously in LT's affairs. However, the GLC lobbied the government over the proposed abolition of the Bus Grant for new vehicles and paid £29 million to reimburse LT for the free travel enjoyed by London pensioners. Nonetheless, there were two significant fare increases during the year, in February and September (or October, for flat-fare schemes) by an average of 16-17 per cent on each occasion.

It was announced in October that the initiative known as the 'XRM Project' – a low-floor double decker on which LT had been secretly working for some time – was likely to be shelved, though confirmation that this was indeed the case did not come until February 1980.

Vehicle news – single deck fleet

The last two Mark 1 Leyland Nationals were taken into stock – LS413 and LS426.

164 single deckers and minibuses were sold during the year. They included sixteen Ford Transits and the last remaining AEC Regal (RF511). The major casualties were the Swifts, with the removal of 147 vehicles; 29 SMs, including SM1, five SMDs and no less than 113 SMSs. Two Leyland National 2s were evaluated during the course of the year, Fishwick of Leyland's WRN 413V and Ribble 841. An order for sixty-nine of the type for delivery in 1981 was subsequently placed.

Fifteen Swifts could be found on Red Arrow services in 1980, acting as cover for Merlins (which were in any case due to be replaced by Leyland National 2s in the none-too-distant future). SMS756 (JGF 756K) waits at Victoria bus station in September 1980.

SMS753 (JGF 753K) had a short but interesting life. New in October 1971, it was allocated to Harrow Weald until withdrawal, which came in August 1978. It was almost immediately converted into an LT Shop and Information bus, for which it received a red and blue livery and was reclassified SPB753. It carried out this role for six years, including a short stint as a mobile plant store, before sale to a preservationist. It is surrounded by several interesting vehicles including RCL2221, still in Shillibeer anniversary livery.

Vehicle news – double deck fleet

The first 250 Leyland Titans were now in service, but production had been slowed by the announcement of Park Royal's closure. It was later confirmed that the Workington plant would become responsible for the Titan, with a resumption in 1981. Meanwhile a further 300 Metrobuses were taken into stock, the highest numbered now being M505.

Almost 350 Fleetlines left the fleet – the highest numbered being DMS1674 – as did nine accident-damaged Metropolitans. Seven RTs were also disposed of, and the six remaining in stock included three for skid bus use, a radio trainer and a mechanical trainer.

Left: It is June 1980 in Wood Green, and while the conductor of the RM strolls nonchalantly back to his bus, DMS142 (JGF 142K) awaits its return journey to Aldgate on the 67. It entered service in August 1971 and after eleven years, was one of 479 Fleetlines sold in 1982, passing to China Motor Bus in Hong Kong in 1984.

Below: Such were the problems with the MD class that it had been planned to withdraw them once their certificates of fitness expired. But the situation improved in 1980 to the extent that when the new Plumstead garage (PD) opened in October 1981, it had a wholly MD allocation. Prior to that, however, whilst still at AM and before a repaint did away with the white upper deck window surrounds, MD22 (KJD 222P) was seen at Bexleyheath garage, about to undertake a short working of the 122 as far as Forest Hill.

LT's 'Green Line' Routemaster coaches, RMC1453-1520, passed to London Country in 1970, but as that decade drew to a close, they were deemed to be surplus to requirements. LT agreed to have them back, and all sixty-eight transferred between the end of 1977 and 1980 with only two, RMC1505/09, found to be unserviceable. The remainder found new vocations as driver trainers, and went on to give several years' more service. Here, another learner sets off in Camberwell's RMC1473 (473 CLT). It retained green livery throughout its career, and was finally withdrawn in 1990.

More Routemasters arrived from London Country; twelve more RMCs and nine RMLs. Three former Northern General RMFs were also received, two directly from the operator and one via Ensign.

Service news

LT was working on an improved form of radio communication, not unnaturally known as BUSCO. The 36 (Hither Green-Victoria/West Kilburn) and 36A (Brockley Rise-Victoria, peaks only) were chosen, but with the likelihood of MDs being replaced in the not too distant future, both routes were converted to Routemaster operation for the trials, starting in mid-January. RMs, which only nine months earlier had ousted the RTs on the 62, formed part of the exchange, the 62 becoming operated by Titans instead.

RMLs also replaced Fleetlines on the 16/16A (Victoria-Neasden or Cricklewood/Brent Cross) in May, while the RCLs from London Country, once they had been prepared for service, were first to be found on Stamford Hill's allocation for the 149 (Ponders End-Liverpool Street/Victoria) from August, with Edmonton following suit between September and November. Uxbridge received RMs for the 207 (Uxbridge-Shepherds Bush Green), replacing DMs, starting in October.

In February, the GLC had proposed that cuts of up to 25 per cent of Saturday services and 33 per cent on Sundays could be made as part of a push towards meeting the budgeted 165 million bus miles for the year. The idea failed to gain traction when it was shown that the target was likely to be met without that sort of intervention, and it was dropped in June.

Another welcome improvement in the area of service planning was an agreement that would allow any bus to operate on any route provided that:

- the type had been cleared for the route in question
- the crew had been type-trained, and
- the correct blinds and other equipment were fitted.

The garage at Turnham Green operated for the last time on 9 May. Vehicles were transferred to the newly refurbished Stamford Brook, which in November was also chosen as the home for the new Airbus fleet. Many years previously, it had been the Chiswick Tram Depot, and was also where the buses operated by LT for British Airways and its predecessors were based.

The British Airways service between Victoria and Heathrow was withdrawn on 14 November. The next day, 'Airbus' was born, based at Stamford Brook and worked by M431-46, which were modified to an H43/9D configuration which allowed more space for luggage. The A1 (Grosvenor Gardens, Victoria-Hyde Park Corner-Cromwell Road-M4-Heathrow Terminal 3) ran every twenty minutes between 0640 and 2140, while the A2 (Eastbourne Terrace, Paddington-Bayswater Road-Shepherds Bush-A4 & M4-Heathrow Terminal 3) operated to a half-hourly timetable between 0635 and 2135. Both routes called at Terminals 1 & 2 before arriving at their final destination.

Airbus M443 (GYE 443W), seen when less than two months old at Paddington on 28 December 1980. Reducing the seating in the lower deck to nine allowed three luggage pens – one for each of the Heathrow terminals at that time – to be fitted.

Other events

Following the resignation of Sir Reg Goodwin as Labour's leader in the GLC, right-winger Andrew McIntosh narrowly beat Ken Livingstone in the subsequent ballot.

The Routemasters still in Shillibeer livery were soon repainted, as was Fleetline DM2646, but RCL2221 did not succumb until the early part of 1981.

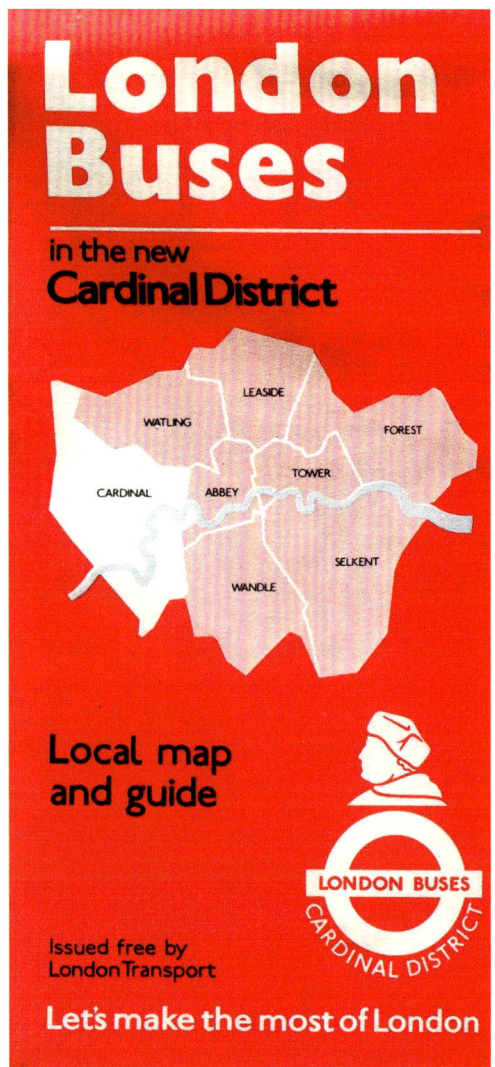

The London Bus Map was redesigned for 1980 and now featured an outline map of the Greater London area, with the eight district boundaries shown. One local map featuring Cardinal was also issued, as pictured here. A novel approach to attracting passengers was a scheme called 'Travellers' Perks'. TV advertising was used for the initial offering in August, which featured the comedian Spike Milligan. Illustrated is the Christmas and New Year edition, which followed the same format. It contained discount and money off vouchers from over twenty well-known establishments, including Barkers of Kensington, Virgin Records, Ronnie Scott's, Swan & Edgar and the Laserium. The offer from Simpson's in the Strand entitled the user to a tin of Savoy Hotel coffee when spending £10 on a Saturday lunch. All that was needed was a qualifying LT ticket – basically a cheap day return, season ticket or bus pass – and everything was available until 31 January 1981.

RM1000 was singled out by Croydon garage for special treatment, receiving an offside blind box, old-style heater and brake-cooling grilles, a gold-underlined fleetname and the word 'Routemaster' above the fleet number. In two years' time it would become Croydon's 'Showbus'.

An unfortunate accident befell M242 within a few weeks of entering service, when it was deroofed in Headstone Drive, Wealdstone. It was however repaired, re-entering service nine months later.

Princess Anne opened the new London Transport Museum in Covent Garden, following its move from Syon Park.

In what might be described as an all too typical sign of the times, LT did not operate any services on Christmas Day for the first time.

EARLY MCW METROBUSES

Having been suitably impressed by the performance of TOJ 592S, the Metrobus used for evaluation at the end of 1977, an order was placed for five, and these duly arrived between April and September 1978. Allocated to Cricklewood, they were to be found on the 16/16A, and were instantly recognisable by virtue of their smaller, three-piece destination display; in addition, M1 (THX 101S) was the only one to sport a black skirt. The photo dates from August 1983 and was taken at Edgware station while it was working the 32 from Kilburn Park. M1 remained at Cricklewood until 2000, although it had been moved to a training role three years earlier, and has subsequently been preserved.

Fulwell received over sixty of the new MCW Metrobuses once production of LTs original order for 200 started to flow. M22 (WYW22T) was photographed in Station Parade, Kew, the starting point for the 90B to Yeading, early in its career. Note the white upper deck window surrounds, and the reflective number plates, features which were perpetuated on all Ms up to and including M55.

Kensington High Street looks unusually quiet, but maybe that is because 29 July 1984 was a Sunday. M31 (WYW 31T), also Fulwell based and often to be found, like M22, on the 90B, has migrated to the 33, and has just left the terminus for the long journey back to base. It has been through the paint shop and has lost the black radiator grille and the white window surrounds in the process. M31 had a twenty-one year service life, being finally withdrawn in 2000.

EARLY LEYLAND TITANS

The first six Titans were allocated to Hornchurch and entered service there in December 1978. When T1 (THX 401S) returned to service after its first repaint in 1983, it retained the white upper deck window surrounds, and had been named *Hornchurch Ambassador*. Proudly bearing the inscription 'A new Leyland Titan for London Transport', it was awaiting its next duty on the 165 to the Mardyke Estate in Rainham on 8 July 1987. I was working in an office on St Edward's Way in Romford that day, and having watched T1 go past, I hotfooted it up to the bus lay-by, had a chat with the driver, and this was the entirely satisfactory result.

T21 (WYV 21T), pictured in Station Lane, Hornchurch on 19 October 1979, was working the 246, which linked the stations at Gidea Park and Hornchurch and had been converted from Fleetline to Titan operation to coincide with the arrival of the type in service. It was advertising the 'Multi-Ride' facility, which started in February 1978 and was in essence an experiment centred on the Havering area which it was hoped would reduce boarding times on one-person operated buses. It seems as though M21 may have been in the wars; it has a non-standard red grille and number plate panel.

The scale of development in the Cranham and Upminster Park area may be judged by the fact that in the 1930s, it only required one T class AEC Regal to operate the 248. By April 1984, when this photo was taken and after any number of extensions, it now required eight or nine Titans. This is T34 (WYV 34T), which was stopping short of the terminus in Cranham at the Upminster Park Estate. It would eventually pass to Stagecoach East London and was withdrawn in 2001.

1981

A left-wing Labour administration took over at County Hall, led from day two by Ken Livingstone, and by virtue of its most controversial manifesto commitment, was almost immediately pitted against a Conservative government whose economic policies were the polar opposite of the new GLC. The promise to introduce lower fares was implemented but was successfully challenged in the courts. It was also the year when Prince Charles married Lady Diana Spencer in St Paul's Cathedral, for which eight RMs were suitably decorated.

The Conservative administration at the GLC introduced a new fares structure in April known as 'Fare Deal'. It worked well in the suburbs, but short distance travellers found that fares of 12p or 24p were increased to 25p, and this was the source of some complaint. It may be that this was one reason why the Conservatives lost the GLC elections held on 6 May. The Labour group was led by Andrew McIntosh, who had narrowly beaten Ken Livingstone for the post the previous year. However, on 7 May, at a meeting called by McIntosh, another leadership election took place, which Livingstone won comfortably. The importance of this to LT could be traced back to a speech he gave on transport policy to the London Labour Party in 1980 that, having been incorporated into the manifesto, could now be implemented. Its central plank was a pledge to make 'Fares Fair', making ticket price reductions across LT, the Underground and British Rail. Pensioners would henceforth enjoy free travel on the Underground, as they already did on the buses. However, the plan met trouble almost immediately when central Government closed the door to there being any additional subsidy to British Rail.

Following its introduction on 4 October, a large increase in ridership was reported during the first month alone.

The 'Fares Fair' deal

In the words of the GLC, this was 'a completely new system that, at a stroke, both cuts and simplifies fares. It not only reduces the number of different fares you can pay but, by linking them to a new structure of fare zones, it also makes them even better value for money.'

Four zones were introduced:

- City (blue), from King's Cross in the north to the Elephant & Castle in the south, Shoreditch in the east and Charing Cross in the west
- West End (yellow), from Baker Street in the north to Pimlico in the south, Trafalgar Square in the east to Kensington in the west. There was an area of overlap between the City and West End zones

- Inner (green), a ring roughly three miles wide between the outer and City/West End zones
- Outer (orange), a ring taking in the remainder of the GLC area

The new fares scale was as follows:

Short hop journeys of up to ¾ mile in central London or one mile elsewhere – 10p
Maximum fare for any ride in one zone – 20p
Maximum fare for any ride across two zones – 30p
Maximum fare for any ride over three or four zones – 40p

The 10p flat fare for children was reduced to 5p, while the maximum Sunday fare anywhere in the GLC area was 20p. Flat fare routes were generally set at 20p, the same as Red Arrows, and the cost of a journey on an Airbus was unchanged at £2. In the accompanying leaflet, TV personality Michael Aspel was brought in to ask various searching questions about the new system, and he signed off on a positive note by asking whether 'Fares Fair' would help all Londoners. The answer? 'It will mean big savings for almost everyone who lives in the GLC area and travels by Bus or Underground.'

It was estimated that this would create an additional 350 million passenger miles, but at a cost of £123 million to be borne by Londoners through a supplementary rate demand. The GLC however claimed that the lion's share of this was attributable to the deficit inherited from the previous administration.

But Conservative councillors were not happy, and those in Bromley led by Dennis Barkway took the issue to court. Central to their argument was that there was no Underground service in their area (only British Rail, whose fares had not reduced), yet their ratepayers were still obliged to pay the extra subsidy. In addition, it was cited that users from outside the GLC boundaries were enjoying the reductions without subsidising them, which was particularly true of tourists, and that government policy required public transport to be self-financing, though in reality this was more of an aspiration than a mandate. Bromley Council lost the argument in the High Court, but won in the Court of Appeal. The House of Lords, the final arbiters, gave judgement on 17 December, for Bromley and against the GLC. The ruling did not go down too well in some quarters; the *Guardian* opined that 'London Transport policy is in ruins. By their judgement yesterday, the five Law Lords have plunged London Transport into chaos'. Even the *Sunday Times* leader writer felt it was a 'bad judgement'. Part of their Lordships' reasoning was based around the view that the GLC had a statutory duty to break even, despite the fact that this was not the way leaders of either party in the GLC had approached the issue of LT funding in the recent past. It is also worth noting that the Lords considered the phrase 'Fares Fair' to be misleading.

The 'Fares Fair' leaflet, double-sided and A2-sized, was a publicity tour de force from the GLC.

The map inside the leaflet gave users a rough idea of which area fell within which zone.

The effect of this will be considered in the chapter on 1982. But by the end of this year, wildly estimated figures of possible redundancies, percentage increases in fares, and service cuts as a result of the ruling were being bandied about.

Vehicle news – single deck fleet

Leyland National 2s LS438-506 were received during the spring and were immediately put to work on Red Arrow routes, replacing MBAs and SMSs, the last of which were finally withdrawn after service on 2 July.

Devon General Bristol LHS6L 93 was assessed in June 1973, leading to an order for six of the type, which on receipt were put into service on the C11 (Cricklewood-Archway) from mid-August 1975. They were followed by a further eleven later the following year, which ousted the FS class from the B1, P4 and W9. With a seating capacity of twenty-six, they were a considerable improvement upon the Transits, but their use proved to be fairly short-lived, as LT invested more heavily in the standard LH6L (the BL class). Route conversions took place in July 1981, the month in which BN13 (OJD 13R) was seen on the W9 in Cecil Road, Enfield. It was formally withdrawn that September and went on to work for both British Caledonian at Gatwick Airport and Western National.

The end came for the LHS6L BS class, with only the last two of the original seventeen remaining, both withdrawn and awaiting sale. FS21 was used to repair FS19 and then sold; all remaining Swifts but only sixteen Merlins, were also sold during the year.

Vehicle news – double deck fleet

Black radiator grilles on Metrobuses were outlawed in favour of red. M427, along with the Airbus Ms, were the first in the revised scheme.

T206 was destroyed by a fire, thought to have been started deliberately, at Barking. 146 new Titans were received during the year, taking fleet numbers T251-396. They were outstripped by the Metrobus once again, with the delivery of M506-728; a total of 223.

The reliability of the Metropolitans was called into question during 1979 and 1980, but it improved to such a degree that it was decided Plumstead should have an all-MD allocation upon opening. The future of the class appeared to be assured in the short term.

For many, the event of the year was that of RM1 being taken back into stock. It had been withdrawn in 1973, when it was sold to the Lockheed Corporation and used for brake testing trials, based at either Chiswick or Aldenham in the interim. It would be seen intermittently at open days and on special services, until it was donated to the London Transport Museum in 1989.

Upton Park's T251 (GYE 251W), numerically the first of the 1981 intake, departing Stratford bus station on 30 October 1981 with a 238 working to Little Heath.

Use of Metropolitans on the 78 at Peckham lasted from February 1980 to October 1981, when they were replaced by Leyland Nationals. On 20 April 1981 MD80 (KJD 280P) stands in Aldgate whilst en route to Dulwich.

The Royal Wedding RMs were designed to look like gift-wrapped wedding presents. Sponsors were found for all eight, and RM219 (VLT 219) carried advertising for Beefeater Gin. It was seen in West End Lane, hotly pursued by 'plain' RM1624 (624 DYE), which is working the full 159 route to Thornton Heath; RM219 will venture only as far as Kennington. It returned to normal fleet livery in October.

Withdrawals hit the Fleetlines hardest once again, with the departure of a further 306. Nine RMAs, ten RMCS, all eleven RMFs and three RTs also left the fleet. Duties of the remaining three RTs were either as skid buses (RT1530, 2143) or as a radio trainer (RT2953). The former Bournemouth Fleetlines were withdrawn, but only one (DMO6) was sold.

Service news

The year's most extensive programme of route alterations, affecting almost ninety services, took place on 25 April.

In preparation for Prince Charles and Lady Diana Spencer's wedding, LT produced 1½ million special 'Royal Warrant' tickets, costing £2 (adult) or 50p (child), allowing travel on all LT buses and most underground services on the big day. Eight RMs were dressed in silver bows and, as in 1979 with Shillibeer and Shop Linker, sponsors were involved, ranging from Heinz to Mothercare to Beefeater Gin. The vehicles were RM219, 519/20/34/59/61/95, 607. RM490 was used to trial the design but did not operate in public service. Buses affected by the wedding day arrangements were diverted or curtailed on thirty-four routes between 0400 and 1400, and another sixteen around Waterloo for a further four hours after that.

1981 saw no services on Christmas Day apart from Airbus A1, which ran from 0730 to 1400.

The front and back of the Royal Warrant ticket issued from early July in readiness for use on the big day. The map, showing all the adjacent Underground stations in the vicinity of the processional route was a useful addition for those visiting from outside the capital.

Other events

In February, a trial started in Barnet and Croydon whereby newsagents were permitted to sell bus passes. Complementing the existing monthly variety was a new weekly pass, available for suburban services at £5.25, or for unrestricted red bus use at £6.50. They could also be bought on buses in the two areas in question.

The first London Marathon was held on 29 March, with much diversion of services along the line of the route, from Greenwich to Constitution Hill. The organisers chartered a number of single deckers from LT to be used as changing rooms at the starting point.

There was much activity during the year so far as LT garages were concerned. Ash Grove (AG) opened in April (receiving an allocation of National 2s for Red Arrow work), leading to the permanent closure of Dalston (D) and Hackney (H). Westbourne Park (X) was next, in August, spelling the end for Middle Row (the original X) and Stonebridge Park (SE). At the end of October, Abbey Wood (AW) and the old Plumstead garage (AM) were replaced by new premises at Plumstead, which became PD. Clapham (CA) re-opened after twenty-three years, having been used as a store in the meantime, to facilitate the closure of Norwood (N), which was to be rebuilt. Work at Edgware and Uxbridge was also planned, while a new bus station at Harrow was opened in May.

On 8 February, the twenty-fifth anniversary of RM1 entering service on the 2 was celebrated with a commemorative run between Golders Green and Crystal Palace. Croydon's RM1000, seen in the chapter on 1980, was one of those taking part.

Over 55 per cent of the fleet had been fitted with two-way radios by 31 December.

MERLINS AND SWIFTS

LT received 665 AEC Swifts with Metro-Cammell bodywork, known as Merlins, between 1966 and 1969. Their basic classification was MB, and MBA signified use on Red Arrow routes, such as here, where the driver of MBA575 (AML 575H) was enjoying a short break from the rigours of the 501 at London Bridge. The decision to start phasing them out came as early as 1973, but MBA575 was not withdrawn until June 1981, when Leyland National 2s took over Red Arrow operations. It was sold for scrap a few months later.

Above: Problems arising from the manoeuvrability of the Merlins, which were thirty-six feet in length and had large overhangs, led LT to invest in the smaller Swift, and 700 were acquired from 1969 to 1972 (London Country had a further 138). This time the proper chassis type name was used! SM31 (AML 31H) was one of the original batch of fifty, bodied by Marshall (not at that time widely known as a supplier to LT), and intended as RT replacements; their capacity (B42F+20), beat the RT (H30/26R+5) by one. SMs were introduced on the 132 (Eltham-Slade Green) in April 1970, and although SM31 entered service on the 270 at Fulwell, by 27 July 1979 it had found its way to Bexleyheath. It was withdrawn the following November.

Below: The Swifts were sadly somewhat unreliable, and LT made the decision to get rid of them, to be replaced by Leyland Nationals. SMS175 (EGN 175J) was spotted in Camberwell Road in March 1980 while working the 42 (Aldgate-Camberwell Green), which for a period of close to eight months in 1979/80 was converted from Fleetline to Swift operation. Soon afterwards, SMS175 was finally withdrawn, after a working life which, excluding time spent stored, lasted just ten years and one month.

DAY AND NIGHT

Above: An early winter morning and LS116 (THX 116S) is en route for Finchley Road station. It would end up with Westlink, while in six years' time, the 268 would be one of the first to be converted to minibus operation. London Country North West was the successful bidder when the contract for the 268 was put out to tender in 1986.

Opposite above: The photographer has made full use of an elevated position at Stratford bus station to photograph RM1744 (744 DYE), arriving from Romford on the 86, closely followed by T590 (NUW 590Y) working the Stratford circular S1. RM1744 was allocated to Seven Kings for eighteen months between September 1982 and March 1984; it spent a further eight months at New Cross before withdrawal. T590 was reported as having been deroofed at Limehouse in January 1985, but was returned to service later in the year.

Opposite below: The N90 came into being in 1960, linking Pimlico and Edmonton, and had grown in importance by 21 May 1981, when this photo was taken, to the extent that it had been diverted to better serve King's Cross, St Pancras, Euston, Charing Cross and Victoria main line stations, and a Saturday service had been introduced. RM1682 (682 DYE) was waiting to turn into Euston Road, with the imposing architecture of St Pancras, which was rescued from redevelopment by being made a Grade I listed building in 1967, dominating the background.

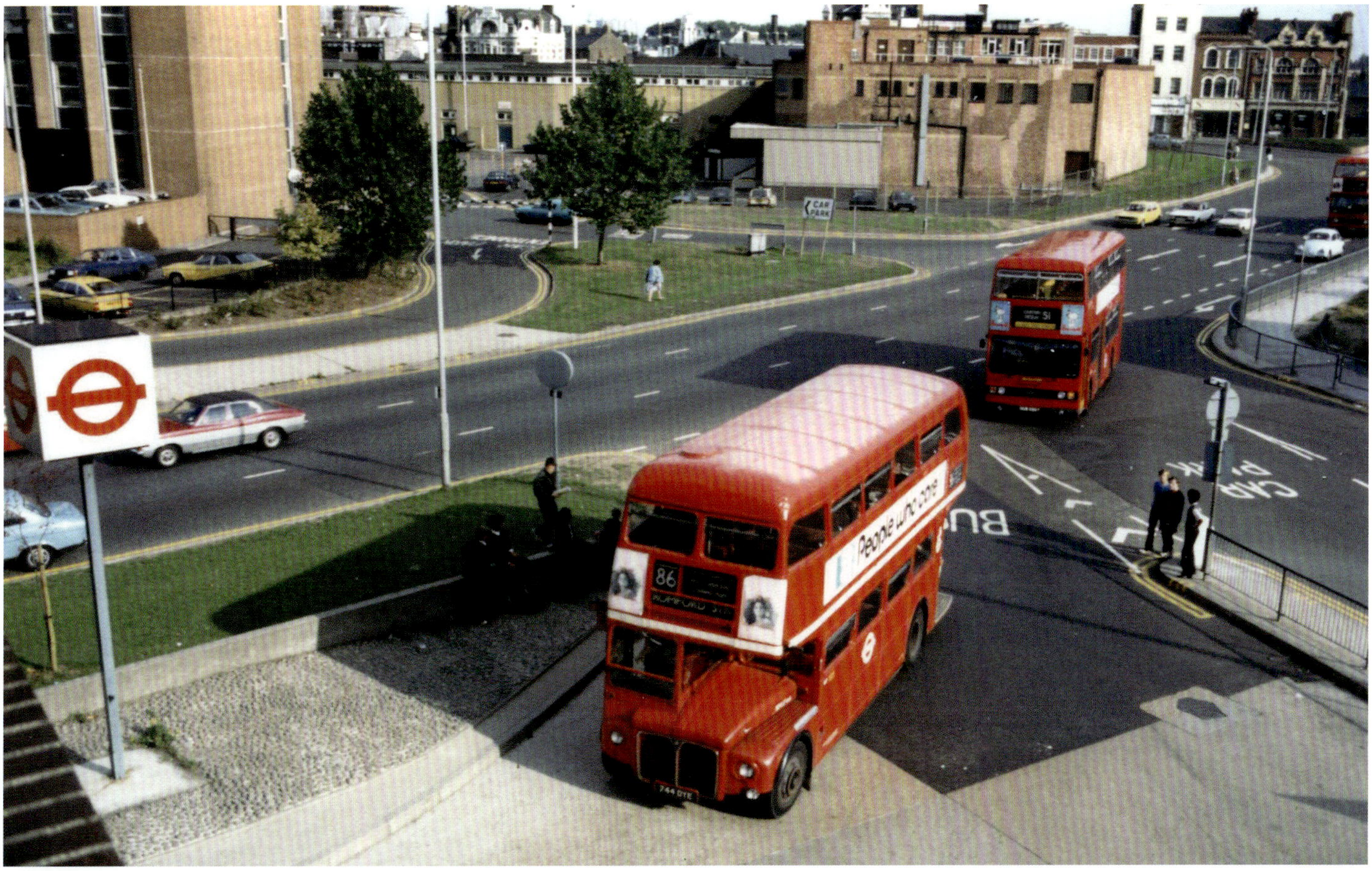
CAR PARK
86
People who care

FARE DEAL 25p.
N90
PIMLICO
FARE DEAL
Any bus ride. Anywhere in the Flat Fare Area.
25p.

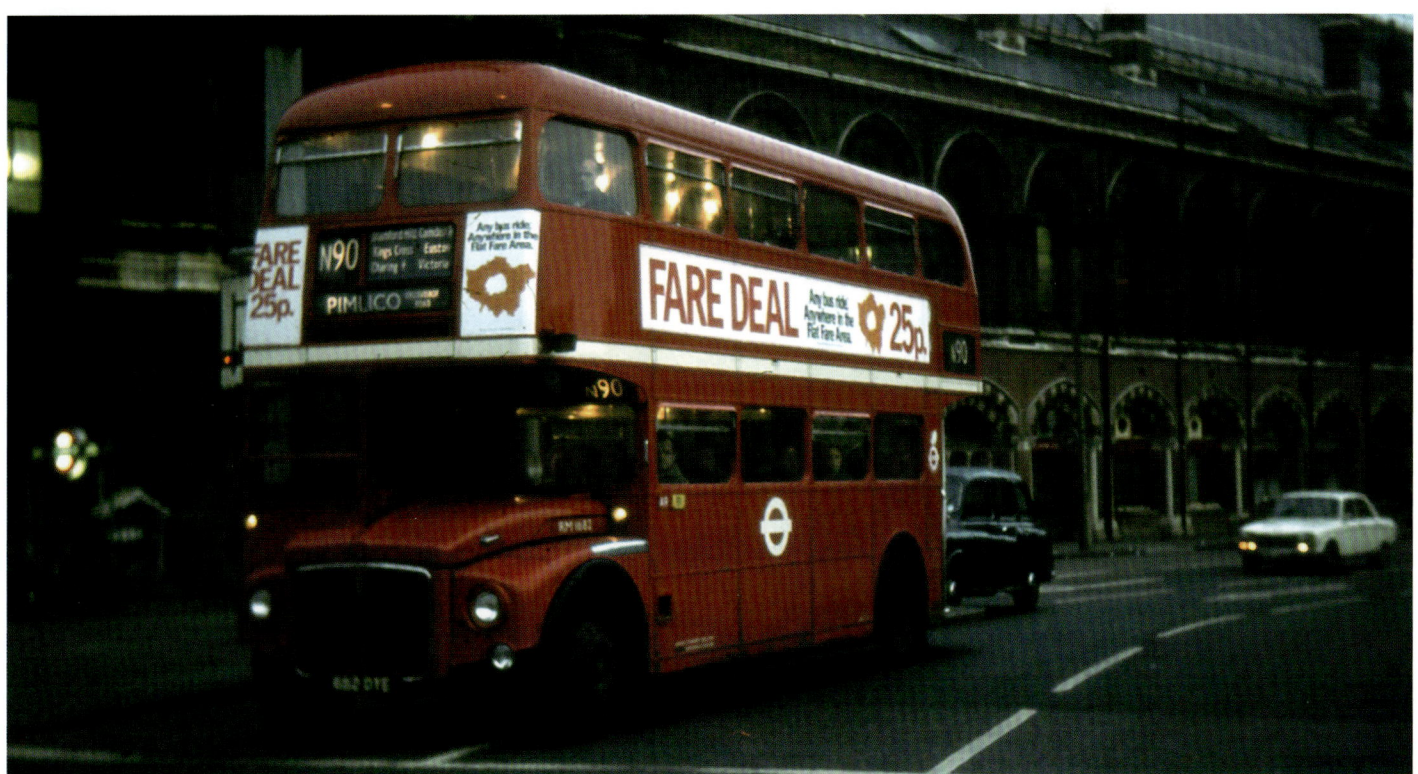

1982

Picking up the pieces after the House of Lords ruling on 'Fares Fair' was the priority, with the effects being felt throughout the area. Condemned in many quarters as being both short-sighted and contradictory (in terms of the Transport [London] Act of 1969 which some felt had been misinterpreted by their Lordships), one thing was for sure; swingeing fare increases and service reductions would be inevitable.

Sympathies were very much with the GLC, to the extent that attempts were made in the Commons to introduce a bill to legalise 'Fares Fair'. Although it passed its first reading, it would proceed no further, leaving the stage set for a one day strike on 10 March, which shut down the entire network, followed by a 100 per cent fare increase on 21 March, which can be summarised as follows:

- 10p, 20p, 30p and 40p fares were doubled, 80p being the maximum; Red Arrow fares were doubled to 40p (although later reduced to 30p), and child fares were increased from 5p to 10p. Airbus fares remained at £2
- the maximum Sunday fare in the GLC area was increased to 40p
- the cost of bus passes was increased by 100 per cent

An LT Service Announcement dated March 1982 spelt out what this would mean for Londoners in the longer term:

Passenger demand is likely to drop by about 20 per cent following the March fare increases. Since the frequency of service provided is geared to the level of demand, London Transport plans to meet the required cost savings by making reductions to the scheduled frequency of most bus services "across the board" – in line with the expected reduced level of patronage; by doing so, the need to withdraw routes is kept to a minimum. A few changes have already been made; others are planned for April, but the bulk of the frequency reductions will take place from Saturday, 31 July…these reductions have been approved, in broad terms, by the Greater London Council…

Overall it is planned to reduce the scheduled level of bus services by 15 per cent during 1982, from 201 million miles per annum to about 172 million. At present, only about 95 per cent of the scheduled service can be manned, but it is London Transport's intention fully to man the new schedules and so increase reliability by keeping to a minimum the cancellations caused by staff shortage. This means that the reduction in actual service provided will be 10 per cent as between the beginning and end of 1982, and the total bus miles to be operated during 1982 will be only about 5 per cent less than in 1981.

Although the QUANTITY of service will decrease, London Transport is determined to improve service QUALITY. This will be achieved by reallocating services to garages where the new schedules can – as far as is practicable – be fully staffed, so that service cancellations are kept to the minimum, and by strengthening supervision of services, ensuring that buses run as close to time as traffic conditions will allow.

The huge increase in ridership that followed the introduction of 'Fares Fair' was lost. A second strike, almost as damaging as the first, took place on 28 June, and this led to those 31 July service changes being deferred. They eventually came into force on 4 September.

The arguments around 'Fares Fair' rumbled on throughout the year, and in the summer, the GLC canvassed the public as to its views on London's transport as a precursor to the submission of its plans for 1983/84 to government. Finding that over 75 per cent of respondents were in favour of 'Fares Fair', a fresh scheme involving a 25 per cent fares reduction was slated for introduction in April 1983.

Bus 237
REDUCED FARE
FROM 31st JULY

The limit of the 20p adult fare on Bus 237 between Feltham Station and Lower Feltham (Three Horseshoes) will be extended to the first pair of bus stops in Sunbury Road (near the footpath to Denison Road) on through buses to and from Sunbury Village. This will bring fares more into line with those charged on Bus 237 journeys terminating at Lower Feltham (Chertsey Road).

In amongst all the news about fare increases, a crumb of comfort was found for passengers on the 237. It might be assumed that representations had been made about the disparity referred to on the poster, so this A4 sized advance publicity panel would have been posted at bus stops along the affected section of route. Copies might also have been found on the Routemasters working the 237; at Hounslow, which was represented on a daily basis, and possibly Stamford Brook, which supplied vehicles on Saturdays only at that time.

Vehicle news – single deck fleet

Two Dodge nineteen seater minibuses with Rootes bodywork, A1 and A2, were the only new vehicles to record in this category in 1982. The pair were despatched to Potters Bar to replace the Transits on the PB1.

Plymouth City Transport Leyland National 22 (SCO 422L) was acquired for conversion to a 'Sales & Information' bus, replacing SPB753.

Disposals accounted for the last BSs and a number of BLs. By the start of 1983, of the sixty-four left in stock, less than thirty were in daily service. Apart from MBS217, which had been resident at Chiswick for experimental purposes, the remaining Merlins and Swifts were awaiting sale.

The two Dodge S56s with Rootes nineteen-seat bodywork were delivered in December 1982, though not taken into stock until the following month and not put into service until 21 March. There were various difficulties which necessitated their return to Dodge, to such an extent that it was the end of 1983 before there was any consistent service from them. A1 (NYN 1Y) was photographed at Darkes Lane bus station in Potters Bar in or around 1984. The PB1 became a non-LT route in June 1986, and the pair were moved onto other work.

Vehicle news – double deck fleet

A further 357 vehicles were added to the fleet; 280 Titans, the highest being T676, and the final Metrobuses from the 1981 order, taking them up to M805. The design of the Metrobus radiator grille was altered from M706 onwards, while Titans lost the circular grille badge in favour of a plain Leyland nameplate from T426 on.

Comparison of the different radiator grille stylings on Titans from T426 on is afforded by these views. In the first photo, T5 (WYV 5T) was working the 165, on its way to Rainham and photographed in Main Road, Romford. This is how the type looked when first put into service; it is 19 October 1979, ten months after introduction. T5 was saved for preservation by Stagecoach, who have it as a special events vehicle based with the West Scotland fleet in Ayr, carrying fleet number 19905. Next, T508 (KYV 508X) demonstrates the revised styling as it makes its way along Minories towards Aldgate bus station on 27 March 1982. The Metrobus in the background will visit there also, then head north to Wood Green on the 67.

Given that London was the largest of the few operators investing in the Titan and bearing in mind the effect on the Workington plant, LT decided to continue with the Titan and Mark 1 Metrobus for the time being, and orders were accordingly placed during the year for delivery in 1983.

The cull of Fleetlines continued at an even faster rate, sales totalling 479. Sixty-one RMs, along with three RMAs and four RMCs were also sold (although around 100 were not officially recorded as disposed of by LT until 1983). In addition, two separate contracts were let for the breaking up of withdrawn RMs, W North of Sherburn-in-Elmet dealing with around sixty, and Vic Berry of Leicester a further 100, at Aldenham itself.

After overhaul and repainting, the much-awaited reappearance of RM1 took place at the North Weald rally at the end of May. The trend for turning RMs into Showbuses continued, with several examples unveiled during the year.

Peckham lost its MDs in September, leaving Plumstead as the sole operator of the type. But with new Titans arriving from November, it was clear there was no future for them, and of the forty-six still licensed for service at the end of 1982, all were withdrawn within the first six months of 1983.

In a photograph taken after 'Showbus' status had been achieved and therefore displaying the results of the work lavished upon it by the staff at Croydon since 1980, RM1000 (100 BXL) was employed on the 60 (Croydon (Sugar Loaf)-Streatham Hill), which was introduced in September 1982.

Service news

In the first three months of the year, no fewer than nineteen routes were converted to one person operation, with Titans replacing Fleetlines. Six more were started, projected to be completed by October, and there would be various other instances as 1982 progressed.

The first set of twenty-one service changes took place on 24 April. Of these, four were completely withdrawn and a further nine lost either part of the route or (in some cases, and) operation at certain times of the day.

This was just the hors d'oeuvre before the main course of events on 4 September, which have been described as 'the biggest overnight transformation [of services in London] ever experienced'. As the pronouncements in March indicated, the changes were to be designed to make more effective use of resources, directing them towards the greatest demand whilst still making the very necessary economies. A total of 210 routes were affected. A small number involved nothing more than a change of garage, though rather more saw type changes, and the RM was one of the bigger casualties, since a reduction in crew operation was one means of reducing costs and mitigating the worst effects of the changes. There were more than 1,300 vehicle movements, and close to twenty route numbers vanished overnight. The net effect was to reduce the overall size of the fleet by around 600, and Fleetlines accounted for the lion's share of these.

However, the decrease in the numbers of passengers was eventually not as great as had been predicted, and planning started once again in the summer to increase provision where it was most needed, with implementation completed by January 1983.

The sheer volume of September changes precludes a more detailed examination in these pages, but a few others of note during the year included the end – for the time being – of LT operation of its northernmost route, the 84 from New Barnet, which passed to London Country, at whose St Albans garage it terminated. LT introduced the 84A (Barnet Church-Turnpike Lane), but also took over London Country's 313 (Enfield Town-St Albans). With the Potters Bar-St Albans section covered by the 84, LT revised the 313 in September to start back from Chingford. In Surrey, reductions in revenue support led to the 164 being cut back from Epsom to Banstead (the slack being taken up by London Country 418) and the 280 from Banstead to Belmont.

One interesting new route introduced on 4 December was the 201. London Underground had axed all but the peak hour services on the Central line between Epping and Ongar, and the 201, extended (except evenings) to Loughton, and on Sundays to Buckhurst Hill station, replaced them. Four years later it would be tendered by Essex County Council and won by West's Coaches, thus ending its association with London Transport.

Finally, the former Midland Red D9s of Obsolete Fleet made a reappearance for the duration of the Christmas Lights displays in central London. Special service 12L ran in the evenings between Trafalgar Square and Marble Arch from 18 November, the final workings taking place on 1 January 1983.

Other events

The front end of DMS963 was removed and installed at the London Transport Museum, allowing visitors the chance to take the driver's seat and work the controls.

Unsurprisingly, there was talk in Westminster of relieving the GLC of its powers in respect of London Transport. At the same time, a Commons Select Committee published a report in July suggesting the formation of a Metropolitan Transport Authority in which the GLC, Department of Transport, London boroughs and councils would each have a role.

A Bus and Coach Council campaign towards the end of 1982 sought to attract more people onto public transport with the slogan 'We'd all miss the bus', which seemed well-timed considering what London had gone through in previous months. It was carried by various London vehicles, each bearing different subsidiary messages:

- D1063 ('We carry more passengers per gallon')
- D2593 ('45% of London households have no car')
- M382 ('Ease the rush, use the bus')
- RM319, 968 and T569 ('Would you rather overtake me or 22 cars?')

M423 was another to be similarly treated.

Plumstead's T569 (NUW 569Y) was one of the vehicles selected to carry the special livery for the Bus and Coach Council. It was parked up in the garage yard in March 1983. The core service on the 177 was from Woolwich Arsenal to Waterloo, with some early journeys extended from Abbey Wood in the east to Fleet Street in central London. It would be a further seven months before the introduction of the peak hours 177 Express (Thamesmead-County Hall), upon which two Titans (T112/13) in a special livery would be employed.

B20 FLEETLINES

The final 400 Fleetlines were ordered for delivery in 1975-76 (although in reality DM2646 did not arrive until August 1978). They comprised a mix of DMS and DM types, but all were to B20 'quiet bus' specification, and received fleet numbers DMS2247-2526 and DM2527-2646. They were easily recognisable from the rear, which had been redesigned to incorporate two chimneys, with angled exhaust grilles and air inlets, and while LT was already disposing of large quantities of the earlier Fleetlines, a sell-off of the B20s would not begin in earnest until 1991.

Shepherds Bush housed over twice as many Fleetlines than Routemasters at this time, and one of the former, DMS2276 (THX 276S), was caught on camera as it headed for Harrow Road and Scrubs Lane, which is about as close as it is possible to get to Willesden Junction where the 220 terminated. The BBC's Television Centre can be seen in the background. DMS2276 entered Aldenham for overhaul in April 1982, after which it was posted away, firstly to Brixton, and then to Stockwell.

On a sunny 22 October 1981 DMS2457 (OJD 457R) was to be found at Arnos Grove underground station on the 34 service that linked Barnet and Whipps Cross (with Monday-Friday peak hour extensions to Leytonstone). It would shortly be stored before heading to Aldenham for overhaul, after which it would move south of the river for the remainder of its career in London. It was sold to Bullock, Cheadle, in late 1991, and had five years there before it was scrapped.

58 • LONDON'S BUSES, 1979–1994

Not all B20s saw regular service, DMS2410 (OJD 410R) being a case in point. After moving from Enfield to Aldenham for overhaul, it was posted to Catford where, eighteen months later, it was relegated to the role of trainer. Stints at Sidcup and Camberwell followed before it received a new paint job (December 1987), after which it went back into service at Stockwell and Merton before withdrawal in June 1991. This view, on 13 July 1986, dates from its days at Sidcup, but I found it hiding at the back of Bromley garage.

THE VIEW FROM THE REAR

Looking somewhat the worse for wear, Metropolitan MD160 (OUC 160R) was found in Holles Street, the stand for services terminating at Oxford Circus, in company with RM1027. It had moved to Plumstead in October 1981; withdrawn a year later, it was one of several MDs to subsequently enter service with Whippet Coaches of Fenstanton, Cambridgeshire.

The distinctive rear end of the Leyland Titan is shown on two consecutively numbered vehicles, T127/28 (CUL 127/28V), pictured when brand new at the Longbridge Road garage in Barking in January 1980. In twelve years' time, they would be sold to Merseybus.

One of the last Fleetlines to retain the white upper deck relief, having been in service for over seven years, D2546 (THX 546S) was photographed on lay-over in York Way in May 1985 whilst employed on the 77A (King's Cross-Putney Heath). The twin chimneys and air inlets, the most obvious characteristics of the B20, can be plainly seen. What is not quite so evident is the wide-angle lens set in the rear window to assist visibility for the driver. D2546 was withdrawn in 1991 and scrapped the following year.

RM113 (VLT 113) would normally have worked through to Victoria, but is in the process of turning short at Drake Street, High Holborn on 14 January 1987. Snow in central London is a comparatively rare phenomenon.

1983

This was the year of London Transport's Golden Jubilee, and various vehicles were adorned in celebratory liveries.

There was some good news for LT and the GLC, in that a proposed fares reduction on this occasion passed the scrutiny of the High Court because the package contained a commitment to a Travelcard scheme which held the promise of a more integrated ticketing system. The Conservatives were returned to power at Westminster in June with a bigger majority, bringing their proposed transport reforms a step closer, for London as well as the rest of the UK. A threat to LT's dominance was posed by the Associated Minibus Operators Ltd (AMOS), but on a lighter note, many events were held to celebrate the organisation's Golden Jubilee.

LT convened a public hearing in March at which the claims of AMOS, to operate four cross-city routes at intervals of between 2-4 minutes between 0700 and midnight were heard. The independent inspector turned down the licence application, which then went to appeal. With LT, the GLC, the unions and taxi drivers' representatives all firmly against the scheme, it proceeded no further.

Fares were reduced by 25 per cent on average across both bus and underground networks and zonal Travelcards introduced from 22 May. It was hoped that this would also produce a beneficial spin-off with regard to British Rail services and ticketing. Zonal changes saw City and West End brought together to form Central, a closer alignment between rail and bus and bus and tube ticket prices. The outer zone 3 on buses was split into separate sections – 3a, 3b and 3c – on the underground. It was hoped that this would transform the estimated loss of one million journeys a day into seventy million new journeys a year across the bus and tube networks. As it turned out, the popularity of these new measures was assured, and receipts were well in excess of LT forecasts. For all zones, the Travelcards cost £12 weekly, £46 monthly, £132 quarterly or £480 annually.

The first session of the new Parliament contained proposals for a Bill, to be preceded by a White Paper, that would transfer LT away from GLC control, the Department of Transport being given the responsibility for oversight of what would be known as London Regional Transport (LRT), with separate bus and underground divisions. Other operators could apply to operate services, either by agreement with LRT or, bypassing the new organisation completely, by application to the Traffic Commissioners. In a further swipe at the GLC, a commitment in the manifesto sought to abolish it by 1986.

It is worth looking in a little detail at this, as here was the start of events that set in train the seismic changes LT/LRT would undergo in the years leading to 1994. The plans as they now stood appeared to please no-one but the ruling party. The GLC felt they would return the capital to the sort of free-for-all last seen in the 1920s. A TV

RM1983 (ALD 983B) was the obvious choice to become a Jubilee bus, and indeed was the only RM to be painted gold. It was allocated to various garages during the ten months (April 1983-February 1984) it carried the livery, initially to Croydon, but subsequently to Stamford Brook, Edmonton, Tottenham, New Cross, Sidcup, Leyton, Seven Kings, Stockwell, Willesden and Ash Grove, finally ending up at Clapham. Each visit would be for one or two weeks, and usually in connection with a local Open Day. That is why it could be found outside Sidcup garage on Friday 1 July, in readiness for the weekend festivities. It was at Stockwell on 21 July, and was photographed whilst working a turn on the 88 outside the Swan public house in Stockwell Road.

documentary in July thought the plans to reduce public spending would hamper any attempt by LT to improve efficiency. *The Times* newspaper recalled the previous year's all-party Commons committee recommendation of a new metropolitan transport authority, while LT's chairman pointed out that 'the views of London Transport – the professional transport operators – should not be obscured by political argument.' For argument, it may be safely assumed that dogma was actually what he meant. GLC opposition to what amounted to a Government takeover was supported by all parties. But displaying an apparent inability to listen to warning voices, the Bill was published in December. To quote the *Surveyor* magazine, in its 8 December editorial:

> … the Government, in its haste to put certain of its policies into force – this one … by 4 April 1984 – is displaying a level of indecent haste that can only be attributed to a lack of forethought and understanding of some of the complexities of some of the policies it is embarking upon.

Vehicle news – single deck fleet

The only movement was of vehicles leaving the fleet. These comprised six of the remaining eight MB class; MBS217 was at Chiswick for experimental use and was not sold until 1987, while Camberwell's mechanical trainer MBA568 was not withdrawn until 1984, being sold for spares the following year. The very last Swift, SMS320, was sold to Blue Triangle during the year.

Vehicle news – double deck fleet

A further 150 Metrobuses arrived, taking their numbers up to M955, but they were dwarfed for the first time by Titans, of which 237 – up to T913 – were taken into stock. These included a number from the 1984 order. It was however decided that once the remaining 212 were received, there would be no more, and trials would be held of the latest types of double deck vehicles.

Seventy-eight RMs were disposed of, along with a solitary RMC, and small numbers of RMCs and RMAs. Numerically the biggest casualties were once again the Fleetlines, with a total of 501, and Metropolitans, with 118, disposals. Fire victims RML2557, T150 and T206 were broken up at Aldenham. Apart from RML2691, sold to a cosmetics company eleven years earlier, RML2557 was the first of LT's original 'red' RMLs to leave the fleet.

The DMO contingent now totalled just one, DMO3, which saw some use in connection with the Golden Jubilee open days but was withdrawn early in 1984 and sold to Guide Friday. DMs 948 and 1102 were converted to open-top at Aldenham.

Service news

Prior to the demise of the Obsolete Fleet operation, which went into liquidation in the autumn, RT1 in wartime livery was occasionally seen on tourist route 100.

Despite having been refused a licence for two years, Culturebus was finally allowed to begin operations in 1983 in competition with LT's own Round London Sightseeing

Tour (RLST) and the newly introduced London Guided Tour. Its vehicles were ex London Fleetlines painted in a yellow livery, and a hop on/hop off reboarding option was included in the offering. LT reduced its fares as a result, to £2 for the RLST and £2.75 for the Guided Tour.

Ten routes (and as a result, six more garages) were converted in full to one person operation in April, with three others on Mondays-Saturdays and two on Sundays only. The nearest any of them ventured to central London was Aldgate (the 225). A new Airbus service, the A3, was introduced at the same time, linking Heathrow with Euston.

The 177 'Thameslink Express' service began on 31 October using T112/113 in white livery with two bold upswept red stripes. It included non-stop sections between Woolwich and Elephant & Castle and limited stops thereafter to Whitehall.

Shoppers' services in the Kingston-upon-Thames area, K1 and K2, were introduced on 12 November. The K1 ran on Mondays, Thursdays and Saturdays, initially to Chessington Industrial Estate but later to Tolworth, Berrylands and Hook. The K2 worked to Tolworth on Tuesdays, Fridays and Saturdays. RM19 and RM23 were the allocated vehicles, receiving distinctive black on yellow blinds but remaining in fleet livery. 1984 was the only complete year of operation as both routes were withdrawn at the end of January 1985.

The final set of changes for 1983 mainly involved the introduction of night buses on Saturday nights/Sunday mornings.

The nearside blind reads '177 Express' but the front blinds read 'Limited Stop Special Service' for Greenwich and the Thames Barrier, so Plumstead's T112 (CUL 112V) is using the time between peak hour 177s on the special service from Victoria which began on 27 April 1985 (Mondays-Fridays) and ran daily from 26 May-8 September. This view dates from July 1985 and was taken in Trafalgar Square, the equestrian statue of George IV dominating the background.

Also visiting Sidcup on 1 July 1983 was RM8 (VLT 8), the first production RM which had been shown at the Commercial Motor Exhibition at Earls Court in September 1958. It would be a further eighteen years before it entered service, being allocated to Chiswick for experimental work in the interim. It looks to be in pristine condition, as though it has just emerged from the paintshop, although it entered service in Golden Jubilee livery in early April.

Resplendent in 1933-style livery, RM17 (VLT 17) was photographed with a 52 working en route to Notting Hill Gate in November 1983. Originally the white lower deck band was not extended around the front, but this later addition significantly improved the look of the vehicle.

Above left: DMS1933 was renumbered DS1933 (KUC 933P) in order to participate in the Jubilee celebrations. It was looking particularly fine as it worked a 109 to Purley in mid-summer. It was stored in 1984 and sold to Stevenson's of Spath in October 1985, who used it for almost a year in this livery before it was repainted.

Above right: There were four 'official' repaints into Golden Jubilee livery; besides RM1983, M57 (named *Aldenham Aristocrat*) and T747, there was T66, (WYV 66T) from Hornchurch, named *Aldenham Diplomat* and seen in Romford whilst on 248 duty.

Below: Finally, Metrobus M359 (GYE 359W) was given 1933-style livery by a painter at Southall garage as a retirement gift to his colleagues! It was photographed at Ealing Hospital in late 1983.

Other events

The Golden Jubilee celebrations were marked by open days at Aldenham, Chiswick, Acton, and several garages during the course of the year. A special logo was designed and can be seen on RM17, although it was RM8 that in April became the first of nineteen vehicles to be repainted into commemorative livery, the list also including RM1933, 2116, DMS1933 (renumbered DS1933), M359, LS194 and LS438. D2593 was given a gold band between decks and anniversary logos to go with its Bus & Coach Council advertising. Finally, D2629 was repainted into Croydon Corporation Tramway livery and was thus celebrating two anniversaries; it earned the nickname 'Chocolate Box'. RM2217, numerically the last RM, was decked out in 1965 livery, being the year it entered service, with period advertisements, and a further five RMs, plus one RML, were brought up to 'Showbus' standard.

While these came about as the result of initiatives shown by individual garages, there were four 'official' versions; RM1983 and T747 (renumbered T1983) were painted gold with a white band between decks; advertisement panels carried the messages 'We've been together now for 50 years' (the RM) and 'Leyland Builders of London's Buses for over 50 years' (T1983). M57 and T66 were given 1933-style livery and were named *Aldenham Aristocrat* and *Aldenham Diplomat* respectively.

Overall advertising liveries resurfaced in 1983 after a few years away. Asda sponsored two, T283 for its store on Tollgate Road, Beckton, and T399 for the East Ferry Road, Isle of Dogs branch. Both locations were among a number of shopping centres for which promotional leaflets and money off fares vouchers were distributed in March and April. Meanwhile, underwear manufacturers Lyle & Scott had RML2412 in a mainly grey and white scheme for Jockey Shorts and RML2444 donned red and white for Y-Fronts. The advertisement panel at the rear read Y-Back! Another Titan, T799, received a cream and brown scheme to promote the Broadway Shopping Centre in Bexleyheath.

T283 (KYN 283X) was repainted into overall advertising livery for Asda in October 1983 and was allocated to Upton Park for the 101 (North Woolwich-Wanstead). Photographed in September 1984 at the former location, it eventually returned to fleet colours in April the following year.

Right and opposite above: The pair of RMLs selected to carry advertising livery for Lyle and Scott.

In the grey and black colours adopted for Jockey Shorts, RML2412 (JJD 412D) passes Piccadilly Circus en route to Putney with a 14 working. It was originally a Country Area bus, returning to LT at the end of 1979. Sporting the red and white Y-Fronts design, RML2444 (JJD 444D) was allocated to Upton Park for the 15, and was photographed in the bus lay-by on High Street South, East Ham. It too was a former London Country bus, transferring to LT during 1978. Both vehicles returned to red livery in early 1985.

Two garages closed during the year, both on 24 June. Mortlake's allocation moved to Fulwell and Stamford Brook, while that of the smaller Riverside was split three ways, to Ash Grove, Victoria and Shepherds Bush. New premises were opened at Bakers Road, Uxbridge in December.

Restrictions on the use of old age pensioner and handicap permits in the evening peaks were lifted in March and May respectively.

The end of year statistics made welcome reading. Passenger journeys were up 11 per cent; passenger miles were up 16 per cent. Pass holders had risen by 25 per cent to 600,000, and while commuting by bus and tube had risen by 7 per cent, car use had fallen by 9 per cent.

Right: Five new bus maps appeared early in 1983, covering north west, north east, south east, south west and central services. The presentation was not liked by the travelling public, and it came as no surprise that a new version of the London-wide map would be issued in 1984.

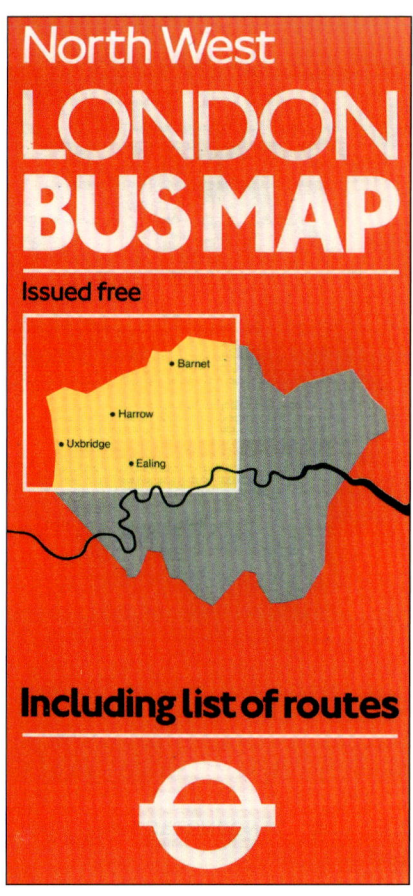

128 – THE HILLINGDON LOCAL SERVICE

On 3 September 1977 a new hourly route 128 was introduced between Ruislip station and Harefield Hospital. Paid for by Hillingdon Council and operated on their behalf by LT, it had three Bristol LH6Ls allocated to it, BL93-95, which carried yellow, rather than white, relief and Hillingdon Local Service fleetnames. A revised livery was introduced in 1981, and fleet strength was increased to four in 1983 when BL56 was refurbished prior to being assigned to the route.

All three photos were taken at Ruislip station.

Above: BL56 (OJD 56R) was brought back from the sales fleet in order to take its place on the 128. This photo, taken on the last day of 1986, shows the 'state of service' indicator above the first offside window, ostensibly to provide information to passengers waiting for the bus travelling in the opposite direction. The revised livery of 1981, with its larger yellow band and fleetname, and the yellow on green destination display, show up well here.

Opposite above: Three LSs, 222/36/40, were painted in this revised livery for the 128, with grey skirts and a greater use of yellow than before, entering service in mid July 1988. Provision of the 'state of service' indicator was discontinued, and standard blind displays were used. It was reported that the vehicles had been sold to Hillingdon Council for £11,000 each and then leased back to LBL. It later transpired that as part of an evaluation process for a new single deck bus, two Leyland Lynxes acquired for the route would be included in that plan. In the meantime, standing in the same spot as BL56, this is LS236 (THX 236S) on 1 November 1988.

Opposite below: The Leyland Lynxes entered service on the 128 from Uxbridge depot on 1 February 1989. They received the same livery as the Nationals, and ownership once again rested with Hillingdon Council. Later in the year, the Council acquired three more, formerly with Merthyr Tydfil, which were numbered LX9-11, but this is LX2 (F102 GRM), photographed on 11 November 1989.

The 128 was withdrawn in August 1991. Earlier that year Hillingdon Council had been forced to withdraw, citing the pressure on local authority finances. The five LXs were taken into LBL ownership and received fleet livery for the 607 'Express' service.

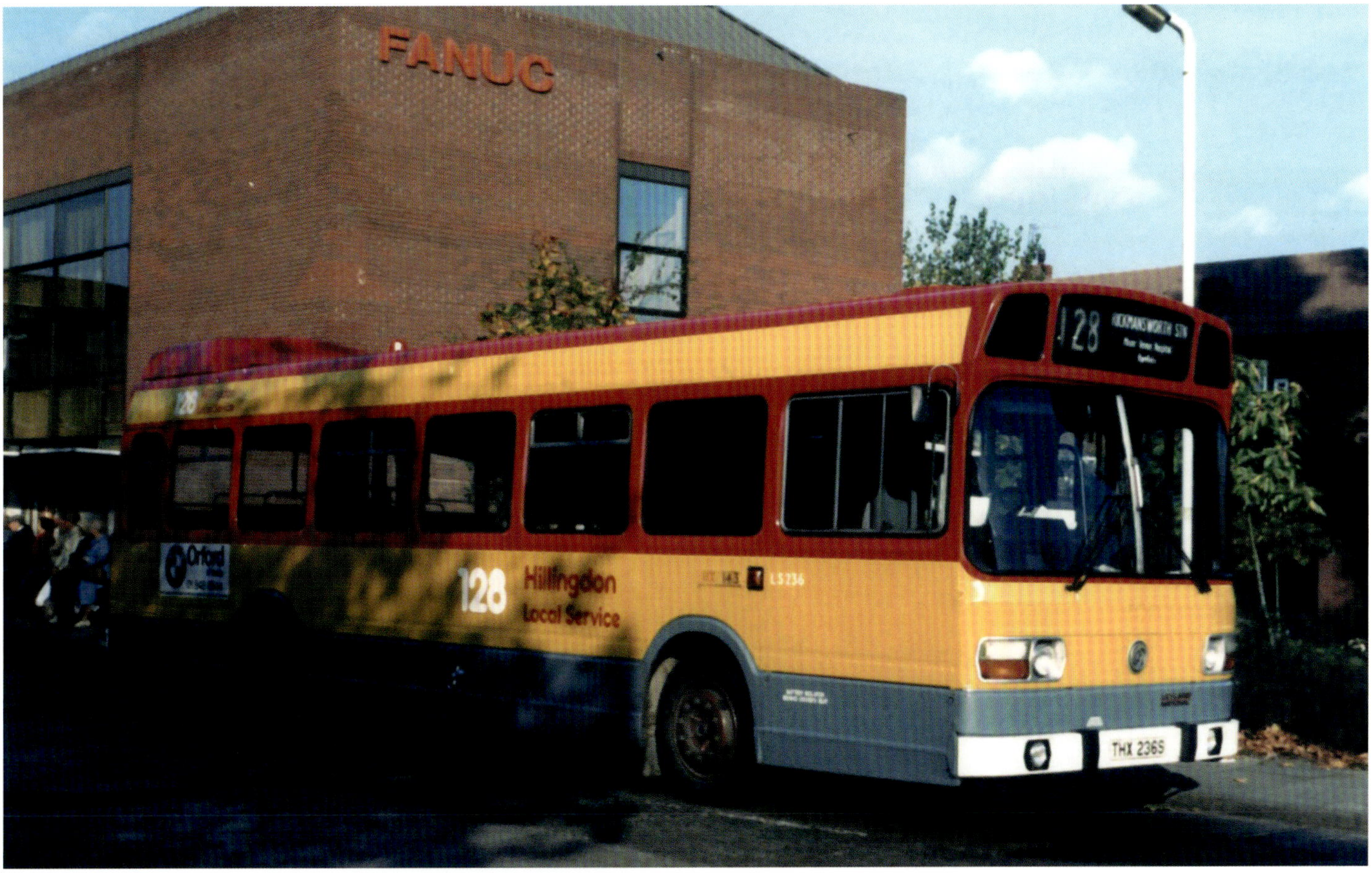
FANUC
128
128
Hillingdon
Local Service
LS236
THX 236S

128
Leyland
F102 GRM

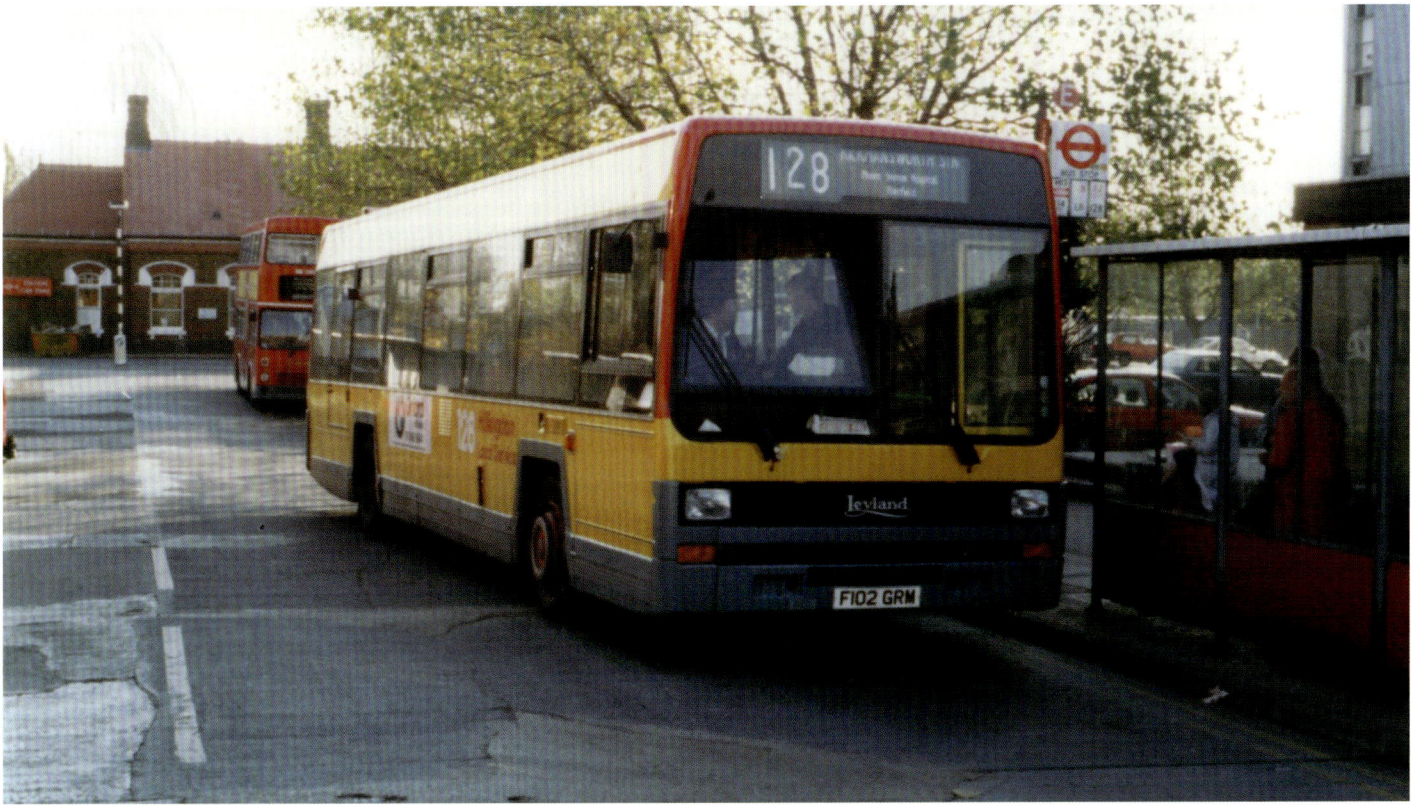

1984

The new London Wide Bus Map reverted to a simple diagram of the Greater London area on the cover, with various locations indicated.

The shape and direction of London Transport governance for the next ten years was determined as a result of measures taken in 1984. The GLC lost its authority over the London Transport Executive, LT became London Regional Transport and route tendering was introduced. .

The London Regional Transport Act entered the statute books on 26 June. Three days later, London Regional Transport was born, thus putting an end to the GLC's period of tenure, which had begun on 1 January 1970. A new Board had already been put in place, and one of its key functions was to separate bus and underground activities into separate subsidiaries. It was further proposed that a tendering process would allow other interested parties to bid to run services to the specifications laid down by LRT; thirteen routes were chosen, although one, the 493, was with London Country and was subsequently withdrawn from the process as Orpington area routes were due to receive a major makeover. All were suburban in nature, geographically remote from each other, and broadly speaking comprised seven north of the Thames and five to the south. Bids were required by November, and the winners would be announced in 1985.

In July, the White Paper 'Buses' was published. Privatisation of National Bus Company constituents was more than just a peripheral issue for LRT. London Country, now split into four separate companies, and others such as Eastern National, whose area bordered Greater London, could be expected to take more than a passing interest in the competition for routes.

The deregulation of bus services that was to take place everywhere else in mainland Britain in 1986 was ruled out so far as London was concerned, where the tendering process was deemed to suffice, but only, it seemed, for the time being. As was regularly pointed out to a Secretary of State for Transport Nicholas Ridley, a man not renowned for listening to advice, the prospect of competition on the capital's most profitable routes and the detrimental effect it would have on already chronic congestion should have been enough to deter even the most ardent free marketeer. But the Conservatives would return to the issue periodically during the next nine years, and eventually it was only when Labour won its landslide victory in 1997 that deregulation in London was kicked into the long grass, from which it has never re-emerged.

A reorganisation of the eight districts took place with effect from 2 January 1984 with the closure of Tower and Watling. Their garages were redistributed into the six remaining districts, and consequentially Stockwell transferred from Abbey to Wandle. The new set-up looked like this:

ABBEY – AF - Putney, AG - Ash Grove, B - Battersea, CF - Chalk Farm, CT - Clapton, GM - Victoria, HT - Holloway, S - Shepherds Bush, WD - Wandsworth, X - Westbourne Park

CARDINAL – AC - Willesden, AV - Hounslow, FW - Fulwell, HL - Hanwell, HW - Southall, NB - Norbiton, ON - Alperton, UX - Uxbridge, V - Stamford Brook, W - Cricklewood

FOREST – AP - Seven Kings, BK - Barking, BW - Bow, L - Loughton, NS - North Street, PR - Poplar, RD - Hornchurch, T - Leyton, U - Upton Park, WH - West Ham, WW - Walthamstow

LEASIDE – AD - Palmers Green, AE - Hendon, AR - Tottenham, E - Enfield, EM - Edmonton, EW - Edgware, FY - Finchley, HD - Harrow Weald, MH - Muswell Hill, PB - Potters Bar, SF - Stamford Hill, WN - Wood Green

SELKENT – BX - Bexleyheath, NX - New Cross, PD - Plumstead, PM - Peckham, Q - Camberwell, SP - Sidcup, TB - Bromley, TL - Catford, WL - Walworth

WANDLE – A - Sutton, AK - Streatham, AL - Merton, BN - Brixton, ED - Elmers End, N - Clapham, SW - Stockwell, TC - Croydon, TH - Thornton Heath

Vehicle news – single deck fleet

1984 was the year of the double decker bus, as there were no new service buses to record under this heading. LRT leased a DAF/Berkhof Esprit coach from Ensignbus for the Tours and Charter division, which became TC1.

Most of the fourteen members of the BL class leaving the fleet this year saw further service in Guernsey.

When first received in September 1984 B593 XNO was not assigned a fleet number. This only came in 1985, along with a livery change; initially the four coloured bands were narrower and were flared out towards the rear. When this photo at King's Cross station was taken it had become TC1, before a further renumbering took place the following year to DB1. It was returned off lease to Ensign in 1990.

Vehicle news – double deck fleet

A further 150 Metrobuses joined the fleet, numbered M956-1105. Twenty-four of them, M1006-29, replaced M431-46 on Airbus services, while a further twelve, M1044-55, were destined for Original London Sightseeing Tour (OLST) duties, ousting B20 Fleetlines. The last batch of Titans, T914-1125, was put into service, and five others, new to the West Midlands PTE in 1978 as 7001-05, were acquired, becoming T1126-30.

The much vaunted trial of new deckers got underway during the year. Of the twelve vehicles, representing four different types, eleven were delivered but only eight entered service in 1984. Allocated to Stockwell for the 170 (Roehampton- Aldwych), N87 (Victoria or Trafalgar Square-Clapham Common or Streatham) and on Sundays, the 44 (Mitcham-London Bridge/Aldgate) were Leyland Olympian/ECW L1-3, Hestair-Dennis Dominator/Northern Counties H1-3, MCW Metrobus Mark 2 M1441/42 and Volvo Ailsa B55 Mk 3/Alexander V1-3. H1-3 and V3 appeared in 1985, and it was V3 that attracted the most interest as its exit door was positioned at the rear rather than the more usual centre, and it would enter service on crew route 77A. It was decided not to introduce a new sub-class for the Ms, whose fleet numbers therefore followed on from the end of the existing order for Mk 1 stock. A third, M1443, designated as Mark 3, was also expected.

Withdrawals accounted for almost 160 RMs, thus outnumbering the DM and DMS leavers by more than fifty. The most spectacular departure was of RM1536, which 'fell' into a quarry in Kent during an episode of the BBC's *The Young Ones*. Early B20 Fleetline casualties were fire or accident-damaged. A single RMC and RMA, but some thirteen RCLs, left the fleet, while the unique rear-engined FRM1, and Fleetline DMS1, joined the London Transport Museum. It was the end of the line for the DMO class with the disposal of DMO3, and twenty-two more MDs were sold, with the remaining six going in 1985.

Aldenham converted RM1288 to give it an offside staircase that might make it attractive to potential overseas buyers.

RML2492 (JJD 492D) joined the ranks of advertising vehicles during the year with this yellow and lime green livery for Underwoods. Though tame by comparison with some modern day schemes, it was considered controversial enough for LRT to stop the practice for several years. It was seen at Liverpool Street, waiting to start the return journey to Hammersmith, in late 1984. It regained red livery in August 1985.

Service news

Six Leyland Nationals were given a special livery for the 'Docklands Clipper' service from Mile End to Cubitt Town via Limehouse which began in January, opening up much of the new Enterprise Zone being built there.

Kingston closed as an operational garage on 13 January, its vehicles moving to Norbiton, but the premises remained in use as a store and the bus station element was unaffected. The new Edgware depot was officially opened on 13 October, with Norwood following a fortnight later, allowing the closure of Streatham.

On 25 February, Hammersmith Bridge had to be closed following the failure of the roller bearings in one of its southern towers. The 9 and 33 were split in two to work either side of the stricken crossing, and the 72 diverted. It was partially re-opened, at least for buses, at the end of March, but weekend closures continued to affect the bridge for the rest of the year.

Considerable changes to night bus routes took place on 13/14 April and 26/27 October, with greater use of one-person operation.

'Stationlink' began in May, a peak hour Mondays-Fridays and all day weekends service, stopping only at King's Cross, Waterloo, Euston and St Pancras stations and worked by Red Arrow LSs. A second route, utilising Titans, began around the same time, namely an all-night route between Euston, Victoria and Heathrow dubbed 'Rail-Air'. They were respectively the 555 and 556, although the latter number could not be displayed on Ts.

Services provided by operators other than LRT included one operated by New Bharat Coaches between Northolt and Heathrow, geared to workers' shifts at the airport, and the link between Victoria rail and coach stations operated by Victoria Shuttle Service Ltd.

As LT introduced its new Metrobuses to the OLST, there was ever-increasing competition from operators that had taken advantage of the plentiful supply of second-hand Fleetlines ... from LT itself! Cityrama, Crouch End Coaches, Culturebus, Ebdon's, London Pride, The Londoners and Maybury's ran more than fifty DMSs, leading LT to introduce a London By Night Tour, operated by Ms from Victoria and Battersea.

Below left: The broad white stripe applied to 'Docklands Clipper' Leyland Nationals such as LS165 (THX 165S) was enough, in London terms, to make them stand out from the crowd. It was waiting at the bus lay-by in Grove Road, Mile End, before returning to Cubitt Town.

Below right: Red Arrow National 2 LS463 (GUW 463W) was pictured at Waterloo whilst working the 555, a new service introduced in May 1984 that was financially supported by British Rail which called at Euston, St Pancras and King's Cross before returning to Waterloo. Whilst the 'Stationlink' logo is clearly displayed, it was the drivers who opted to also show the route number 555, which had been originally intended for internal purposes only. The service was withdrawn on Friday evenings from the start of 1986, and completely in the following June, after British Rail withdrew its subsidy.

ALTERNATIVE VEHICLE EVALUATION – DOUBLE DECKERS

Left: Having already amassed 1,440 Metrobuses, the arrival on the scene of the two Mark II examples was felt to be special enough to merit a trial along with the Olympians, Dominators and Volvo-Ailsas. Differences between the two types were not particularly visible from the outside, apart from the restyled front end (note there is no dropped windscreen on the nearside). M1441 (A441 UUV) was fitted with a Gardner 6LXB engine with a Voith D851 gearbox; M1442 received the Cummins L10 engine and a Maxwell gearbox. Eleven of the twelve triallists were mainly assigned to the 170 (Aldwych-Roehampton), and M1441 has just left the former location in May 1985 and will shortly turn into the Strand; Australia House is on the left.

Below: The Hestair-Dennis Dominators were expected in the spring of 1984, but production delays meant that it was November before they arrived at Chiswick. H2 was the first to be licensed for the necessary type training, followed by H3, and this led to their being the last to enter service on the 170, in February 1985. They were bodied by Northern Counties, fitted with Gardner 6LXB engines, and were not dissimilar in design to the Greater Manchester PTE standard. This is H2 (B102 WUW) crossing Westminster Bridge on its way back to Aldwych early in its career; County Hall can be seen in the background, where at this time the GLC would be playing out the last twelve months of its existence. It would be fair to say that the Dominators came out of the trial the least well of the four types, and their use was, to say the least, spasmodic.

Above: The Leyland Olympian was the replacement for the Bristol VR and by the time LT started looking for successors to the Mark I Metrobus and Leyland Titan, around 1,000 were already in service around the country, built at Bristol at first before construction was moved to Workington in 1983. Bodied by ECW, the three entered service in March and April 1984. L1 had a Leyland TL11 engine with the Hydracyclic gearbox, while L2 and L3 were fitted, like M1441, with the Gardner 6LXB coupled to the Voith D851 gearbox. L3 (A103 SYE) was seen in Trafalgar Square in June 1985.

Below: By virtue of its rear staircase and door, the most notable of all the deckers taking part in the Alternative Vehicle Trial was Alexander R bodied Volvo-Ailsa V3 (A103 SUU). Confined to crew-route 77A because of safety concerns around the operation and oversight of the rear door, it entered service on 18 March 1985. It was seen in Kingsway, having just passed Holborn underground station whilst on its way to Clapham Junction. Note the extra panelling at the rear for the staircase. This stretch of road formed part of my daily commute at the time; unusually, it appears relatively uncongested.

ON THE TOURIST TRAIL

> As LT sold off its Fleetlines, various operators saw an opportunity to give them a second career in the capital. LT bolstered its sightseeing fleet with them for a while, but a variety of liveries would now enliven the central London tourist scene.

Culturebus began operations in 1983 with six Fleetlines acquired that April. They were painted in a distinctive yellow livery and twenty-one places to be visited en route were listed on the panels between decks. In its former life, this had been DMS1476 (MLH 476L), new to Turnham Green in August 1973 and seen here in 1983 on the Victoria Embankment, having just emerged from the Blackfriars underpass. The apparent absence of any customers leads one to suspect that it was making its way into the centre to start work for the day. Culturebus was taken over by Trathens during 1984 and by Ensignbus in July 1985. The name lingered on for a while, but MLH 476L returned to Ensignbus and worked for them, and briefly for Southend Transport, for a further five years before making its final journey to the scrapyard.

Below left: London Pride tour buses were not difficult to spot, owners Emmerheath Ltd having opted for this pink, orange and white livery. They first took to the streets in 1984, with a fleet that would ultimately comprise seven Fleetlines, three of which had been converted to open-top format. This is DMS648 (MLK 648L), new to LT in May 1973 and withdrawn in June 1982, which had already seen service with Culturebus before donning London Pride colours. This view in Piccadilly Circus dates from 1984; within twelve months the company had merged with Ensignbus, at which point its blue and silver livery became the order of the day, but the London Pride name was retained. MLH 648L was eventually sold in 1987, and was later acquired by Thames TV, appearing in 'The Bill'.

Below right: DMS2101 (KJD 101P) entered service at Thornton Heath in May 1976 but after less than 5½ years in service it was withdrawn in October 1981, passing to Ensignbus. It was sold in November 1982, along with a number of others, to London Cityrama, which was an operating unit of Limebourne Coaches. By the summer of 1986, Cityrama had amassed seventeen DMSs, of which three were open-top examples. In 1993, Cityrama was acquired by Ensignbus, and the fleet merged with that of London Pride. Grosvenor Gardens, opposite Victoria bus station in SW1, was an important focal point for sightseeing tour buses, and that is where KJD 101P was waiting for the off in the summer of 1985.

Still in Grosvenor Gardens but in August 1984, and quite a queue has built up behind Ebdon's TGX 813M, the former DMS813. New in January 1974, it was finally withdrawn in August 1983, passing to Ensignbus at the end of the year. It was converted to an open-topper and then sold on to Ebdon's, a Sidcup based coach operator. A fleet of fourteen DMSs was quickly built up during 1984, but operations passed to Ensignbus at the end of 1985. Nonetheless, TGX 813M had several more years servicing the tourist population before being exported to the USA in late 1991.

The Bristol VR was a far from common sight in London, unproven as it was in the capital's traffic, but Cityrama clearly felt confident enough to acquire a couple of Series 1 models from APT (Lincoln) for their sightseeing fleet in April 1984. New to West Yorkshire in 1969, they were the former VR10/11, and it is the latter, XWX 56G, pictured as it turned into Parliament Square on 4 August 1984. Still in APT livery, it would be repainted in time for the 1985 season, and it was withdrawn and scrapped in 1991.

The 1984 vehicle order included twelve Metrobuses for an upgrade to the Sightseeing fleet. M1044-55 received branding to emphasise that this was *the* original tour, and were kitted out with public address systems, racks for publicity leaflets, and tachographs. M1055 (A755 THV) was caught on camera in St Paul's Churchyard as it passed an interesting array of coaches, including Southdown's Plaxton Paramount 3200 bodied Leyland Tiger 1002.

1985

The Government's Transport Act received Royal Assent on 30 October. LRT received the results for the twenty-three of its routes put out to competitive tender, and discovered that it would not be responsible for fourteen of them. However, one positive was that deregulation and privatisation would not be coming to LRT yet, as it was decided that the tendering process was sufficient for now. But Nicholas Ridley ensured that he had the powers to introduce it in London at a later date if necessary. Another Act, passed in July, spelled the end for the GLC, which would be abolished in April 1986. And on a lighter note, rumours abounded as to the mystery over the non-appearance of a Metrobus Mark 3.

Work proceeded on meeting the demands of the 1984 London Regional Transport Act, which required an annual business plan, reductions in staff numbers, more driver-only routes and a cut in the projected annual deficit (for which the Government was setting a limit of £95 million by the end of the 1987/88 accounting period). The GLC took the Government to court over a demand for £280 million to run the bus and tube

RM666 (WLT 666) creates a mini tidal wave as it makes its way along Lea Bridge Road with a 38 bound for Leyton Green one November in the mid-1980s. Given the proximity of the River Lea, this is an area that has been prone to flooding in the past, most recently in October 2018.

network and won; it was deemed "unlawful, irrational and procedurally improper". That did not stop the Ministry of Transport reinterpreting the Act to allow it to retrospectively determine what should be paid by the GLC. Plans to reorganise the districts once again were also being worked upon, although the fruits of these labours would not be seen until 1987/88.

The separation of the bus and underground divisions of LRT took place on 1 April; the bus side of the operation would now be run by London Buses Limited (LBL).

It was a year of books, reports, policy documents and even a video about the direction in which the combined efforts of the Government and LRT were taking London Buses. Many emanated from the GLC, which, freed from its everyday responsibilities for LBL, could comment frankly upon the work its new masters were doing – usually in an uncomplimentary way! Mindful of the need to cut costs, coupled with an anticipated fall in bus mileage and increase in driver-only operation, LRTs business plan raised the prospect of five depot closures: Battersea, Edmonton, Poplar, Southall and Walworth. Strikes took place at certain of these, and at others, at various times during the year. Battersea, Poplar and Walworth did in fact close in early November, and the situation at Southall was exacerbated by an arson attack.
LRT was granted a two-year operating licence (instead of the usual five) when a significant proportion of its vehicles checked by Department of Transport inspectors were found to have defects.

Coming to terms with tendering

The first set of results were disappointing for LBL. It is instructive to see the issue from the point of view of LBL management, which was in little doubt as to what was needed. The December 1985 issue of the staff newsletter, *Bus Talk*, described it as 'the crunch of competition', and pulled no punches in pointing to the weaknesses LBL had to address:

> London Buses is losing its battle for jobs, that was the message, loud and clear, when half of the first 'package' of twelve tendered LBL routes went to other operators earlier this year. By 1987 a quarter of all our routes will have been put out to tender; if we carry on losing half of them some of the outer garages won't just be in trouble – they will have vanished.
>
> Tendering is all about efficiency. Each route is awarded to the operator who offers the lowest tender price for providing the service. London Buses is losing out because it can't match the prices quoted by other operators. Our costs are too high.
>
> Part of London Buses' problem is that it picks up a lot of staff benefits: from the pension scheme, through subsidised canteens and free family travel to sports and social clubs. Partly, it's because of history. LBL pay and working practices have always been the same no matter where you work in the London area. As a result we are vulnerable to competitors on the outskirts of our area who base their tenders on outer London costs. Who took those first six routes that LBL lost? Small private companies took only two. The others went to London Country and Eastern National. They were able to offer lower prices because they operate more efficiently with lower-cost crews out of lower-cost garages outside the London area.
>
> And they will go on grabbing routes unless London Buses finds ways of getting its costs down to the same kind of level.

The report was equally blunt about the steps that needed to be taken to level the proverbial playing field.

> There have been dramatic headlines about £40 pay cuts. The £40 is not an ultimatum. It is a measure of how uncompetitive we are. Certainly we need higher productivity. Certainly we need to cut overheads. Certainly we need flexibility. We probably need a graduated pay scheme to reflect the true costs of recruiting and retaining staff in the central, inner and outer areas ... There are many ways in which we *might* cut costs; they need to be evaluated thoroughly in the areas where the threat is imminent. Most of our routes which cross from London into Essex, Herts and Surrey are out to tender. Others will follow. What we all have to work on is making sure they are not lost for want of a determined effort to compete.

Another tendering round was announced in July, debated for the next few months, and finally put out for tender towards the year end with a closing date for applications in January 1986. London Country's 493 was removed from the process as it was intended that the Orpington network should undergo major revision.

Vehicle news – single deck fleet

The only new vehicles in 1985 under this heading were three Carlyle bodied Ford Transits, FS27-29, for the H2.

Greater Manchester PTE loaned one of its Dennis Domino minibuses, 1760, which received the temporary fleet number DMB1, in December for trials on the C11, though it did not enter service until the following month.

Five of the first six Leyland Nationals were sold for further service, LS1 going to Red Rover, Aylesbury, and LS2, 4 and 5 to British Airtours at Gatwick. There was only one other disposal during the year, that being the last but one Merlin, MBA568.

Vehicle news – double deck fleet

New Metrobuses received this year totalled 284, reaching fleet number M1424. There was no sign – or even news – of M1443, the Mark 3 Metrobus.

Of greater interest was the arrival of a solitary Volvo Citybus/Alexander R, C1, on a three-year lease. A fuel saving of up to 30 per cent was claimed for similar vehicles operating in Stockholm; a reservoir stored power generated by braking, which was then released when the bus was once again in motion, with the engine only cutting in when the reservoir became exhausted. Taken into stock in September after an appearance on the BBC1 science programme *Tomorrow's World*, it would be prepared for service from Palmers Green in the New Year.

Fleetline DMS2456 had been sent to Ogle Designs, Letchworth for work that would make it more passenger-friendly. This included a split-step entrance, green handrails to aid the partially sighted, a straight staircase, repositioned rear exit and glider doors and a revised, ergonomic cab design (though this was not successful, and the original cab was reinstated). It could be found on the 77/77A, though it was known to stray onto other Stockwell garage routes.

The solitary Volvo Citybus/Alexander R C1 (C101 CUL) was being prepared for service at Palmers Green in the final few months of 1985, but the extent of the modifications required to satisfy the licensing authorities meant that it did not take up service on its intended route, the 102 (Golders Green-Chingford) until July 1986. Although leased for three years, it was taken out of service and returned to Volvo in September 1987. After a brief spell in Scotland with one of the A1 Service participants, it passed to Black Prince of Leeds, and in 2007, Lord, Hull.

This offside view of DMS2456 (OJD 456R) shows the revision necessary to accommodate the new straight staircase. Based at Stockwell, which was also at this time playing host to the Olympians, Mark II Metrobuses, Hestair-Dennis Dominators and Volvo-Ailsa B55s on the Alternative Vehicle Evaluation, it was normally assigned to the 77. In this view, however, taken in Holles Street, it was on a short working of the 88 (Acton Green-Mitcham), a route I used on many occasions that was plagued by late running and bunching and which would be split before the decade was out.

Titans were being returned to British Leyland for various improvements at the rate of two a day. The former WMPTE examples, T1126-30, moved to Selkent where they were put to work on tour and express work.

On the disposals front, the Routemaster was the hardest hit class of 1985; 370 RMs left the fleet, many for scrap, along with ten RCLs and one RMC. RM1288, with its offside entrance conversion, was exported on loan to China in March, along with 'normal' RM1873. DM/DMS withdrawals were well down at just over sixty, and as previously reported, the MD class became a thing of the past. Two of the last three RTs were disposed of, leaving only RT1530, the erstwhile Chiswick skid bus.

A fire started deliberately at Southall depot on Christmas Day either destroyed or rendered completely beyond repair a total of nine Metrobuses (M23/53/71, 104/16/52/75, 235/53). Several more needed considerable repair work before they could be returned to service.

Service news

Details of tendering wins and losses are henceforth given in an appendix.

Significant route alterations took place on 2 February, 27 April, and the two biggest, on 3 August and 2 November. They were driven by the imperative of reducing costs as has already been described, although the November changes were to some extent also dictated by the need to reallocate the work from the closed depots.

The Dennis Dominators entered service on the 170 from February. When the 77A on which it had been employed since March was converted to one-person operation, Volvo-Ailsa V3 moved to the 77. The trials ended on 31 December and it seemed that the Olympians had emerged victorious, as an order for 260 was placed for delivery in 1986.

There were large scale changes to the Night Bus network in April, most notable of which was the withdrawal of the Inter-Station service and the 'Rail-Air' 556, which were replaced by the new N50, N51 and N56.

A move to display the tourist potential of certain routes more prominently began with the 15 and 23, the East Ham- Ladbroke Grove services, the 15 operating via Bank and the 23 via the Tower. Under the new arrangements, these became the 15A (Mondays-Fridays only) and 15 respectively while the 23 was dropped. Two other routes, the 52 (Victoria-Mill Hill Broadway) and the 188 (Euston-Greenwich) were similarly treated later in the year. Special summer services were run to Thorpe Park and to various seaside resorts, and closer to home, to the Thames Barrier and a 'Touristlink' service between London Zoo and the Tower.

Six new mobility routes began during the last week of October, numbered 921-926.

Various Christmas shopping services were introduced with varying degrees of success, that at Lewisham being well received, but the only route to operate on Christmas Day was once again Airbus A1 to Heathrow.

Opposite: Two views of Routemasters on the 15A. In the top picture, RML2450 (JJD 450D) in Haymarket sports the yellow between decks band and 'Via Bank' detail in the destination display in this April 1986 view. No tourist will fail to spot the large yellow advertisements now dominating the front.

Only a few RMLs received a yellow roof in addition, and the practice was quickly stopped. The only one I ever saw was RML2737 (SMK 737F), in a typically congested Trafalgar Square on 20 May 1985 when I thought my luck was out, being stranded on the wrong side of the road. Little did I realise how useful this photo could be to me thirty-five years later.

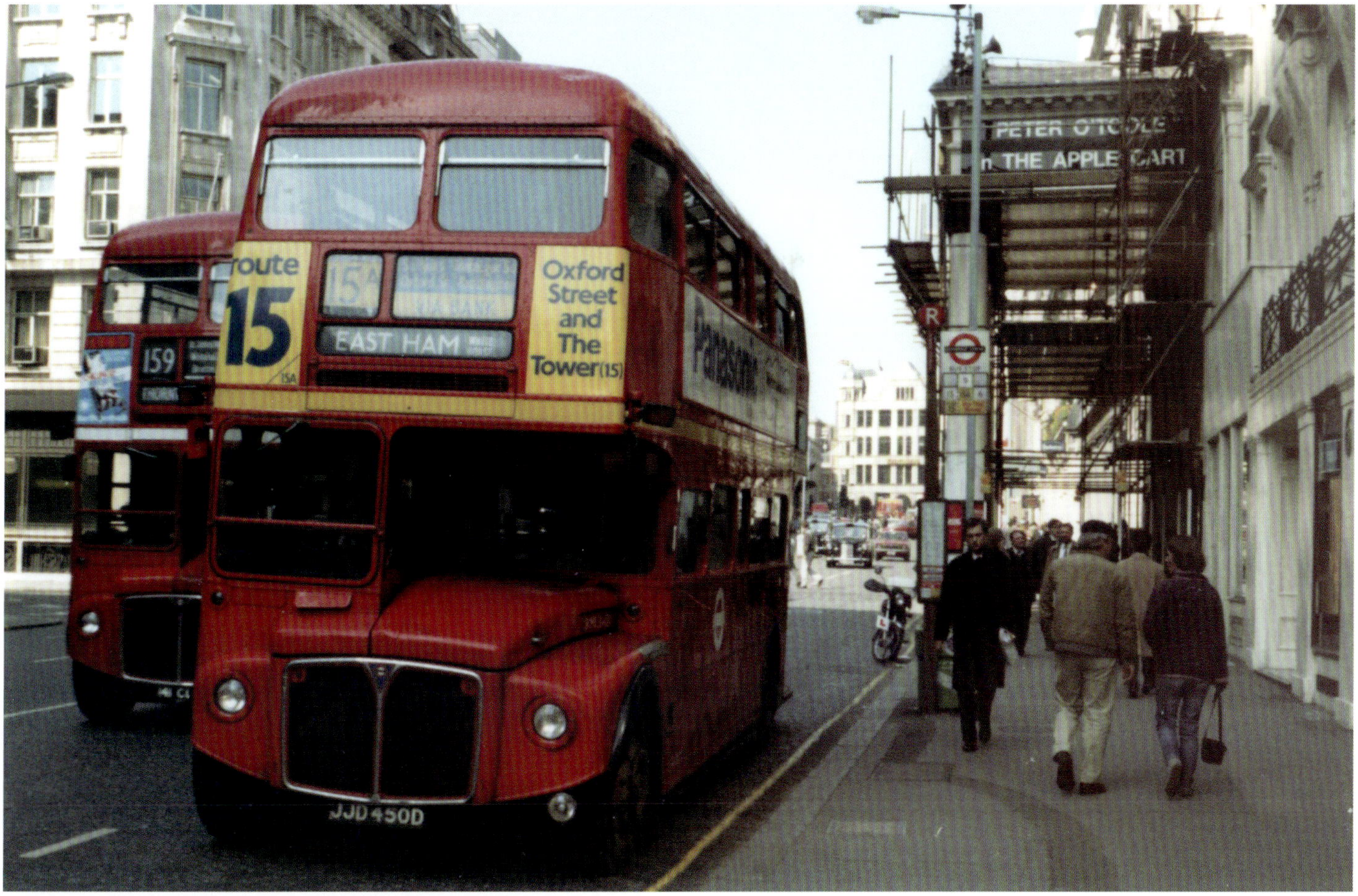
PETER O'TOOLE
in THE APPLE CART
route 15
EAST HAM
Oxford Street and The Tower(15)
Panasonic
159
JJD 450D

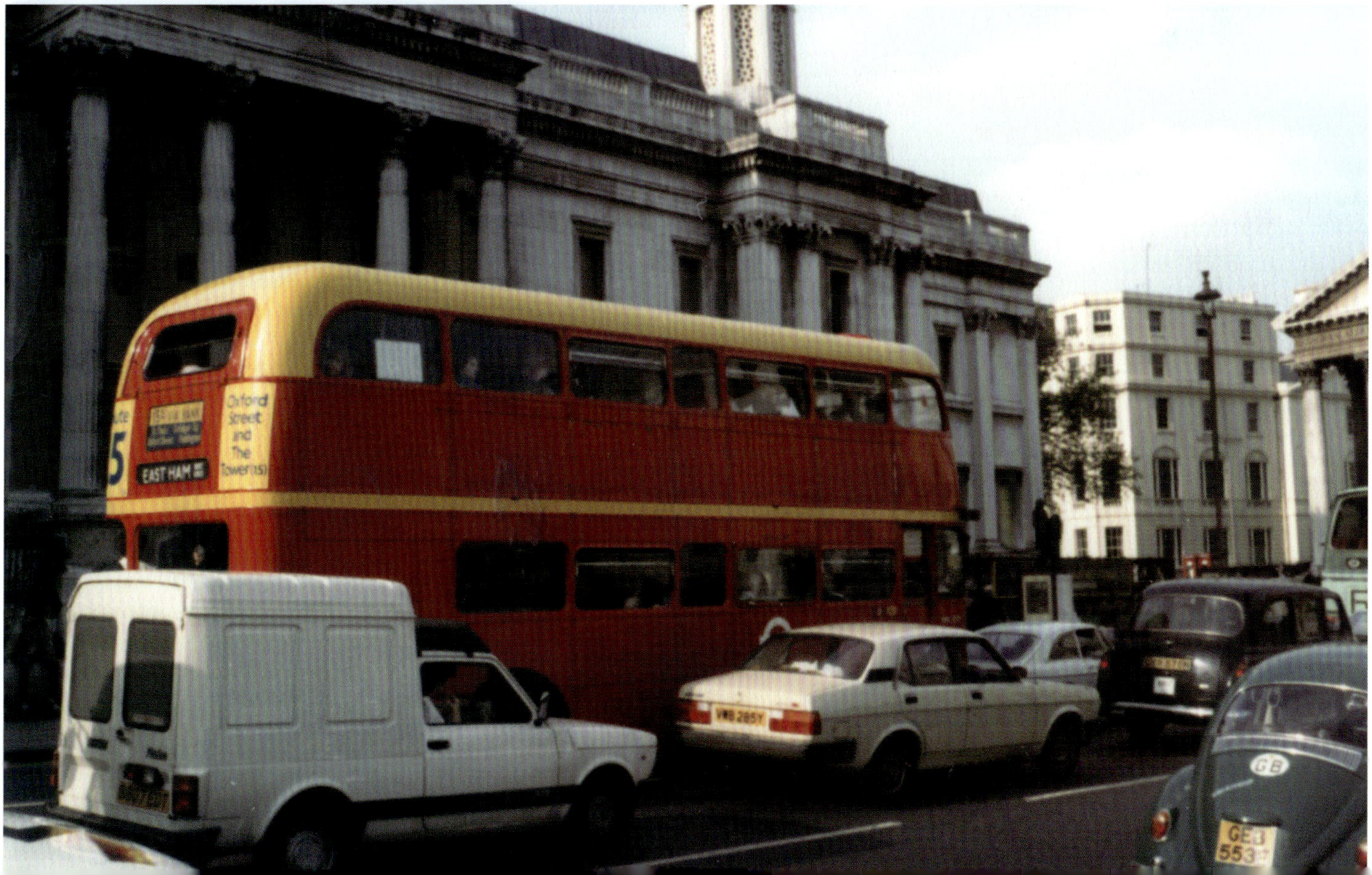
Oxford Street and The Tower(15)
EAST HAM
GB

Other events

The three RMLs and two Ts sporting overall advertising liveries, and the Croydon Tramway Centenary 'Chocolate Box' D2629, were all repainted during the year.

With an even greater need to make use of ticket machine technology to improve data recording, Timtronic, Farestram and Wayfarer machines began to appear at some depots during the year. A move to having fares represented by letters rather than figures was an issue with Gibson and Almex E machines, leading some depots to adopt their own ad hoc solutions which were then adopted across the fleet! The wide range of travelcards was further expanded by the introduction of the Capitalcard, the joint brainchild of British Rail and LRT. Available for 2, 3, 4 or 5 zone travel and in weekly, monthly, quarterly or annual versions, they joined the ranks of the Off Peak Travelcard, the Bus Pass and the Explorer, which for a one day ticket remained at £3 (adult) or £1.30 (child).

Examples of alphabetic fares on Almex E and Gibson machines, and the poster which light-heartedly attempted to explain the codes to the travelling public.

LEYLAND NATIONAL 2 – THE RED ARROWS

Above: It's February 1984, and LS438 (GUW 438W) is making its way along Aldwych with an early morning Red Arrow 513 from Waterloo to London Bridge. The first of the Leyland National 2s, it was selected to carry Golden Jubilee livery, as a result of which it was given a white roof and lining and was named *City Belle*. It went back into standard red in January 1985, and then clocked up another seventeen years on Red Arrow work before its withdrawal in 2002.

Below: LS457 (GUW 457W), pictured outside Broad Street station in 1985. Broad Street had been run down for many years, and by this time had only one service, to Watford Junction, in the peaks. It was no surprise, given the general state of dilapidation, that it closed in 1986 and was demolished before the end of the year. The 502 was introduced in September 1968, linking Waterloo and Liverpool Street, and lasted until July 1992, both stations then being linked by Red Arrow 505 though by a different route.

88 • London's Buses, 1979–1994

Meanwhile, on 25 October 1985 LS462 (GUW 462W) was picking up in Holborn, outside what at that time was the HQ of Mirror Group Newspapers during the Maxwell era. The 501 began life at the same time as the 502, in September 1968, and initially linked Waterloo with Aldgate, though this was changed in 1970 to London Bridge station, and its final outing came on 31 May 2002. LS462 had been sold to Parfitt's of Rhymney Bridge eight years previously.

'SORRY I'M NOT IN SERVICE'

The traffic is beginning to build behind M233 (BYX 233V), en route to Kew Green with a short working of the 65. The reason is plain to see, as M431 (GYE 431W), which had been heading in the opposite direction until the need to display the mysteries of its Gardner 6LXB engine to passers-by could no longer be ignored, blocks the other lane. Hopefully aid will not have been too far away.

Sometimes there is no way a bus is going to make it back into service, or even back to base, without some heavy duty assistance. That was the fate that had befallen RML2527 (JJD 527D), which had been employed on the 15 on 11 August 1987 before being laid up in Aldgate bus station. Relief was being provided by 2418L (B734 XJD), one of four Leyland Freighter T45 recovery vehicles acquired in 1984.

Completing this trio of casualties is RML2648 (NML 648E), which had been pulled up short at Euston on 8 April 1988; the seat squab is a giveaway that something is amiss. It appears to have been working the 14, which was extended from Tottenham Court Road to Euston during Monday-Friday peaks, and was blocking the boarding point for the 68, on which Croydon's Olympian L244 was employed. RML2648 was one of the fifty Routemasters given gold livery for the Queen's Jubilee; it was not withdrawn until April 2005 and was later exported to the Czech Republic as a mobile restaurant.

1986

Deregulation was finally introduced to all of Great Britain except for the area over which LRT held sway, and the first NBC company to be privatised, Devon General, was sold to its management. For LBL, it was a year of further tender losses, the end of the training school at Chiswick and the complete closure of Aldenham Works. And, as of 1 April, the GLC ceased to exist, leaving day-to-day control of the network in the hands of LRT.

First, those infrastructure changes. Training responsibilities passed to the districts, so there was no longer a need to retain the driving school at Chiswick, with its famous skid-pan. Conductor training was centralised within Abbey district. Aldenham, by contrast, no longer the centre for fleet overhauls (as doing a body/chassis separation as part of that process, as had occurred with RTs and RMs, was either impractical or impossible on newer types), had been encouraged to seek work from outside LBL, and had done so quite successfully.

But in July the axe fell, LRT announcing its closure, and Bus Engineering Ltd (BEL), created at the same time as LBL in April 1985, had the task of transferring its remaining Aldenham functions to Chiswick, something that took up much of the autumn, until Aldenham finally closed on 15 November. On the same day, certain other, lesser aspects that had been administered by LBL at their 55 Broadway HQ became the responsibility of the districts.

A new division, the Commercial Operations Unit, was set up in January, to concentrate on something more glamorous than service bus work. The Round London Sightseeing Tour was rebranded as the 'Official London Transport Sightseeing Tour' (OLTST), and weekend breaks and excursions were brought into the fold from the Tours and Charter organisation, whose coaches also moved into the new set-up, which occupied the reopened Battersea depot. In October this became London Buses Ltd (Tours & Charter), which took over the ownership of the fleet.

New subsidiaries were established following tender successes in the south west and south east. Stanwell Buses Ltd, trading as Westlink, began operating the 116, 117 and 203 from 9 August. Its principal base was in Pulborough Way, Hounslow, and twenty-eight Leyland Nationals were transferred in to form the opening allocation. A week later, Orpington Buses Ltd, trading as Roundabout, started work on the R1-R6 network with a fleet of new minibuses; the depot (though it did not offer much in the way of facilities) was on the Nugent Industrial Estate in Orpington. This was the first attempt by LRT to put the services of an entire area out to tender, and its perceived success would lead to similar schemes being put forward in future. LBL did quite well out of it all, with only the 51 (to London Country South East) and 61 (Metrobus) changing hands, although cost issues post-award led to the 261A being surrendered to Metrobus.

Five depots were closed during the year: Edmonton from 1 February; Loughton on 24 May; Southall from 9 August; Bexleyheath from 16 August; and Elmers End on 25 October. The closure at Loughton was particularly poignant, as virtually all of its routes had been lost on tender to other operators, despite the fact that the staff there had done so much to try to protect their jobs by readily accepting more flexible working practices.

Vehicle news – single deck fleet

Delays in receiving the stock for London Liner operations led to the Commercial Operations Unit leasing five coaches; LD1/2 were Leyland Tigers, while DD7-9 were DAF MB200s. All carried the Duple Caribbean 2 body. They were retained once the Metroliners and Olympians were active, receiving London Coaches fleetnames for work on tours and private hires.

No full-size saloons joined the fleet in 1986. Instead, and following the trend that was developing at speed around the rest of the country, forty-eight minibuses were put into service. Twenty-four Robin Hood bodied Iveco Daily 49.10s, RH1-24 arrived for the Orpington scheme, with the final two having dual purpose seating. Four of them – RH14/19/20/22 – were loaned to Eastbourne Buses in connection with their new minibus operation; two had returned by the end of December. The remaining twenty, along with five Volkswagen LT55/Optare City Pacers, OV1-5, were put to work on the Orpington network, for which they received a smart new maroon and grey livery and large Roundabout fleetnames on the side panels. Contrary to usual practice, they were all named, the Ivecos after birds, and the City Pacers after winds.

LRT acquired nineteen Optare City Pacers which LBL operated on their behalf on the new C1 and C20/C21 services. They wore plain red livery and were initially known

DD8 (C28 MCX) has not yet lost its London Liner branding, even though by 30 June 1986 the MCW Metroliners had taken over on the Birmingham route. Instead, it was working the IPC (International Publishing Corporation) staff bus, picking up outside the Waldorf Hotel in Aldwych for its short journey to SE1.

only by their registration numbers, D338-56 JUM, until they were welcomed into the OV class as OV6-24 in 1988.

DP1 was a Plaxton bodied DAF hired for just a week in March as a driver trainer. Unusually, this fleet number would be used again in a few years for another London Coaches DAF/Plaxton combination, and by Metroline, on a Dennis Javelin.

DAF MB200 TC1 was renumbered to the more logical DB1.

Withdrawals were few, claiming just six BLs, six Leyland Nationals (five for further service elsewhere and one following accident damage) and Transit FS19, the former radio trainer.

Vehicle news – double deck fleet

The last sixteen Metrobuses, M1425-40, took to the streets this year. Meanwhile the order for 260 ECW bodied Leyland Olympians was largely completed; a total of 229 were delivered, the highest numbered being L242. Six, L166-71, were fitted with coach seats, though this did not affect their seating capacity, which remained at sixty-eight.

With the Alternative Vehicle Evaluation complete, and the decision made to invest in the Olympian, attention turned to the remaining types. The future for Dennis Dominators H1-3 was unclear, and they remained stored at the year-end. Volvo-Ailsas V1-3 were to be retained, and moved to Potters Bar for service there, but the non-standard V3 spent much of the year out of use. It finally became plain that the Mark 3 Metrobus, which would have been M1443, was not going to materialise.

ML1-4 were the MCW Metroliners acquired for the London Liner service to Birmingham. The two further Olympians for the Eastbourne service were bodied by East Lancs, becoming LC1/2. Like the Metroliners, they were fitted with toilets.

I had to wait for three years after its arrival before I caught a glimpse of the superbly turned out Leyland PD2/East Lancs LE1 (AED 26B), which was standing outside Wandsworth depot in company with brand new DAF SB3000/Van Hool DV11 (F611 HGO).

A fascinating acquisition in July was that of a 1964 Leyland PD2/East Lancs, numbered LE1. Operated initially in Warrington Borough Transport livery, its purpose was to provide manual gearbox training.

M205 was fitted with a Deutz water-cooled engine for a trial period; this led to a further three inches being added to create a rear bustle. It re-entered service in September at Brixton. M597 received an experimental Maxwell gearbox later in the year.

The Commercial Operations Unit received thirty-nine Routemasters that had otherwise been earmarked for disposal for the revamped OLTST, twenty of which were converted to open-top. They were repainted into traditional livery, with gold fleet numbers and names, and a cream band. Eleven RCLs and six RMAs were also taken in for refurbishment. Closed-top RMs took up duty on 22 March, open toppers and RCLs in April. The Metrobuses dedicated to sightseeing assisted during the transition period but were subsequently stood down to begin their new life as service buses.

Nonetheless, 321 RMs were disposed of during the year. Of these, 142 were scrapped, but an almost equal number went to the Scottish Bus Group, where they were placed in service with Clydeside, Kelvin and Strathtay. In England, six were acquired by Blackpool Corporation.

A pair of RMCs was also sold, along with a single RMA and DMS. The latter, DMS2080, operated for a short time with Olympic Coachways before being acquired by Filers of Ilfracombe. After a further five owners, it passed to the Big Bus Co. who in 2001 exported it to Philadelphia. By 2006 it was with Double Deck Sightseeing Tours in Las Vegas.

Six Metrobuses leaving the fleet were all victims of the fire at Southall depot the previous December.

Illustrating the new OLTST order on closed top Routemasters, RM710 (WLT 710), and behind it, RM479 (WLT 479) on the Victoria Street stand. The date is 3 April 1986; the relaunched Tour has been in operation for just thirteen days, and the open top and RCL examples will shortly hit the streets as well.

94 • LONDON'S BUSES, 1979–1994

Open-top conversion RM752 (WLT 752) shows off its new OLTST identity as it waits in Haymarket on 25 June 1986 for the next complement of tourists.

Meanwhile there was still plenty of work for older Routemasters, and RM23 (VLT 23) was very much on the move. Starting 1986 at Stamford Brook, it went to Hounslow, then Camberwell, before ending up at New Cross with only half the year gone! This was however its last posting before becoming a driver trainer in 1987, but on 13 October 1986, I found it at the Somerset House stop on the Strand, preparing to take the 1 to Greenwich.

Service news

It is possible to regard the number of invitations to tender in 1985 as a tentative step on the franchising road. Not so 1986. Over forty routes were involved, often on an area basis, and included among the batch of nine advertised in mid-summer were the first three that penetrated central and/or inner London. The tenders were also notable for the number of alterations to the routes in question. Once again, LBL successes were few.

There were no huge service-wide route alterations, as in previous years. Large though they undoubtedly still were, the vast majority of changes resulted from conversions to one person operation and the programme of operator changes and garage closures resulting from the tendering process.

Mid-March heralded the introduction of a two-hourly service between London and Birmingham, operated jointly with the West Midlands Passenger Transport Executive (WMPTE) under the name 'London Liner'. Both operators suffered delays in obtaining vehicles to operate the service, as detailed above. On 17 May, another express service, this time to Eastbourne, was launched, and once again, the intended Leyland Olympians were late in arriving.

More 'Touristlink' services appeared; last year's London Zoo-Tower of London became the T1, from 22 March; the T2 ran between Victoria, Trafalgar Square and the Tower of London (returning via Baker Street and Notting Hill) from 7 June, and the T3 linked Lancaster Gate with the Thames Barrier, from 4 May. The T1, T3 and the returning Thames Barrier shuttle from Greenwich (Cutty Sark) operated on Saturdays, Sundays and Bank Holiday Mondays, while the T2 was a daily service.

Leaving Victoria bus station on its next outing to the Tower of London, M1172 (B172 WUL) from Gillingham Street was one of three vehicles dedicated to the route (the others being M1035 from Holloway and M1350 from Westbourne Park). Note that instead of a garage code, the route number is displayed.

The opening of Heathrow's Terminal Four in April led to several changes. The 105, 140, 202 and 285 were extended accordingly, while the Airbus A1 and A2 were rerouted, the A2 having also been rerouted from Bayswater Road to Euston to replace the A3.

A new service which encroached upon Eastern National territory began in August. Numbered X99 and named 'The Forester', it ran from Harlow and Basildon and utilised six Leyland Nationals, LS27/30/71/76/79, 435, which received a dedicated livery of red, green and white.

The 68 (Chalk Farm-South Croydon) provided a particularly notable service alteration arising from its conversion to one person operation. Particularly susceptible to delays from congestion, and with the two depots supplying the route being some fifteen miles apart, it was split in October, with the new 168 taking over between Waterloo and Chalk Farm (Mondays-Saturdays). The 68 continued in parallel as far as Euston, but a new peak hours express service, the X68, was also introduced on Mondays-Fridays, running from West Croydon to West Norwood the non-stop to Waterloo, terminating in Russell Square, in the mornings, with a reverse working in the evening. This called for the six coach-seated Leyland Olympians, which did work on ordinary 68 duties outside the rush hour.

A new departure was a central London minibus service, the C1 (Westminster-Kensington), beginning in October. As a daytime route, it allowed the Optare City Pacers employed on it to be allocated to the C20/C21, which worked in the evenings between Victoria, the West End theatreland and Waterloo. They were operated from Victoria Basement.

Coach-seated Olympian L170 (D170 FYM) has arrived at Russell Square in this photograph taken on the morning of 31 October 1986. Nowadays the X68 only operates during the morning peaks.

Other events

T613 was given West Ham Corporation Tramways livery to celebrate the borough's centenary.

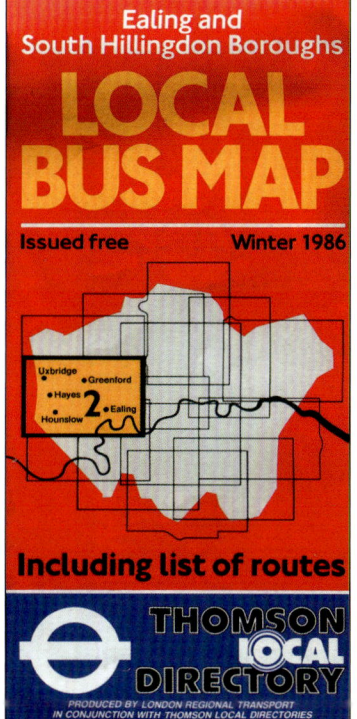

Above: T613 (NUW 613Y) was seen in Green Street on the S1 Stratford circular. The lines of the West Ham Corporation Tramways livery suited the Titan particularly well.

Left: As well as London-wide maps in Spring and Summer 1986 a series of local maps was produced, of which this is 'Ealing and South Hillingdon No. 3', printed in October and sponsored by Thomson Local Directories. It covered a considerable area of west London, from Heathrow and Uxbridge in the west to Shepherds Bush and Ladbroke Grove in the east, Harrow in the north to Hounslow and Richmond in the south.

Fare increases in January saw 10p added to most cash fares, although the end came for the Red Bus Rover, which was replaced by the One Day Travelcard. In June, the One Day Capitalcard was also introduced, costing £2.50 for an adult and £1.25 for a child under sixteen. As regards ticketing equipment, LRT henceforth required the use of Wayfarer 2 machines on all its tendered services.

Despite an LRT-imposed ban on vehicles in 'Showbus' condition, the practice was not completely wiped out, with Norwood and Muswell Hill/Stamford Hill RMs and even a Metrobus at Ponders End continuing to flourish.

Six of the remaining eight RMCs still sporting London Country's green livery were repainted this year, the exceptions being RMCs 1480 and 1516.

Yet again there was no Christmas Day service except for the A1, but there was sponsorship for free travel on New Year's Eve after 2345.

WESTLINK AND ROUNDABOUT

The distinctive liveries chosen by the two new subsidiary companies are well illustrated here.

In Westlink colours, which were altered during 1988 to those seen here – originally the white/green stripe was not swept upwards – LS40 (KJD 540P) was found in London Road, Hounslow, with a 117 working to Hounslow.

The livery for the Roundabout network based on the Orpington area sat very well on the Optare City Pacers, of which five were operated. OV2 'Hurricane' (C526 DYT) waits at the Rose & Crown in Green Street Green, before returning on the R3 to Petts Wood station.

LONDON LINERS

There was another joint venture under the London Liner name which began on 17 May, this time in conjunction with Eastbourne Borough Transport, to that operator's hometown. This required two vehicles, and LC1/2 appeared in May and August 1986 respectively. This is LC1 (C201 DYE), pictured in Terminus Road, Eastbourne, at the start of its journey back to London, while in the background, Eastbourne's 23 (GHC 523N), a Leyland Atlantean/East Lancs. loads for a local service. This version of the London Liner was intended to finish at the same time as the Birmingham route, but it continued until October 1987.

Three DAF MB200/Duple Caribbean 2 Executive coaches were hired in for the start of the London Liner service in March 1986 operated jointly by London Coaches and the West Midlands PTE. DD9 (C29 MCX) was awaiting departure from Wilton Road in the upper picture. All three moved onto other work when the MCW Metroliners ordered for the work were finally received in May; ML3 (C103 DYE), in the same spot, will also soon be Birmingham-bound. B3 is the Metroliner's operating number; fleet numbers were not carried. LBL left the partnership in March 1987 and ML3 was sold to Busways Travel.

1987

It was in one respect a good year for LRT, with the opening on 31 August of the Docklands Light Railway, linking Tower Gateway and Stratford with Island Gardens. However, tragedy struck in the shape of the fire at King's Cross underground station on the evening of 18 November, which claimed the lives of thirty-one people. It was not a particularly good year for LBL, plagued by industrial action over proposed new employment conditions for staff at Norbiton. Despite tender wins at Harrow and Bexleyheath, implementation at the former location was bedevilled by the late arrival of the Mark 2 Metrobuses and the unsatisfactory performance of hired-in Fleetlines. By the end of the year, it was being widely reported that deregulation and privatisation would come to London perhaps as early as 1990, and that the districts would be reorganised (yet again) into smaller units to this end.

The devolving of responsibility from 55 Broadway to local level, briefly mentioned last year, came a step closer with the announcement of a new structure within London Buses. Changes began in August and September, with the appointment of the first Garage General Managers, a process it was hoped would be completed by April 1988. These new post-holders would be responsible for specified services on routes operated by their depot, preparation of budgets and monitoring financial and operational performance, in an attempt to ensure that targets were being met. Although there was some better news so far as tender wins were concerned in 1987, the threat of deregulation of London services had not gone away, and so cutting costs wherever possible was essential if LBL was to continue to compete with the private sector.

It was announced that Abbey district would be disbanded, in a move begun in August and completed during November. A Central Traffic Division was created to oversee this congested area, but it would have no responsibility for garages on its patch. In the ensuing redistribution, Wandle took Putney and Victoria, Forest got Ash Grove, Chalk Farm and Holloway joined Leaside and Cardinal received Shepherds Bush and Westbourne Park. The two garages remaining were already due to close; Wandsworth on 11 July (though it passed to the Commercial Operations Unit) and Clapton on 15 August.

The effects of industrial unrest were felt most keenly at Norbiton, where the start of the Kingston Buses scheme had been delayed past the original date of 27 June. By early September, and with a continuing loss of operating staff, LBL was ready to hand back the 65, 71, 85 and 213 to LRT, a move that would have inevitably led to the closure of Norbiton. However, by the middle of the month the unions agreed to accept the altered conditions of service, LRT was told that the contracts would be met, and a management/union team was set up to look at all aspects of route tendering.

The Harrow scheme got off to a particularly poor start, with large numbers of passenger complaints. Among the many grievances were over-optimistic running

Metrobus M547 (GYE 547W) shows off the revised Leaside livery whilst standing in Goswell Road, near Angel underground station, on 17 November 1987. This would have been a short working of the 43 (London Bridge-Friern Barnet).

times, vehicle shortages and capacity issues. The leased Fleetlines broke down with alarming regularity; they were not a type that Harrow depot had had experience of in the past. With no radios or anti-vandal screens, they were taken off the road at 1900, with LSs substituting. The Mark 2 Metrobuses had at least started to appear by the year-end.

Leaside district started to introduce a revised livery, comprising a black skirt and white band at cantrail level. M1253 was the first to display it. But it was overtaken by events in late autumn when LBL decided to update the plain red fleet livery. In came a two-inch white band and grey skirt, and the London Transport 'roundel' was revamped; out went the plain white circle and bar, to be replaced by a red circle outlined in white, with a yellow bar carrying the words 'London Buses' in red.

Vehicle news – single deck fleet

The two remaining Ivecos on loan at Eastbourne were returned early in the year and repainted into fleet livery.

Selkent evaluated an AA Motors Leyland Lynx on the 70 in February.

LRT-owned Optare City Pacers in all-red livery started work on the London Country North West C2, the Camden Hoppa, which was the replacement for the 53 north of Oxford Circus. Implementation was partially achieved by 24 March, and in full by 4 April. They were numbered MBV27-51.

Westlink MR17 (D477 PON) waits outside Surbiton station on a dull winter's day before its next outing on the K1 to New Malden.

New Carlyle bodied Freight Rover Sherpas for the Chelsea Harbour Hoppa were SC1/2. SC1 had an automatic gearbox for performance comparison with SC2. Along with RH19/22 (see below), they carried a blue and white livery.

London Coaches took three new DAF MB230/Duple 340, DD1-3, and three bodied by Van Hool, DV1-3. More second-hand acquisitions were DD5 (DAF MB2300/Duple 340), AD1 (AEC Reliance/Duple Dominant II) and LP1-3 (Leyland Leopard/Plaxton Supreme).

The MCW Metroriders for the Kingston-upon-Thames scheme to be worked by Westlink were MR1-22. The final four had dual-purpose seating. A further thirty were received for Harrow Buses, M23-52 and twelve for Bexleybus (MR53-64 but carrying local fleet numbers 29-40). A further twelve to the new lengthened specification were ordered for the Roundabout network and would enter service in 1988.

Leyland Nationals on the move included six for Westlink and thirteen to the LRT Disabled Unit following an increase in Mobility Bus work. A further eleven were sold. Two Ford Transits and Merlin MBS217 also left the fleet.

Vehicle news – double deck fleet

No new buses were said to be on order for 1987, yet staff in one district were told that there would be no second-hand acquisitions either! As things turned out, this was not the case, as the *Evening Standard* reported in February that 209 buses would be acquired in 1987/88, and Potters Bar depot, which was now operating as a self-contained entity, was allocated thirteen ex South Yorkshire Volvo Ailsas, in batches of nine and later, four. Twelve of them took fleet numbers V4-15, and the unlucky thirteenth was used for spares only. Potters Bar already had V1/2, with V3 as a driver trainer, though it later returned to service with the rear door removed and a seat in what was the doorway. The experimental L1-3 were at Norwood, the two Metrobus Mark 2s at Brixton and at the start of the year the Dennis Dominators were stored but moved from Stockwell to Brixton in June.

The remaining Olympians were received; the last four, L260-63, were coach seated and given Selkent Travel livery for the 177 Express. They were named: L260 Renown; L261 Buccaneer; L262 Invincible, and L263 Conqueror. Following on from these were a further twenty-eight with Northern Counties bodywork; so far as the official London system was concerned, they were L264-91, but they would actually carry Bexleybus fleet numbers 1-28 in public.

Twenty-seven new MCW Metrobus Mark 2s, M1452-78, finished in red and cream, were received for the Harrow scheme. To overcome a delay in delivery, a similar number of former Greater Manchester PTE Northern Counties bodied Fleetlines were leased from Kirkby Central in time for the start date.

As well as the aforementioned South Yorkshire Volvo Ailsas, West Midlands Travel – formerly the PTE – supplied another fifty, which became V16-65. V20 was a late arrival in March 1988, but they were all put to use in either Harrow Buses or Leaside livery.

V4 (LWB 389P) looks particularly smart in this view at Potters Bar bus station on 26 May 1987. Note the board advertising that this is a Hertfordshire County Council contract service.

Outside the bus station in College Road, Harrow, ex Greater Manchester Fleetline 7363, now temporarily re-numbered LF318 (YNA 318M), is loading for Pinner on the 183. To say the type was unpopular during this short stay in London would be an understatement; they were not in the best of condition internally, externally or mechanically, and were widely disliked by drivers and passengers. LF318 was taken out of service before the end of 1987; in fact, only nine of the twenty-seven were used in 1988, and the last to return to Kirkby Central was LF340, in mid-March.

The last of the fifty former West Midlands PTE Volvo Ailsas, V65 (JOV 765P) went to Leaside, and on this occasion, was parked up at the Station Road depot forecourt in Edgware after service on the 107 (New Barnet-Queensbury).

Mark 1 Metrobuses came from Greater Manchester PTE (M1443-47) and West Yorkshire PTE (M1448-51) via dealers, one of which, Ensignbus, also leased the original Titan demonstrator back to LBL which now took fleet number T1131.

In December, fourteen Daimler Fleetlines, once new to London Transport, returned to the capital from Clydeside Scottish for use with Bexleybus. As they did not pass to the new unit until January 1988, details of all the vehicles in that fleet will appear in the next chapter.

Metroliner ML3 was sold to Busways. ML1/2 were hired to Devon General, still in London Liner livery, for work on National Express services between Devon and London. Volvo Citybus C1 was returned off-lease.

Routemaster withdrawals totalled nearly 350, many finding their way to former NBC and Council companies which saw them as a useful tool in the newly deregulated era. Disposals of RMAs totalled twenty-six (all bar two being sold by BEL), two RMCs, and nine DMSs. But RMC1515 in its new open-top state at Forest district received red and green livery and was found on short workings of the 15 between Aldwych and Marble Arch from 16 November, for passengers to experience the Christmas lights in Regent Street and Oxford Street.

Yet another arson attack, this time at Sidcup, two months before its intended closure, caused severe damage to four Titans – T708/34/58, 900 – which were scrapped early in 1988.

Service news

Results on the tendering front were mixed. Six routes that had already been won by LBL were put out to tender again because the costings were said to be incorrect (the full costs of operation were not being met under the existing contract prices). Those involved were the 79A, 84A, 125, 179, 179A, 228A/C and 261. The 233 was also included, even though it had not been tendered before. The results made depressing reading for LBL, which won just one.

The focus in 1987 was to invite tenders for area schemes, and the Kingston network was one of three chosen. LBL did very well, winning all bar one of the routes on offer, but the changes did not take effect on 27 June as planned. LBL wanted to renegotiate new contracts which would pay less (£185 for an increased working week of 43 hours. Nearly all London buses came off the road as a result of a one-day strike on 11 May, and the issues surrounding change of conditions went to the High Court. The ramifications for LBL were enormous. Success could mean a better chance of winning more LRT tenders; defeat would undoubtedly impact upon attempts to achieve economies, which might in turn allow other operators with a lower cost base in to run services. As it turned out when the case was heard on 13 July, LBL won.

Adding to the overall sense of dismay at Norbiton was the fact that services were now expected to be run using DMSs, most of which had been withdrawn for a long time or were ex trainers, in place of more modern Ms. Thirty-four DMSs and one DM were due to move in during June/July, having been overhauled in previous weeks, but they were slow in arriving, and when they did, it was realised that they were too tall to fit inside the entrance to Kingston bus station. Until the new bus station opened, they were kept away from the 65, and the Ms that had been due for transfer elsewhere, had to stay longer than anticipated to help out. Kingston Buses Ltd was set up to operate 65, 71, and 85 from Norbiton, while the K1/K2 and 213 (now the K3) were to be operated by Stanwell Buses (Westlink), which would also take over the 216 on 27 June and open a base for new minibuses at the old Kingston depot. In the meantime, it was agreed that Kingston Buses Ltd would not start up until the end of December.

The second scheme was centred upon Harrow, and initial proposals were put forward in March, but the services tendered bore little relation to them. The whole network, now totalling twelve routes, was won by LBL and operated under the name Harrow Buses, starting on 14 November, with minibus routes becoming Harrow Hoppas

The Bexleyheath scheme involved twenty routes, of which LBL won seventeen. The remaining three, the 132, 228A/C and 233, went to Boro'line Maidstone. Minibus services were to be marketed as Bexley Hoppas, with Bexley Bus fleetnames on larger vehicles, and the entire fleet was given an attractive blue and cream livery. The contract start date was set at 16 January 1988.

Otherwise, there were significant service alterations at various times of the year, mainly in connection with the redistributions which accompanied depot closures, the taking-up of new tenders from the 1986 round or the implementation of the Kingston and Harrow schemes.

The X99 'Forester' service ceased from 7 February. The six coach-seated Leyland Nationals used on the route transferred to London Coaches. Their new owner won a contract to provide services for a Japanese school in West Acton and five LSs, Ford

DMS1890 (GHM 890N) had spent over three years as a driver trainer, latterly at North Street, before being despatched to British Leyland in Nottingham to be spruced up in readiness for a return to passenger service. Seen in Victoria Road, Surbiton on a 71 working to Chessington Zoo, it sports the red-on-yellow Kingston Bus fleetname instead of the LBL roundel but is still recognisably a London bus.

Transits FS25/26 and Dodge A1, along with some single deck coaches, were used on the ten services involved.

Berks Bucks, the new name of Alder Valley North, ceased its operation of the Careline service for passengers with disabilities which had worked between the main London rail termini, Victoria Coach Station and Heathrow. It was put out to tender by LRT later in the year.

Involvement with London Liner services to Birmingham ceased after 28 March. The Eastbourne route carried on until 11 October.

The new C3 Chelsea Harbour Hoppa (Earls Court-Chelsea Harbour) started on 13 April. It used two of the Ivecos that went to Eastbourne (RH19/22) and the aforementioned Sherpas.

Alder Valley North operated Leyland National, 243 (LPF 601P), rebuilt to a DP21F configuration and in a livery that owed more than a little to British Rail, on the Careline service. This photo, taken in late December 1986, preceded the company's name change to The Berks Bucks Bus Co Ltd by some two weeks; four weeks after that it pulled out of this service altogether.

The T3 (Lancaster Gate-Greenwich) continued but the T1/T2 were rolled up into a new Z1, a circular service based on London Zoo's North Gate. It began on Good Friday, 17 April and operated every Saturday and Sunday until 6 September, as well as daily between 26-29 May and 20 July to 4 September.

Other events

Apart from Clapton and Wandsworth, other depots closed during the year were Clapham (7 February), when Streatham reopened after rebuilding, and Hendon (6 June). Walworth reopened on 15 August for Red Arrow operations and plans to reopen Bexleyheath were put in train in readiness for January. Kingston re-opened as a base for Westlink minibuses, but ultimately for big buses as well following the transfer of the 216 from Norbiton. Harrow Buses opened a new minibus outstation at

Chalk Farm had charge of the Z1, and with a combination of windscreen and blind displays, T607 (NUW 607Y) works the circle in Baker Street in a photo taken in the summer of 1988.

L43 (C43 CHM) demonstrates not only the advertising for the 'Autocheck' ticketing equipment but also the 269 in its complete form (Bromley North-Woolwich) before it was cut back as part of the Bexleyheath tender scheme. I found it leaving Bromley North on 16 July 1987.

North Wembley on 14 November. Sidcup was slated to close on 16 January 1988 with the reopening of Bexleyheath.

When Selkent Olympian L261 was registered 2 CLT, RM1002, now OYM 368A, had the distinction of becoming the first LT vehicle to wear an A-suffix registration. By the end of the year, RM9/12/14/20, 2001 had also parted with their original registrations, which passed to L263, M1437, L262, L260 and T1000 respectively.

Wayfarer 2 machines continued to be introduced, but the trialling of a ticketing innovation began in Plumstead, New Cross, Sidcup and Catford. Called 'Autocheck', it comprised two readers and new-style passes, permits and Travelcards, the size of a credit card, which magnetically stored (and therefore also transmitted) details of usage. A bleep would sound to confirm validity, but a louder noise would indicate that the card had expired.

The redesign for the Winter 1987/88 London Bus Map differed in several respects from its predecessors. M1387 was featured on the cover working a fictitious route 23 to the 'Shopping Centre', and the slogan 'That's our bus' accompanied the new-style roundel. For the next issue in Summer 1988, M1421 was featured in the latest livery, along with a brand new set of passengers.

SECOND-HAND METROBUSES

In early 1987, given the short-term absence of any new vehicles, the undoubted popularity of the Metrobus led to second-hand examples being sought to further aid conversions to one person operation. The first five to appear were M1443-47, which came from Greater Manchester PTE. After repainting, and the fitting of London destination screens, they were despatched to Potters Bar depot, whose locale, it was felt, would better suit their single door layout. M1444 (GBU 4V) has moved on however, from London Northern to Leaside, and was seen making the turn into Bounds Green Road on a 221 working between Edgware and Turnpike Lane stations. All five were sold to County Bus, part of what was the former London Country North East, in 1997.

The next four were new to the West Yorkshire PTE, and comprised two Alexander and two MCW bodied examples, M1448/49 and M1450/51 respectively. They too were sent to Potters Bar after the necessary modification work, which is where we see M1450 (CUB 539Y) after it has completed its latest duty on the W8 (Chase Farm Hospital-Picketts Lock Centre). The four did not have long service lives in London, and M1450/51 moved on to Mott (Yellow Bus), Stoke Mandeville in 1994 where they enjoyed a further ten years' service.

Fleet numbers M1451-80 were taken up by the orders for Harrow's new Mark II Metrobuses, but in 1988 the last of the second-hand contingent appeared. These were five MCW bodied examples from Busways Travel, formerly the Tyne & Wear PTE. Like their predecessors, they were initially attached to Potters Bar, but in 1989 four of the five moved on to Holloway, and so brought their single door configuration to central London. Seen at Centre Point on 1 April 1990, M1484 (VRG 418T) was one of the twenty Ms Holloway used on the 14 on a Sunday. But the presence of an RML in the background, also on the route, suggests that the theory and actuality of vehicle allocating were not always synchronised.

THE HARROW SCHEME

To operate the scheme introduced on 14 November 1987, Harrow Buses took twenty-seven new MCW Mark 2 Metrobuses and thirty new MCW Metroriders. Leyland Nationals were provided from within LBL, along with Alexander bodied Volvo-Ailsa B55s acquired from West Midlands PTE. But to cover a potential shortage owing to delays in Metrobus production, twenty-seven Leyland Fleetlines ex Greater Manchester PTE were leased from Kirkby Central. All photos were taken between November 1987 and April 1988 at Harrow bus station.

Mark 2 Metrobus M1458 (E458 SON) was taking a breather prior to working a 340 to Edgware station. The section of the 140 from there to Harrow Weald depot was withdrawn as part of the Harrow scheme.

Two of the Volvo-Ailsas I witnessed on the 183 to Golders Green had to rely on handwritten route number displays. V24 was one, seen in December 1987, and surprisingly, fifteen weeks later, V29 (JOV 779V) was still relying on a piece of paper to inform passengers that it was on the 183 bound for Golders Green.

Parked up behind M1458 was one of the new Metroriders, MR33 (E133 KYW). Five new minibus routes were introduced with the Harrow scheme, and the next outing for MR33 will be on the first of these, the H11 to Northwood station.

1988

Unfortunately, newly-founded Bexleybus witnessed similar problems to those already experienced at Kingston and Harrow. Sutton and Hornchurch area services were also under the tendering spotlight, but outcomes there were nowhere near as surprising as the loss of central London route 24 in another exercise. The threat of deregulation had still not gone away, and during November and December, the five districts were reorganised into eleven operating units of between 350 and 500 buses each. And in what might be thought of as a lack of short-term,

Grey-Green adopted a new livery which drew on the company name before enlivening it with a bold orange stripe. Volvo Citybus/Alexander 131 (F131 PHM) cuts a fine sight as it picks up in Charing Cross Road on 23 November 1988, in the third week of the new contract. The RML following on the 22 was able to drop off one or two passengers and depart before 131 had finished loading.

joined-up thinking, it emerged that after all the time and expense incurred in setting up the likes of Roundabout and the Kingston, Harrow and Bexleybus schemes, these were now to be subsumed within their appropriate new unit.

Bexleybus took to the streets on 16 January. The fleet had been repainted into the smart new blue and cream livery prior to commencement and was fully available from day one. But complaints started almost immediately and centred on reliability and overcrowding. Notwithstanding the experiencing of yet another problematic area scheme introduction, LRT announced a further two for 1988, in Sutton and Hornchurch.

The reorganisation of LBL was first announced in the LRT business plan for 1988/89 which appeared in January. The remaining five districts would be broken down to form a larger number of smaller, commercial units that would have their own identity and build upon their experiences of the tender process to date in readiness for deregulation and privatisation, both of which were still being actively considered, despite the fact that the timeline had now slipped to 1993 or thereabouts, blamed officially on a 'lack of legislative opportunity'. More likely, since it had already been widely commented upon, it was the growing realisation that to mount a free-for-all during weekdays (excluding evenings, if the experiences of the provinces were anything to go by) on the most remunerative services with second- or third-hand buses, driver-only Leyland Nationals and Daimler Fleetlines no doubt, would reduce central London to a state of almost permanent daytime gridlock. Nonetheless, a 'Statement of Strategy' emanating from LRT HQ in June reiterated that preparing for deregulation was one of its key objectives for the future.

At around the same time its plans for the role of LBL once it had been reconstituted into privatised units were laid out. There could be little to argue about in terms of the proposed requirement to oversee registration of commercial bus routes, to seek multi-operator ticketing arrangements – imagine the chaos if this was not a given – plus the identification of socially desirable services and the provision of travel information, concessionary bus schemes and disabled facilities.

While the original plan had been to effect this major change in 1989, it was brought forward so that eleven new operating units came into being on 7 November (London Central and Selkent) or 5 December (the remainder). They were, in alphabetical order and with their allocated depots and codes:

CENTREWEST (logo – stylised arrow)
HL - Hanwell, ON - Alperton, UX - Uxbridge, X - Westbourne Park

EAST LONDON (logo – Thames sailing barge)
AP - Seven Kings, BK - Barking, BW - Bow, NS - North Street, U - Upton Park, WH - West Ham

LEASIDE BUSES (logo – swan)
AD - Palmers Green, AR - Tottenham, E - Enfield, SF - Stamford Hill, WN - Wood Green

LONDON CENTRAL (logo – the Cutty Sark)
NX - New Cross, Q - Camberwell, PM - Peckham

LONDON FOREST (logo – oak tree)
AG - Ash Grove, T - Leyton, WW - Walthamstow

LONDON GENERAL (logo – London General B-type bus)
A - Sutton, AF - Putney, AL - Merton, GM - Victoria, RA - Red Arrow Unit (Walworth), SW - Stockwell, VB - Central Minibus Unit (Victoria Basement)

LONDON NORTHERN (logo – Houses of Parliament)
CF - Chalk Farm, FY - Finchley, HT - Holloway, MH - Muswell Hill, PB - Potters Bar

LONDON UNITED (logo – City of London coat of arms)
AV - Hounslow, FW - Fulwell, NB - Norbiton, S - Shepherds Bush, V - Stamford Brook

METROLINE (logo – four stripes encasing the fleetname)
AC - Willesden, EW - Edgware, HD - Harrow Weald, W - Cricklewood

SELKENT (logo – hops)
BX - Bexleyheath, OB - Orpington Buses, PD - Plumstead, TB - Bromley, TL - Catford

SOUTH LONDON (logo – Tower Bridge)
AK - Streatham, BN - Brixton, N - Norwood, TC - Croydon, TH - Thornton Heath

London Coaches and Westlink were unaffected by the changes.

Vehicle news – single deck fleet

Only two new vehicles arrived in 1988, and these were Leyland Lynxes LX1/2 that were operated by LBL on behalf of Hillingdon Borough. LX2 was illustrated on page 71.

The mini- and midi-bus revolution continued apace with the bulk of new vehicles being MCW Metroriders. Normal and lengthened versions, numbered in the same range, following on from MRL73 in 1987, were:

- MRL74-77, 89-92, DP33F
- MRL78-88, B33F
- MR99-103, B23F
- MR104/05, DP23F
- MRL106-31, B28F
- MRL132/33, DP28F

Similar B25F examples operated for Wandsworth Health Authority were originally numbered SG1-6, but these were later incorporated into the main run as MR93-98. MCW loaned one further Metrorider in January which was not taken into stock until the end of the year at Westlink; it became MR134.

Thirty-six of the first thirty-nine Mercedes Benz 811Ds with Alexander B28F bodywork were received, numbered between MA1-39 with MA28, 36/37 still to arrive. The Optare Star Rider, which was also based on the 811D, appeared as SR1-28, while five Mercedes 709D with Reeves Burgess B20F bodies that incorporated tail-lifts, MT1-5, were operated on behalf of Ealing Borough.

Above: Catching a glimpse of a short-term loan or demonstrator vehicle can be difficult if its stay with LBL is of short duration. No such problem with this Iveco 49.10/Robin Hood, which remained with the Central Minibus Unit in Victoria Basement for almost eight months between April and November 1988. E629 AMA does not appear to have gained a fleet number during that time, and as this view in Terminus Place, Victoria demonstrates, its approach to route information is unconventional, to say the least.

Opposite above: The last of the initial batch of Star Riders, SR28 (F928 YWY) has received its London Central branding and carries it prominently beneath the windscreen. The P11, on which it was working, linked Waterloo and Peckham and was one of four new P-prefixed 'Peckham Hoppa' services introduced on 19 November. It was photographed at the terminus on the Waterloo station taxi road.

Opposite below: Optare City Pacer E998 TWU pictured on Carelink duty at Euston station on 8 April 1988. It would receive fleet number OV50 later in the year.

WATERLOO STATION P11
hoppa
SR 28
LONDON CENTRAL
F928 YWY

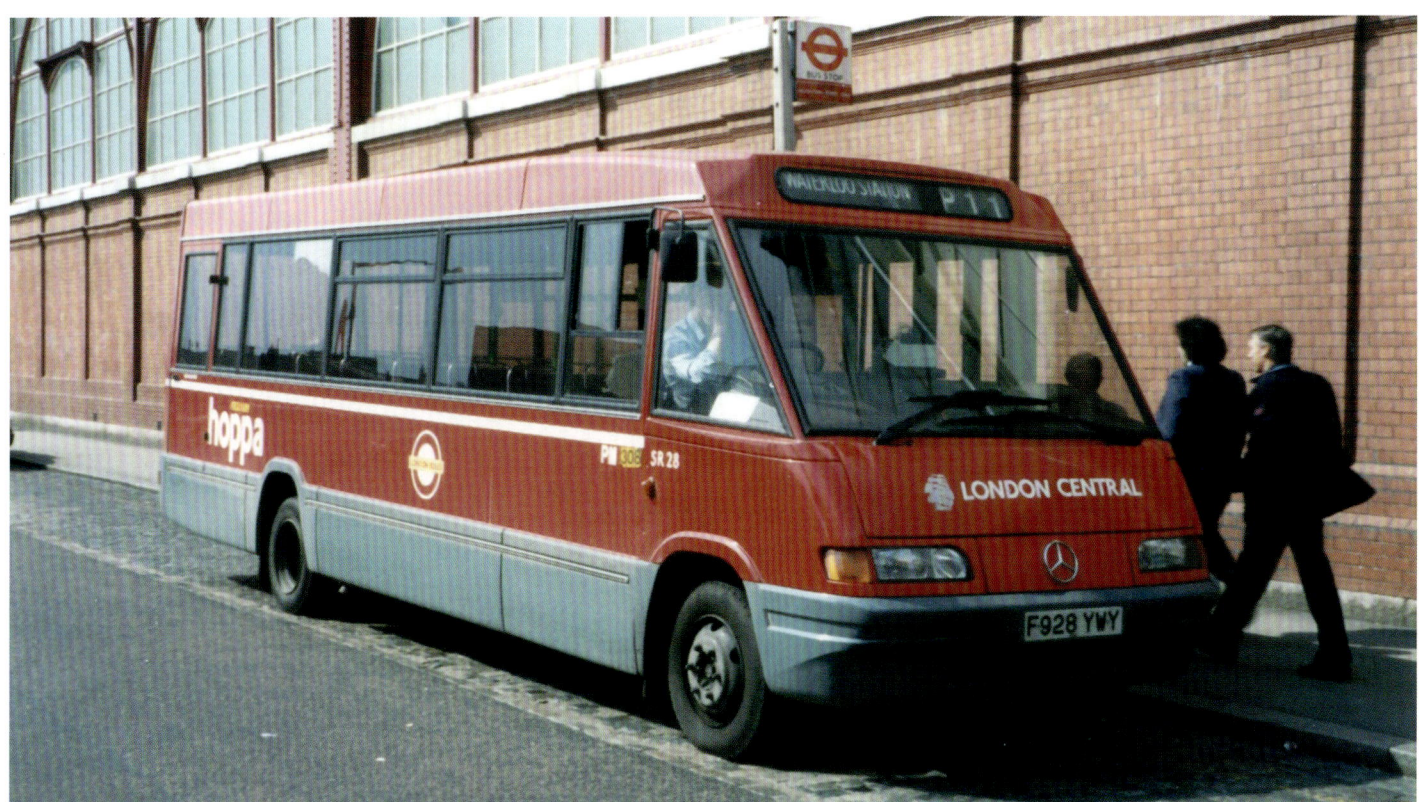

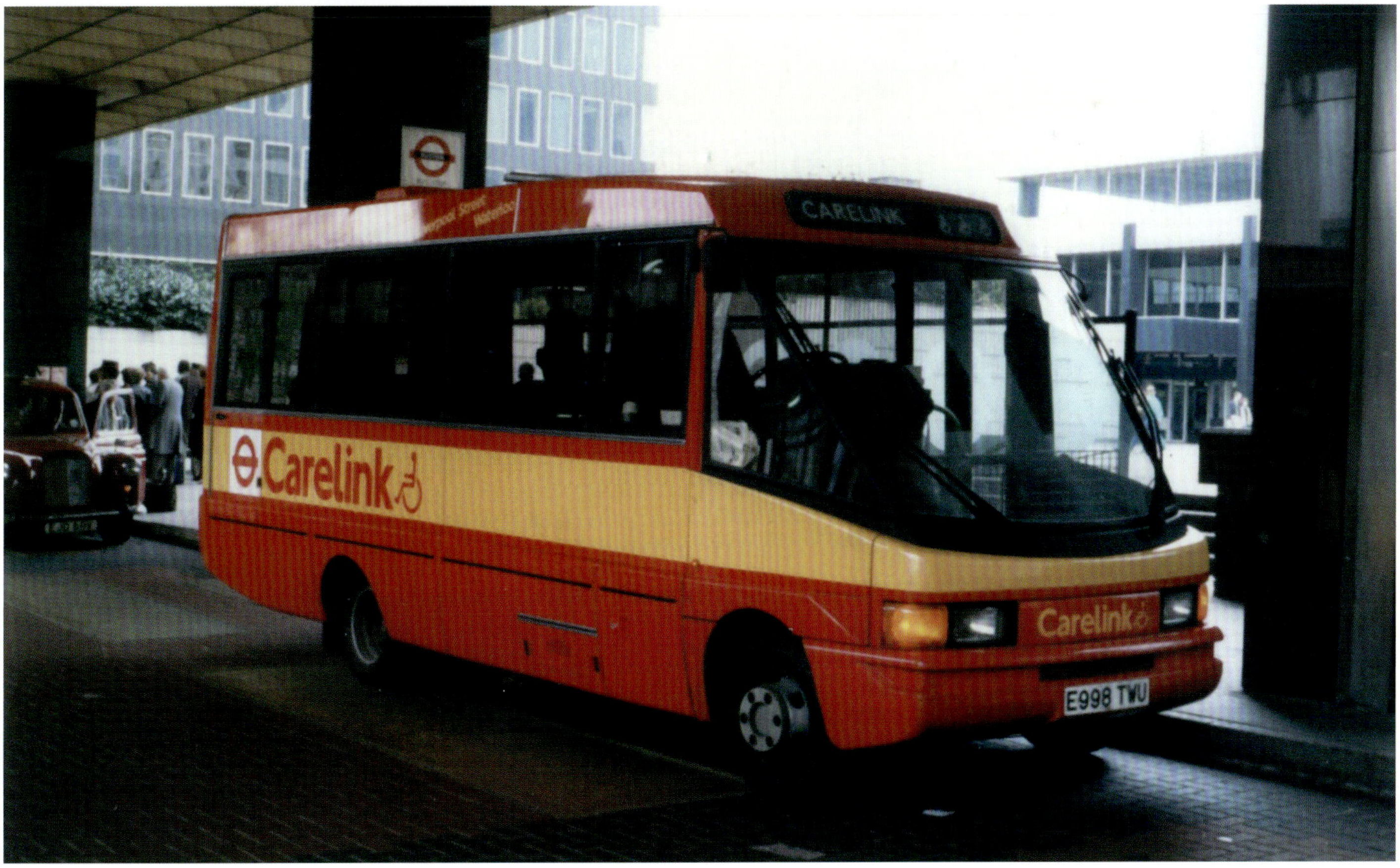
CARELINK
Carelink
Carelink
E998 TWU

Finally, three Optare City Pacers were acquired for the Carelink contract. They too were fitted with tail-lifts and DP seating for fourteen and room for three wheelchairs and received fleet numbers OV50-52 before the year was out.

Four new coaches were acquired for the burgeoning operations at London Coaches. DV4/7 were DAF MB230LB, DV5/6 DAF SB2305; all were Van Hool Alizee bodied. Three second-hand purchases were LD3/4 (Leyland Leopard/Duple) and AP2 (AEC Reliance/Plaxton).

Withdrawals accounted for five BLs. One had been held in a derelict state for some time, but the others were the Hillingdon 128 buses which, when replaced by Leyland Nationals, were taken by Trimdon Motor Services. Fourteen Leyland Nationals were sold, along with a single Ford Transit (FS26). The remaining three Metroliners also departed, appropriately enough to West Midlands Travel.

Vehicle news – double deck fleet

As with the single deckers, there were just two new arrivals, these being MCW Metrobuses at Harrow that took fleet numbers M1479/80. Busways Travel supplied a further five, though these had already seen ten years' service in the north east. They became M1481-85. West Midlands Travel sent the single missing Volvo-Ailsa, V20.

A Leyland PD2/MCW Orion was leased for six months of the year. It was numbered LM2 during its stay.

The last nine former Greater Manchester Fleetlines that had supposedly been helping out at Harrow were returned to Kirkby Central by the end of March.

T512 was converted to open-top following an upper-deck fire. Rather appropriately, it received the name *The Phoenix*.

Withdrawals saw another 191 RMs leave the fleet. RML900, which suffered accident damage in 1987 and was deemed to be beyond repair, was sold to Clydeside Scottish who promptly restored it to working condition (with parts from RM1984) and, as if to rub salt into the wound, brought it back to London in June when it performed on the 13 and the 26, resplendent in its 'Oor Wullie's Special' livery. Five RMCs and two RMAs were also sold, along with the remains of seven DMSs.

Vehicles transferred to the new operating units 1986-88

STANWELL BUSES LTD (WESTLINK)

1986   Leyland National (28 LS)
1987   Leyland National (6 LS)
        MCW Metrorider (22 MR; 11 returned and 4 to Suttonbus in 1988)
1988   AEC Routemaster (1 RM)

BEXLEYBUS

1987   Daimler Fleetline (14 DMS ex Clydeside Scottish, new to LT)
1988   Leyland Olympian (28 L)

Daimler Fleetline (19 DM/DMS)
Leyland National (24 LS, 10 returned during the year)
MCW Metrorider (12 MR)
Iveco Daily 49.10 (13 RH)

KINGSTON BUS

1988   MCW Metrobus (40 M)
Daimler Fleetline (36 DM/DMS)
Leyland National (24 LS)
Leyland Leopard (1 LP)

SUTTONBUS

1988   Daimler Fleetline (87 D/DMS)
MCW Metrorider (4 MR, ex Westlink)

Service news

Boro'line Maidstone had a very good year. As well as the three routes acquired when the Bexleyheath scheme was introduced, it took over the 422 (Bexleyheath-Woolwich) and 492 (Sidcup-Dartford) in November, part of a package of measures including contract renegotiations to aid the struggling Bexleybus. It also achieved a major tender win in the shape of the 188 (Greenwich Cutty Sark-Euston), which brought it into central London.

It was however a mixed year for LBL, which achieved only two wins from the Hornchurch scheme – both minibus routes, and three of the four 'Peckham Hoppas' (Kentish Bus took the fourth). However, it did better in Sutton, taking every route tendered, with the area operations becoming known as Suttonbus. Three out of five minibus routes were won in Walthamstow, and as part of that process, new routes 34A (Upper Edmonton-Walthamstow Central), 215 (Walthamstow Central-Yardley Lane Estate) and 257 (Stratford-Walthamstow Central/Chingford Mount), along with re-instated 97 (Leyton-Chingford), were introduced.

Ensignbus consolidated its position with four wins in the Hornchurch area, which also marked the appearance on the London scene of Frontrunner (East Midland). Another newcomer was Pan Atlas Coaches, trading as Atlas Bus, which took the 112 (Ealing Broadway-Palmers Green). But the major talking point was Grey-Green's success with the 24 (Pimlico-Hampstead Heath), which brought about a £2.5 million investment in thirty Volvo Citybuses for the route.

There were plans to put parts of routes out to tender. These might have involved all-day Sunday work on the 89, 113, 119, 186, 240; Sunday evening work on the 267; Saturday operations on the 91 and 187, and weekday evenings on the 202. But in the absence of any meaningful interest, the work stayed with LBL.

The Carelink service began on 21 March using three Optare City Pacers in a dedicated red and yellow livery. The vehicles were leased by LRT, which then sub-let them to LBL.

L260 *Renown* (VLT 20, *D260 FYM*) waits in Regent Street on 20 June before its next run out to the Thames Barrier and Greenwich. Selkent certainly knew how to publicise their private hire and excursion vehicles.

The weather on 29 December 1988 was not conducive to photography but having made the eighty-mile trip to Kingston, I did not intend to go home empty-handed. 'Kingfisher' branded LS324 (AYR 324T), which also carries an interesting arrangement of advertisements not seen on other LSs, was laying over in the Cromwell Road bus park in Kingston. I noted at the time that the K10, at 23 miles, was LBLs longest route.

A new daily route that began on 20 April was the 400, which ran from Oxford Circus to Tower Hill, then non-stop to the Thames Barrier (on weekdays) and Greenwich. Since 1988 was the 400th anniversary of the Armada, the numbering was apt.

Kingston Bus launched a new commercial service, the K10, between Kingston-upon-Thames and Staines. It was marketed as 'Kingfisher'.

Conversion of the 28 and 31 from Routemaster to midibus operation, to be branded as 'Gold Arrow' was announced. This was connected to the future possibility of deregulation and not to the tender process.

A new network of routes centred on Docklands was proposed. These would run for around two years until the development of the Canary Wharf area was completed. It was introduced in March 1989, but in the meantime, and given that the plan was for full-size buses only, Harry Blundred, the MD of Devon General and minibus pioneer, announced that his Docklands Transit Ltd would operate several routes separate from, but complementary to, LBL services, using sixteen-seater Mellor bodied Ford Transits which would be brought in from Devon. A start date in March 1989 was mooted.

Conversions to driver-only operation continued as a means of achieving savings, the 25, 29, 53 and 135 being important examples, but the success of the Routemasters acquired by some of the privatised companies in England and Scotland appeared to be the catalyst for a rethink about the continuing use of the type in the central area should a competitive need arise.

As previously mentioned, Sidcup depot closed on 15 January with Bexleyheath reopening the following day. Battersea was finally vacated and sold when London Coaches fully moved to Wandsworth. An outstation at the Kentish Bus Dartford depot was introduced in April. Hornchurch closed on 23 September as a result of losing most of its work to Ensignbus and Frontrunner.

The Sutton area scheme was introduced from 26 November, having been deferred from 29 October, although a special service, the 213 between Sutton and St Helier, was introduced solely between those two dates.

Other events

Plans for a Croydon tramway advanced with a report favouring the conversion of the Wimbledon-Mitcham-Croydon BR line and new sections from Croydon to New Addington and Elmers End.

BEL was sold to Frontsource Ltd in January. In September, plans to redevelop the site, to be known as Chiswick Park, were announced.

Fares across the LRT domain rose in January by an average of 9.5 per cent. Area bus passes were introduced from 10 January, and a series of fourteen leaflets were issued to coincide with the event. The Winter 1987/88 London-wide map was finally issued that same month, although it was already two months out of date.

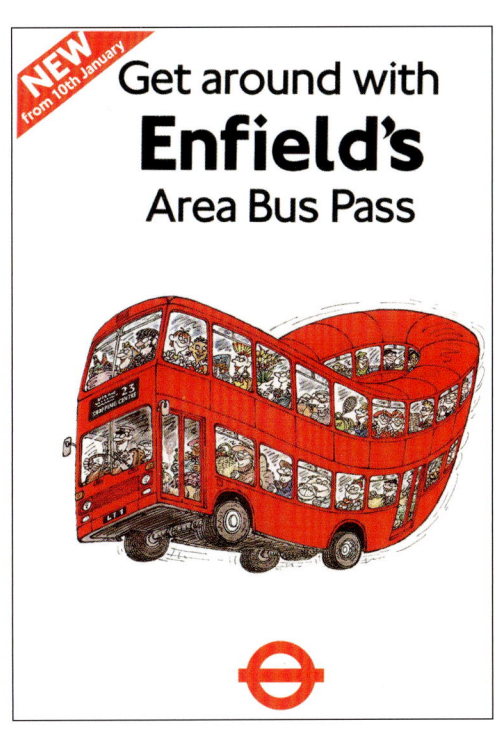

Enfield's version of the Area Bus Pass leaflet.

THE BEXLEY SCHEME

Of the twenty routes in the Bexley area that were put out to tender, LBL won seventeen, the other three going to Boro'line Maidstone. Bexleyheath depot was reopened, at the expense of Sidcup, which was briefly retained as a storage facility. Bexleybus operations began on 16 January 1988; a new livery of blue and cream was used, and buses were numbered in a new series, although LBL fleet numbers were also allocated. All photos were taken between January and March 1988.

Above: There were twenty-eight Olympians which emanated from an order cancelled by Greater Manchester, bodied by Northern Counties and leased from Kirkby Central. This is 8 (L271, E908 KYR) in Sidcup on a 229 working to Foots Cray.

Opposite above: LBL exchanged a number of RMs with Clydeside Scottish in return for fourteen DMSs which took numbers 77-90. Here 86 (DMS1678, THM 678M) loads for Woolwich on a Lewisham-bound 178. The fleetname has been applied below the first offside passenger window rather than the more usual position demonstrated by 102 below.

Opposite below: The DMs and DMSs from LBL stock had been idle for some years and had to go to Ensignbus for overhaul and refurbishment first, but all were in place in good time. 102 (DM1160, KUC 160P) was photographed in Bexleyheath on a 96 working to Woolwich, ahead of Kentish Bus Leyland Tiger 102.

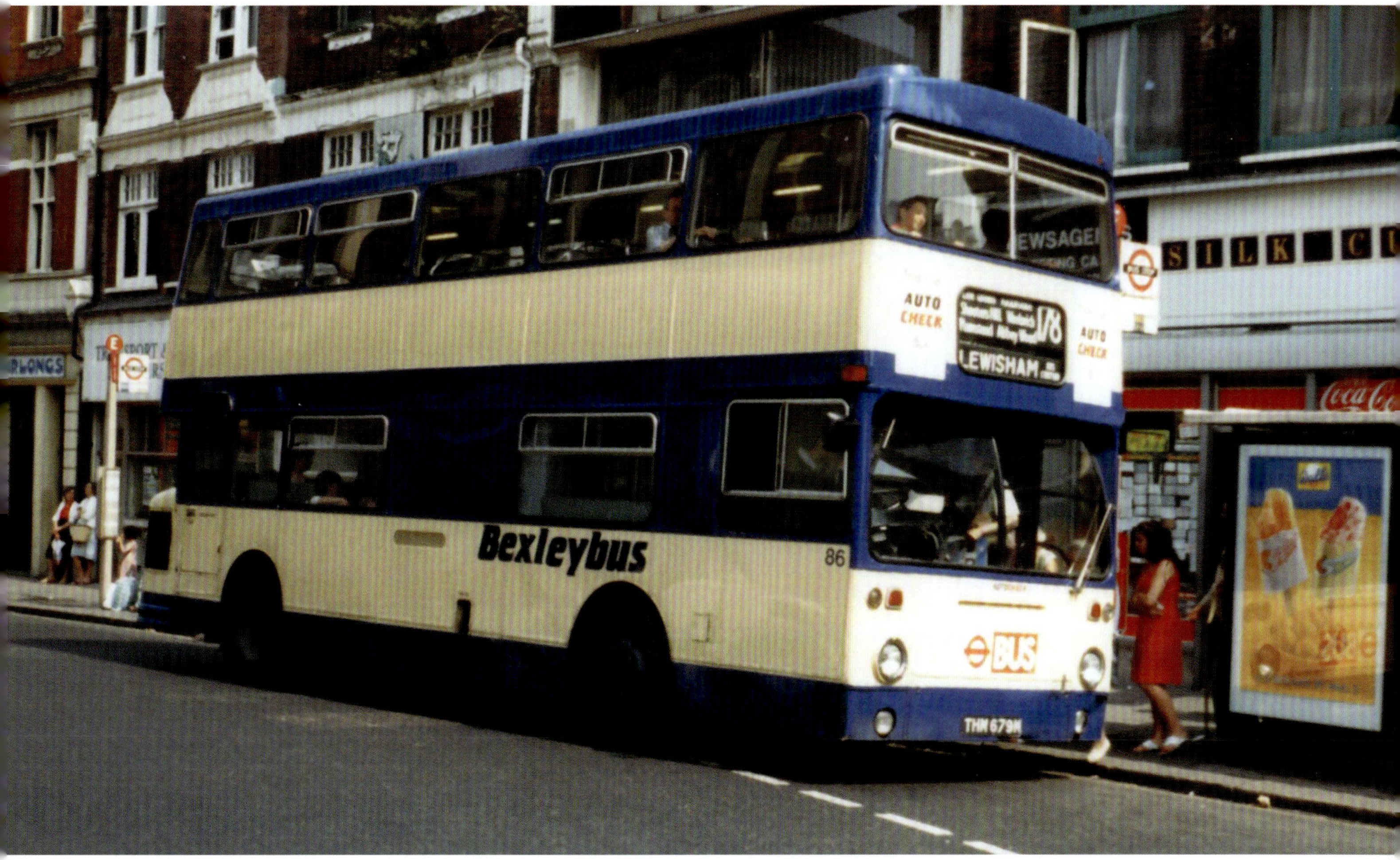
AUTO
CHECK
LEWISHAM
Bexleybus
86
BUS
THM 679M

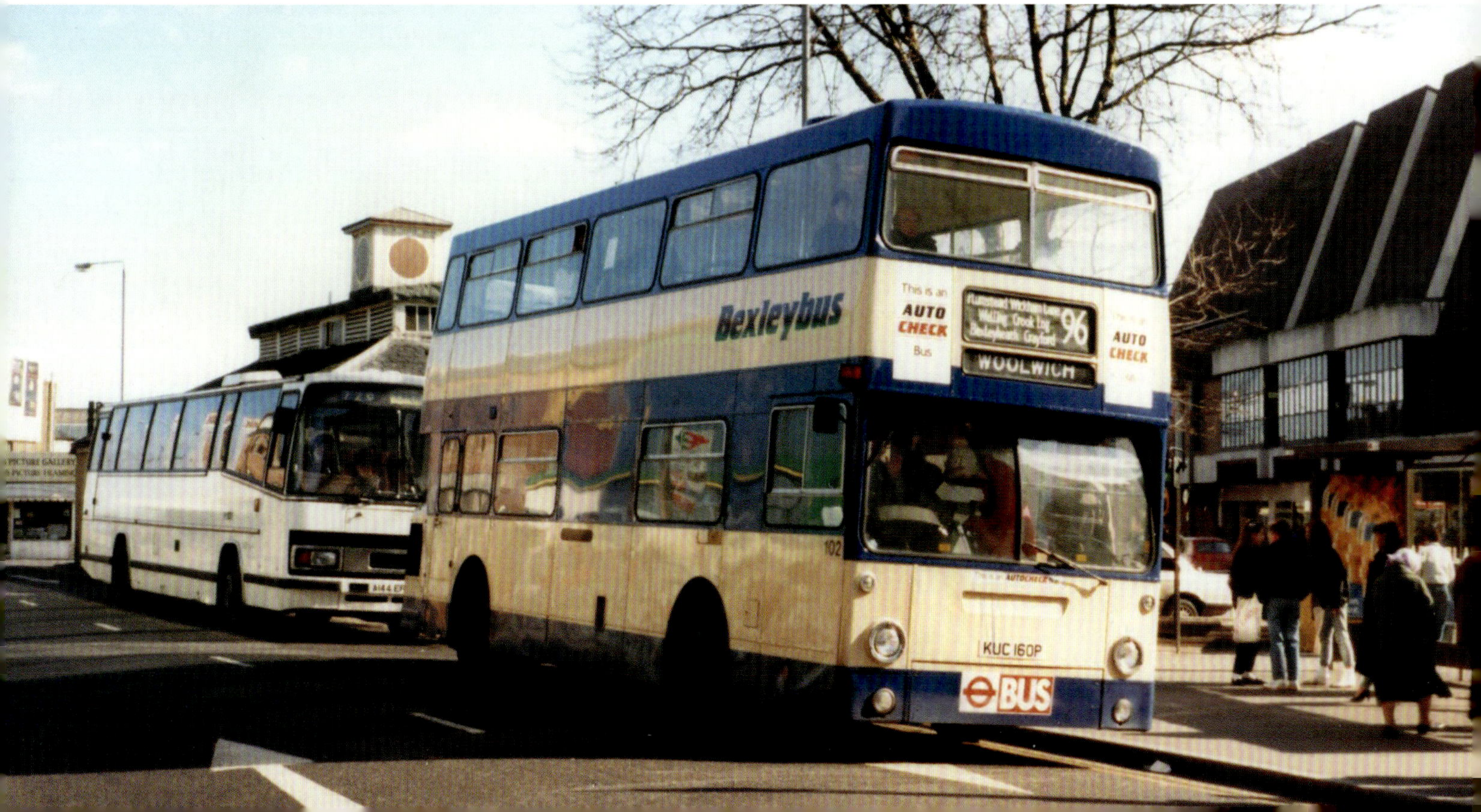
Bexleybus
This is an
AUTO
CHECK
Bus
96
WOOLWICH
102
KUC 160P
BUS

Bexleybus required twenty-four Leyland Nationals, and these were drafted in from across the network. Standing in General Gordon Place in Woolwich, 50 (LS135, THX 135S) is soon to depart on the 422, a new Monday-Saturday route linking Bexleyheath and Woolwich.

Minibus requirements were dealt with by the acquisition of twelve new MCW Metroriders (29-40. MR53-64) and the transfer of twelve RHs from Orpington (65-76, RH11-18/20/21/23/24). RH20 had been on loan to Eastbourne Buses, where it was painted in their blue and cream livery. On return, it gained the Bexleybus name, although this was some months before LBL's tendering wins were announced, so it was stood down until the appropriate time! Now as Bexleybus 73 (D520 FYL), it was about to work to Erith on another new service, the B12. Later in 1988 it was transferred to Catford, and in common with the other eleven, it was sold in the early part of 1991, ending up with Midland Fox.

FOREST, GENERAL AND UNITED

With a name like London Forest, it was hardly surprising that the oak tree would become the company logo. Parked up on the Strand, in between two buildings I knew particularly well in my working days, Bush House and Somerset House, RML2359 (CUV 359C) is suitably decorated for the 6 (Kensal Rise-Hackney Wick), whose route through central London was deemed to have tourist potential.

London General DMS2404 (OJD 404R) in Aldwych in November 1990 displays as its logo the B-type bus which the London General Omnibus Company (LGOC) operated in droves from 1910 onwards. The 77A (King's Cross-Wandsworth) clung on to its Fleetline allocation until quite late, considering that it was a central area route on which Metrobuses had started to appear from May 1990.

The insignia chosen by London United as its logo was that of the former London United Tramways, which had been founded in 1894, and was based on the coat of arms of the City of London. It appears on M327 (EYE 327V), seen in Hammersmith bus station on a 33 working to Fulwell on 27 April 1989. Whilst at that time overall advertisements were still not favoured, wrap-around versions such as this for 'System Text' which M327 had carried since 1985, were acceptable. It also acquired the name 'Stripey' whilst so decorated.

1989

Docklands Transit, a 100 vehicle minibus operation covering seven routes, was launched. It was the brainchild of Harry Blundred, who had pioneered the use of high frequency services using Ford Transits in Devon. A new service of a more luxurious kind came with the introduction of the X15 'Beckton Express', using a fleet of beautifully refurbished RMCs. Trials of the most up-to-date saloons began, and it was fifty years since RT1 first took to the road, giving rise to much celebrating. However, a series of strikes paralysed the network on several occasions between May and July and staff shortages were still an issue, not least for Boro'line Maidstone and their services in and around Bexley.

There was still no word from central government as to future deregulation, although in amongst the additional finance made available for safety and infrastructure improvements on the Underground following the King's Cross fire was some extra funding to be directed towards promoting competition between the various LBL units.

The new Docklands Transit operations required approval from LRT, but, in reality, they were allowed only after the appropriate licences had been obtained from the Metropolitan Traffic Commissioner. LRT then announced that Travelcards and passes would not be valid on Docklands Transit services, a move that was condemned by the new operator. Nonetheless, the first two routes were launched at the end of March, with others following both north and south of the river as the year progressed.

Vehicle news – single deck fleet

Following the decision to mount an 'experimental' trial of the latest saloons, three new vehicles were acquired. Unlike the double deckers five years earlier, these would operate for different companies on a wide variety of routes.

DA1 was a DAF SB220/Optare Delta B49F+24 which went to Selkent and entered service on the B1 in August after coach seats had been fitted. Also entering service that month was DA2, with a B30D+52 configuration, for London General. It was put to work on the Red Arrow network.

SA1 was a Scania K113CRB/Alexander B51F+23 which appeared for South London in August at Thornton Heath for the 59.

RN1 was a Renault PR100/2/Northern Counties B51F+22 that operated out of East London's Seven Kings depot from November, mostly on the 150.

Six more Leyland Lynxes LX3-8, were acquired by London United for the 283, while three former Merthyr Tydfil examples, which became LX9-11, were put to work on the Hillingdon 128. It was decided to include the original Lynxes, LX1/2, in the trial with the other three types.

130 • LONDON'S BUSES, 1979–1994

DAF SB220/ Optare Delta DA2 (F551 SHX) was allocated to Red Arrow routes and was working the 502 when seen at Waterloo at the turn of the year.

It would be stretching credulity to suggest that the Omni/CVEs were attractive vehicles. Of the Hounslow vehicles, only CV2 carried Westlink livery; the other two were delivered in this white with green stripes scheme while the fourth received the red and yellow of Carelink. CV1 (F265 WDC), with its somewhat startling destination display, was discovered in Lampton Road, Hounslow, outside the Civic Guest House and opposite the Civic Centre, on 20 July 1989.

Turning to the mini-and midibus scene, the most interesting - and indeed unusual - minibuses received in 1989 were four Omni/CVEs, CV1-4, of which the first three were operated by Westlink on the newly introduced H20 (Hounslow-Ivybridge Estate).

Seventy-one more Alexander bodied Mercedes 811Ds took the total number to 107. MA101-107 were dual-purpose seated, as was the solitary Reeves Burgess bodied 709D, MT6, which was distinguished from the rest of the class by not having a tail-lift fitted. MT7/8, operated for the London Borough of Ealing, and MTL1, were further Reeves Burgess bodied examples on 709D and 811D chassis respectively, while MW1-16 began a new sequence for Wright bodied 811Ds notable for having Northern Ireland registrations. But the largest intake of all involved the Optare Star Riders, with ninety-three newcomers, SR121 being the highest fleet number to date.

New coaches abounded. DV8-22, 51-60 were various Van Hool Alizee bodied DAFs, while Plaxton Paramount bodied Leyland Tigers were TPL1/2. All were leased, as was DB2, a second Berkhof bodied MB200 new in 1985. Three more second-hand examples were acquired; LP5/6 were Plaxton bodied Leyland Leopards which had worked for Eastern Counties, Ambassador Travel and latterly Cambus, while TP1 was a Leyland Tiger/Plaxton which when new was London Country's TP14.

Leyland National sales gathered momentum as a result of the influx of smaller vehicles, with a total of thirty-eight leaving the fleet. There were just two minibus disposals to record – Freight Rover Sherpa SC2 and Ford Transit FS25.

LS431 received an unusual overall livery in silver and blue for Surrey County Council's centenary. Metrorider M134 was given a white and blue scheme for its Kingston Polytechnic contract work.

Vehicle changes – double deck fleet

London Northern put new Alexander bodied Scania N112DRBs, S1-9, into service on the 263 in July.

One of London Northern's new Scanias for the 263, S8 (F428 GWG), at the Macdonald Road (Archway) terminus of the 263 on 28 September 1989.

December saw more new double deckers arriving with London United and London General that would not be entering service until 1990. For the former, Leyland-bodied Olympians L292-314 carried 'Riverside Bus' fleetnames for the 237; the final three were coach-seated. Conversely, it was the first three of London General's twenty-seven Northern Counties bodied Volvo Citybuses that were similarly treated. Numbered VC1-27, all bar one, VC24, had arrived by the year-end, and were destined for the 133.

After the excesses of the two previous years, there were no second-hand double deck acquisitions in 1989, and the number of withdrawals and sales was lower than in previous years. Fifty-nine Routemasters (including four RMCs and a solitary RMA) and eighteen Fleetlines departed, as did ten of the Volvo Ailsas that had spent just a couple of years at Potters Bar.

Six Titans that went to Bexleybus to replace Fleetlines were given the blue and cream livery, but future transfers to here and to Harrow remained in red.

Service news

Two of the more notable road closures this year included Battersea Bridge, struck by a river barge, and the Strand underpass (Waterloo Bridge-Kingsway), which remained closed all year for long-term repairs. Pedestrianisation schemes were also instituted in Kingston-upon-Thames, where crowds turned out to watch Routemasters ply Clarence Street for the last time, Croydon (on what was already a buses only road) and Bromley, where the proposal was to close the High Street from 1000 to 1600 Mondays-Saturdays, but in the end buses were diverted away at all times.

The H20, upon which the eye-catching Omni/CVEs were used, began on 20 March. Westlink operated the route on behalf of the London Borough of Hounslow, who retained ownership of the vehicles. Westlink also took on three new minibus routes, K4/5/6, in

RM138 (VLT 138) stands at Golders Green station on 30 January 1989 before making the journey back to Wandsworth on the 28. In around five weeks' time, the 'Gold Arrow' era will begin, and Londoners would discover whether important trunk routes like the 28 and 31 were suitable for high density midibus operation.

Kingston-upon-Thames, and were successful in gaining six Surrey County Council services in October, which took their buses to such faraway places as Virginia Water and Bagshot.

Centrewest began their new 'Gold Arrow' operations on the 28 on 4 March and on the 31 on 15 April and followed up with a new four route network in the Uxbridge area marketed as the 'U-Line' on 27 May. The new Mercedes 811D MAs were used in both cases, but the conversion of the 28 and 31 was dogged by reports of overcrowding and bunching, resulting in long gaps in headway. Despite the fact that ridership was said to have increased by 10 per cent, a survey of passengers on the 'Gold Arrow' routes found that over 65 per cent wanted a return to the trusty Routemaster. A 'Night Arrow' service, the N31, was added in November, also utilising the MAs.

East London revamped its Docklands network to reflect the continuing expansion of the area (and perhaps also the forthcoming competition). While the D1 from 1984 was withdrawn, three new routes were introduced:

- D5 (Becontree Heath-Isle of Dogs-Mile End)
- D6 Hackney Central-Isle of Dogs
- D7 (Mile End-Poplar)

There was also the X15, which linked Beckton with Aldwych in the peaks, inaugurated on 6 March. Within a fortnight it was extended at the western end to Oxford Circus in the morning, with evening returns from Trafalgar Square. Outbound morning and inbound evening journeys were operated as ordinary 15s. Customer service was key, and as part of this, conductors would buy newspapers to sell on to passengers. Refurbished RMCs and an RMA were used from Upton Park, and the 'Beckton Express', as it was known, was deservedly a success from day one. It was stressed however that the X15 existed to fill the gap until the DLR extension to Beckton was opened, not as competition to Docklands Transit.

East London LS395 (BYW 395V) carried the gold lining and fleetnames for the Docklands Shuttle, but was seen at Grove Road in Mile End on a D5 working to the Isle of Dogs Asda on 11 July 1990. The company's logo is prominently displayed.

The timing of my morning commute into London made it difficult for me to photo one of the RMCs in the Strand, where I was working, so the decision was made to head out to Paddington, to where the 15B had been extended from 20 March, in the hope of seeing one there. I found RMC1496 (496 CLT) parked up in Chilworth Street, the blinds set ready for the return journey on the 15B. It is 3 April, so this was the start of the fifth week of operation, and enormous credit must go to the staff at Upton Park for preparing the RMCs to such a magnificent standard.

Finally, having been postponed because of ongoing roadworks, the D4 (Mile End-Poplar) was finally introduced on 20 May.

The 400 received sponsorship from Heineken and two Olympians, L260/62, were given wrap-around advertising which included the name 'Bounty Bus' to reflect a 200th anniversary exhibition being held at Greenwich.

Clapton depot reopened for the first time in almost two years for the operation of the 236 (Finsbury Park-Hackney Wick). It also housed the MRLs for the 100 'Wapping Citylink' which began on 10 June.

London United was successful in winning the 283 (West Brompton-East Acton) from Scancoaches in July and introduced its new Leyland Lynxes after a couple of months delay. These were not included in the experimental vehicles trial.

Above: London United Lynx LX3 (G73 UYV) in Old Oak Common Lane on 11 November 1989. Their late arrival meant that there was a substitution by LSs for the first two months. This was the first time Nationals had worked from Shepherds Bush depot. When the Lynxes did appear, there were issues involving small streets and unhelpful car parking around East Acton station which led, three days after this photo, to the terminal point being moved to the Goldsmiths Arms, a short distance away in East Acton Lane.

Right: Major changes to the Night Bus network took place in September and October with ten new routes reflecting the realisation that London was becoming a city that never sleeps.

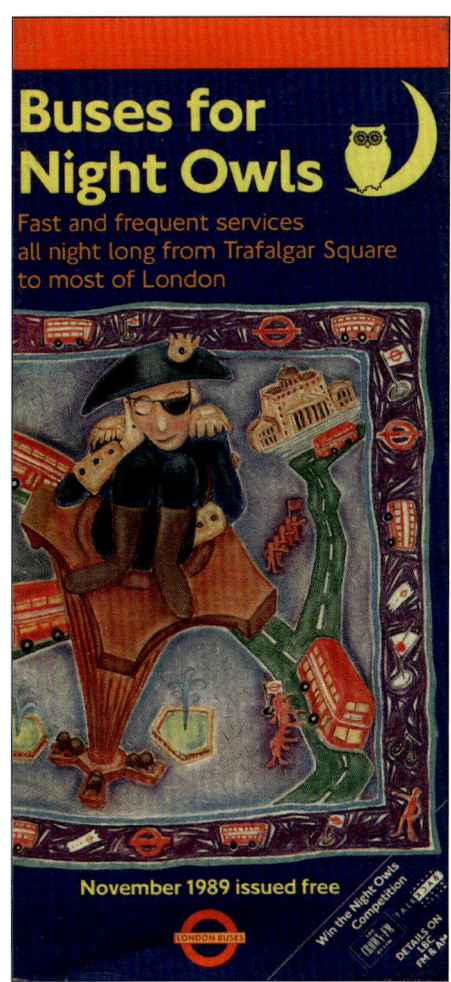

Selkent management sought to introduce more midibus workings, resulting in the introduction of new routes 225 (Rotherhithe-Lewisham), 273 (Lewisham-Lee (Horn Park Estate) 284 (Lewisham-Grove Park) and B16 (Bexleyheath-Eltham), plus the conversion of the existing L1 (Lewisham-Honor Oak Estate). Optare Star Riders and Wright bodied Mercedes 811Ds were used.

The Airbus A1 was yet again the only Christmas Day service. On Boxing Day, unusual workings included Kentish Bus on the 96 and 272 in place of Bexleybus, and BTS instead of Harrow Buses on the 140 and 183. Ensignbus managed to combine three routes into one with a special 86B (Barking-Noak Hill), incorporating parts of the 169, 86 and 174.

Other events

The annual fares increase equated to 12.4 per cent. Adult single fares ranged between 40p (short hop) and £1.30 (four zones). Red Arrow journeys now cost 50p, a rise of 25 per cent.

The 'Autocheck' trial that began during 1987 ended in February.

There were several events to mark the fiftieth anniversary of the entry into service of RT1. The highlight was on 9 August, when it retraced its movements on the exact day fifty years earlier when it emerged from Putney depot to work the 22, then as now linking Putney Common and Homerton.

Repainting of vehicles in order to launch two of the new units added a welcome splash of colour. London General decorated RM89 and RM1590 with traditional 'General' livery for the party at Victoria on 3 April. Also that day Stamford Brook marked the beginning of London United by returning M1069, an arson victim in 1988, to service in a tram-style livery. It was followed by RML880 (later renumbered ER880) in LUT trolleybus colours.

Finally, if I might be forgiven, a record of my brief time behind the wheel of a London Routemaster. In April 1989 the Leaside Training Officer wanted to try out an interesting theory. Driver trainer RMs generally stood idle at weekends, but with a properly organised programme of events, they might usefully be used to give members of the public the paid opportunity to drive one of these iconic vehicles for an hour or two. He and I travelled into London on the same train, he knew of my interest in buses, so I was an obvious candidate for the role of guinea pig, and I spent an afternoon at North Weald airfield carrying out the various possible manoeuvres. RM819 (WLT 819) performed beautifully on the day, and although the idea came to nothing in the end, I'm happy to remember the instructor's comment that he would have no trouble in getting me through a test if I ever wanted to leave my office job and work on the buses! RM819 lasted another year as a trainer – on top of the three it had already clocked up – and was withdrawn in July 1990 and scrapped the following year.

SINGLE DECKERS – EXPERIMENTAL TRIAL

Left: Optare Delta DA1 was received in April 1989 with the registration F54 CWY but was given the plate from RM400 the following month. Having started life at Bromley, it went to Thornton Heath for six months in early 1990, and then in early 1991 Bromley passed it on to Plumstead, where it joined the Private Hire fleet. This photo at Russell Square shows it in the smart DP livery it received in October 1991, but it would not be long until it moved again, to East London and Seven Kings before ending its London career with Westlink.

Below: The evaluation of the Renault RN1 (G276 VML) was split into two phases, the first with East London, working from Seven Kings, and secondly at Leaside's Stamford Hill garage. It was loading in Waterloo Road in November 1990 when I caught it on camera, on a 149 service to Ponders End (which was extended to Waterloo from Liverpool Street station in the peaks). RN1 lasted five years in London service and re-appeared in mid-1993 working for Parfitt's of Rhymney Bridge.

The Scania N113, SA1 (F113 OMJ), alternated between Thornton Heath, where it worked the 59 and 109, and Bromley, in a swap with DA1, seeing service on the B1. It was with Bromley when I saw it resting in a car park on Twickenham Road, Richmond in May 1990. There was to be no happy ending for SA1; it was not deemed to be suitable for London and was returned to Scania in October 1990. It eventually found its way to Black Prince, Morley, where it would stay for fourteen years.

A photo of one of the Leyland Lynxes involved in the trial appeared earlier in the section on the Hillingdon 128s.

TRADITIONAL GENERAL AND UNITED LIVERIES

One of the two Routemasters repainted in traditional livery by London General, RM1590 (590 CLT) in Victoria Street on 6 April 1989.

A modern take on London United Tramways livery adorns M1069 (B69 WUL), pictured in Chiswick High Road on 28 April 1989.

1990

London welcomed a vehicle that was already taking the provinces by storm, the Dennis Dart. Unlike times past, however, when (for example) LT could ask Metro Cammell to body 700 RFs, these 220 arrivals in 1990 represented the work of three different bodybuilders. Better housekeeping was also the order of the day, with improvements mooted in several areas of LBL operations. Liveries were in the news again; LBL proved to be more successful than in previous years where winning tenders was concerned, and with an uncanny prescience, the chairman of LBL went on record to support the idea of road-pricing. Ken Livingstone, elected Mayor of London ten years from now, was probably listening, as congestion charging was introduced in 2003, during his first period in office.

It would seem that the attention paid to some basic elements of running a bus service had been somewhat lacking since responsibility was taken away from the GLC. Two principal aspects singled out for improvement were that vehicles should be cleaned inside and out on a daily basis, and information provided at bus stops should be up-to-date, accurate and relevant. It is not widely known, but at that time, 18,000 bus stops were being served, 1,000 bus stands were in use and thirty-five bus stations were under LRT control – a mammoth undertaking. A Bus Passenger Infrastructure Unit was set up by LRT to oversee it all.

Congestion remained an enormous problem, and a new initiative was unveiled during 1990 in a further attempt to mitigate its effects. Variously dubbed 'clearways' and 'red routes', certain stretches of road would be subject to strict enforcement of parking, loading and unloading conditions. The first three identified were the A1 between Highgate and Angel, the A13 between Aldgate and Limehouse, and the A501 (Angel-Shoreditch-Aldgate).

LRT decided to return to red corporate livery, thus spelling the end of the Harrow Buses and Bexleybus colour schemes and Leaside's black skirt. Some variety was nonetheless retained as Westlink and Suttonbus were allowed to remain as they were. Other operators on LRT contracts could retain their current identities, though it was expected that advice would be given where appropriate.

Tender losses meant the end for Kingston Bus, and the return off-lease of Metrobuses and Olympians. The Harrow and Bexleybus networks had been put out to retender in full, but so far as the former was concerned, only five routes were retained. London Central took all of the work at Bexleybus, and in a move designed to maintain some sort of continuity, took over the network, and the garage site, seven weeks earlier than originally planned. It was described in the November edition of the staff newspaper, *The Clipper*:

> The company's original plan was to open a new garage on a greenfield site at Belvedere, but following representations from the staff at Bexleyheath garage,

Four months before Docklands Transit ceased trading, albeit temporarily as it turned out, former Devon General Mellor bodied Ford Transit, now numbered 222 (E222 BDV), was waiting for custom at the Isle of Dogs Asda on route D56, the result of an earlier split of the D11 from Liverpool Street at Limehouse, on 11 July 1990.

London Buses Ltd will transfer Bexleyheath garage to London Central from 24 November, commercial director Robin Young told *The Clipper*.

'We will operate the existing services, less the 272, which is going to Boro'line, until 19 January. From that date we will run the routes that we were planning to run from Belvedere, plus the B16 route and part of route 89, currently allocated to New Cross.'

London Forest won a contract from the Department of Health to facilitate the movement of staff between various central London sites, requiring two second-hand Freight Rover Sherpas.

Docklands Transit ceased trading on 17 November. Prior to this, LRT had finally allowed just two of the company's routes, the D12 and D15, to be included in the integrated ticketing pool.

Vehicle news – single deck fleet

The only new full-size saloons were seven DAF SB220/Optare Deltas, DA3-9.

London followed the national trend by taking the Dennis Dart to its heart. It was the most popular type of 1990, with 181 new arrivals during the year. In the DT class, the first twenty-seven were bodied by Duple, but following the parent company's decision to close operations, Carlyle took over and was responsible for the remainder, taking fleet numbers up to DT155, although DT134-143 would not appear until 1991. The other thirty-six were bodied by Wright, the thirty-seaters being DW1-14 and DW44-51, while those with thirty-six seats became DWL1-14.

There was still room for more mini- and midibuses. A further eighteen Optare Metroriders, MRL135-152, were received, most going to Selkent. East London had thirty-three Reeves Burgess bodied Renault 50s (RB1-33), but numerically the biggest new class was the Renault 75/Wright (RW), of which Centrewest took all ninety. The Mercedes Benz 811D was again well-represented, with examples bodied by Alexander (MA108-124), Carlyle (MC2-5), Optare Star Rider (SR122/123) and Reeves Burgess (MTL3-5). Last but not least, eight new Iveco 49.10/Reeves Burgess came to London United, FR1-8, operated on behalf of the Borough of Hounslow and which could be adapted to take two wheelchair passengers.

There were six second-hand arrivals: Duple bodied Dennis Dart DT168, a pair of Freight Rover Sherpa/Dormobile new to West Riding and London Country South West respectively (SD1/2), Mercedes Benz 811Ds bodied by Carlyle (MC1) or Reeves Burgess (MTL2) and LSL1, a former Southdown Leyland National that was destined for the disabled unit.

There was considerable activity again on the coaching front. New in 1990 were nine DAF SB2305s, four with Duple 320 bodywork (DD1-4) and five Van Hool Alizee (DV62-66). Three new Plaxton Paramount bodied Leyland Tigers received fleet numbers TPL3-5; the former London Country North East TPL31 was also taken into stock, becoming TP2. Second-hand acquisitions were DAF MB230/Duple 320 (DD42) or Duple 340 (DD91-93), the latter trio having already served here until February as DD1-3 before being rehired in May, and three Volvos from the Digby Stewart College, DS1-3.

In terms of withdrawals, the Leyland National was the major casualty, with 149 sold in the year. Dodge S56 A2 left, as did a pair of BLs; just BL81, at Westlink, survived in service at the year-end. SR10, a fire victim early in the year, was scrapped after being cannibalised, and SA1, which was part of the experimental trial, went back to Scania. Various coaches were either sold or returned off-lease; DD1-3 (see above) and DD5, DD42, DV51-54, LC1/2 and TP1. The coach that started it all in 1984, DB1, went back to Ensign.

Vehicle news – double deck fleet

By contrast, only twelve of the new arrivals in 1990 belong in this category, bringing the total number of Volvo Citybuses with London General to thirty-eight. VC24 completed the batch for the 133; the remaining eleven, VC28-38, were allocated to the 196, although being based at Stockwell, they could (and did) appear on either route.

Some of the Fleetlines no longer required at Bexleybus were returned to service by London General for a short time, carrying a hybrid livery the likes of which it is doubtful London had ever seen before.

Withdrawals accounted for fifty-one Fleetlines, including a couple of B20s DMS2320, DM2552, sixty-five RMs and four RMCs. After three years of service, forty-one of the sixty-two second-hand Volvo Ailsas were sold; six were former South Yorkshire PTE

Fleetline working at Bexleybus ended in February, when the type was replaced by Titans, although withdrawals began a little earlier. DMS2143 (OJD 143R) was stored for a short while before being resurrected and despatched to Sutton where, along with three others, it was given a partial repaint and returned, albeit briefly, to service. Described as 'bizarre', its new guise was part LBL (red front with the white stripe and grey skirt) and part Bexleybus (everywhere else). I found it waiting to cross Euston Road into Upper Woburn Place on 10 May 1990; the driver's resigned expression rather implies 'is this what it's come to?' It appears to have been used on both the Wimbledon tennis and Hampton Court Flower Show services, and was then sold, but it saw another fourteen years' service with two other operators before it was sold for scrap.

vehicles, the remainder were ex West Midlands PTE and were drawn from both the Potters Bar and Harrow Buses allocations. Finally, returned off-lease were seventeen of the Bexleybus Olympians and twelve Metrobuses from Harrow.

A start was made on the replacement of worn-out AEC engines in Routemasters by Iveco units, the work taking place at Battersea. But undoubtedly the most newsworthy event so far as the RMs were concerned was the conversion of open-top RM163 to a five-bay vehicle and thus its renumbering as ERM163, the 'E' standing for 'Extended'. The consequent increase in seating from sixty-four to seventy-six improved the

Showing off its new, five-bay body is London Coaches' ERM90 (VLT 90), on the stand at Victoria. It gave eleven years' service in this form and was then sold to Mac Tours, Edinburgh, eventually becoming part of the Lothian Buses fleet.

competitiveness of the London Coaches offering, and its success meant nine more were converted during the year, becoming ERM80/84/90/94, 143, 235/37/42/81.

Almost forty vehicles of all sizes except double deckers were loaned or used as demonstrators during the year.

Service news

Whilst Harrow and Bexley names might have been consigned to the history books, another new name was taking to the roads in west London. The London United Olympians and Lynxes received in 1989 put to work on the 237 and 283 respectively were given 'Riverside Bus' logos.

London General received new Volvo Citybuses with Northern Counties bodywork at the end of 1989, so they were ready to start work on day one of the renewed contract for the 133, 6 January 1990. My photo, taken a few weeks later on 30 March, shows VC18 (G118 NGN) in Finsbury Circus; my notes suggest that for some reason it was not able to access the usual stand at Liverpool Street station that day, but I have been unable to corroborate this.

A similar thing was taking place at London United's Stamford Brook garage, where all-Leyland Olympians had appeared before Christmas 1989 but were first seen out on 6 January when the new contract for the 237 (Shepherds Bush-Sunbury Village) started. A new trading name, Riverside Bus, was adopted, and the opportunity was taken to include the 283 (West Brompton-East Acton) in the scheme, vehicles being transferred from Shepherds Bush to Stamford Brook for the purpose. L304 (G304 UYK), seen in London Road, Brentford on 3 March 1990, was only working as far as Lower Feltham.

There was more to come. Centrewest introduced the 'E-LINE', a network of routes in and around the Ealing area, namely:

E1 Greenford-Ealing Broadway (Brentford-Ealing Broadway section replaced by the E8)
E2 Greenford-Brentford/Syon Park (Ruislip-Greenford section replaced by the E7 and E9)
E6 – a new service between Hayes and Greenford (Mondays-Saturdays excluding evenings)
E7 – a new service between Ealing Broadway and Ruislip (Mondays-Saturdays)
E8 – a new service between Ealing Broadway and Brentford
E9 – a new service between Ealing Broadway and Yeading (Mondays-Saturdays)

The E3-E5 remained unchanged, although they were converted from Metrobus to midibus (RW) operation, as was the E1 outside Monday-Friday peaks, and the E2. The E6-E9 were RW-operated from the start.

On 12 May, London General introduced the 'Streetline' brands on its fleet of new Mercedes 811D/Alexander midibuses, which were allocated to the 39 and 239. This was another conversion from Metrobus operation, with the 39 working Putney Bridge-Clapham Junction, with the onward section to Victoria forming the 239.

The 39 was one of a number of routes around this time to be split, in an attempt to combat the evils of congestion and to take advantage of the smaller vehicles now available. The Victoria to Clapham Junction section was renumbered 239 and rerouted at Clapham to serve the Gateway (now Asda) superstore. Mercedes 811D/Alexander midibuses were introduced, bearing the new Streetline identity, and MA122 (G122 PGT) was waiting for departure time in Terminus Place, Victoria on 31 August 1990.

London United used Duple bodied Dennis Darts and the 'Harrier' fleetname for its new services in the Richmond area, the R69 and R70. They were less well known on the H24, introduced on 29 September 1990, which linked Feltham and Hatton Cross Underground station, which was normally operated by three Metroriders. DT17 (G517 VYE) has recently arrived at the latter location not long after commencement. There was a switch to the FR class early in 1991, and the H24 itself lasted until August 1993, when it was incorporated into the H25.

Other names applied during the year were the 'Barnet Hoppa' for the new 384 and the 'Harrier' at London United for the R69/R70, which received new Dennis Darts, both in April. More 'Harriers' turned up that same month for Hounslow area services H21-H23. The addition of the H24/H25 in September marked the return of the Hoppa – because these were LRT contract services and that's what LRT wanted! 'Skipper' was the name chosen by Metroline, applying it to new Dennis Darts on the 206 (Neasden-Kilburn High Road) in September and the 251 (Arnos Grove-Edgware/Stanmore Broadway) and 288 (Edgware circular) in November. Also that month, new route P5 (Elephant& Castle-Brixton) was named the 'Camberwell Clipper' by London Central.

The 400 service to Greenwich, which lost its weekend operations later in 1988, the year it was introduced, was withdrawn on weekdays on 26 May.

Most of the LBL subsidiaries were developing small, dedicated fleets for private hire and special services work, and the five former West Midlands Travel Titans were leading players. They were separated in 1987, with T1128 moving to East London and T1129 to London Central; the others remained at Selkent. T1129 (WDA 4T) looks well cared for in this photo in Aldwych on 24 May 1990. The two Fleetlines to the rear are also of interest; DM1102 (GHV 102N) was converted to open-top at Aldenham in 1983, and two years later was named 'MV Royal Daffodil', joining the Selkent charter fleet in 1988. Further back, outside Bush House, the home of the BBC World Service, is the corporation's own Fleetline, the former DMS25 (EGP 25J). Owned by Ensignbus from the mid-1980s and originally part of its sightseeing fleet, it was fitted with a canvas roof and began its stint with the BBC in 1989.

An express version of the 207 (Uxbridge-Shepherds Bush), numbered 607, came into being on 21 July. The new route called at just fifteen stops en route, with an allocation provided by the consequent reduction of vehicles on the 207.

First proposed by East London in 1989, LRT went on to seek tenders for a new express service between Waterloo and Docklands, which was won by London Forest and introduced on 28 August using ten Titans. The branding and route information contained on broad white panel between decks was commendable.

A bold new night route initiative in October saw New Cross supply a coach-seated Olympian for the 'Medway Night Express', the NX1, on Fridays and Saturdays, leaving

Trafalgar Square for Gillingham at 0100 and 0345, returning at 0235, and 0525 to New Cross Gate only. A major selling point was that it left London later than the last services provided by Maidstone & District's 'Invictaway' coaches, and British Rail.

It would be fair to say that the abrupt departure of Docklands Transit from the London scene, temporary though it turned out to be, was an acrimonious one. Chairman Harry Blundred was in no doubt that the unwillingness of LRT to grant the company access to the Travelcard market was the key issue, and his ire was also directed at the Office of Fair Trading – he felt there was nothing 'fair' about the way the company had been treated. The end came on 17 November 1990.

As examples of what London bus managers and drivers have to contend with, 1990 saw:

- various demonstrations throughout the year, but most notably that against the poll tax on 31 March
- high winds in January, similar to those experienced in 1987, which saw double deckers replaced by saloons in some cases. Only one LBL vehicle suffered material damage
- terrorist activity – real or intended – causing disruption in May, July and September
- a large hole which appeared in Wimbledon Broadway, necessitating diversions from mid-June until late July, and
- water main bursts in Acton, Malden, Stanmore, Tooting and Tottenham during the summer and autumn, with the 123 suspended between Tottenham and Wood Green for three weeks in October.

Waterloo Bridge was closed for maintenance work during the first week of 1990, so the 501 was diverted via Blackfriars Bridge and Victoria Embankment. Making the turn from the latter into Temple Place was LS500 (GUW 500W), providing a rare photographic opportunity. In fact, this was the first day, 2 January, that the manoeuvre was possible. By 1990, London General had responsibility for the Red Arrow services, as it does for the two remaining routes, the 507 and 521, to this day.

Other events

Fares were increased from 4 February by around 10 per cent overall. Although some were unchanged, rises were generally between 5p and 20p. The Original London Sightseeing Tour charged £8 for an adult, half that for a child, with a £1 discount for buying in advance of travel.

BEL moved from Chiswick to Willesden, and the remaining buildings were demolished in preparation for work to commence on phase one of the 'Chiswick Park' development. Acton, a former tram and (briefly) trolleybus depot, reopened its doors in May for the first time since 1937. In the interim it had been used by London Underground for stores but was now brought up to speed to house vehicles on the E3.

There were garage closures, at Muswell Hill (July) and Walworth (October), the vehicles at the latter moving to the new Red Arrow base in Cornwall Road, near to Waterloo. London Coaches acquired a new home at Northfleet, replacing temporary facilities in the town and at the Borough Green, one of Maidstone & District's depots.

Left: The latest version of the London Bus Map (Summer 1990) carried advertising for the 'Beatles' Revolution', an exhibition being held at the Trocadero in Piccadilly.

Below: Chiswick Works closed its doors for the very last time when BEL moved to new premises in Willesden. Prior to that, 14 November 1986 witnessed the end of the famous training school and skid patch, and the three vehicles retained for this special purpose, RMs 1740, 1921 and 1932, were sent to nearby Stamford Brook to work as trainers. This is RM1740 (740 DYE) in full flow on 5 August 1984, at this point still in its first season in the role. It was withdrawn in 1991 and was exported to Uruguay.

To help with its publicity of the Travelcard, an extraordinary vehicle was constructed using the cab sections of DMS1515 at the front and a Network South East Class 321 at the rear. Sandwiched in between them was a section of a 1973 tube stock carriage. Completed by December, its first appearance was on a television advertisement.

Services from 2345 on New Year's Eve to 0500 on New Year's Day were sponsored this year by Foster's Lager. Around fifty services and over 350 vehicles were involved.

MINIS AND MIDIS GALORE

All five of the Carlyle bodied Mercedes Benz 811Ds went to Orpington for the Roundabout network, where the aim was to increase capacity on the R3. MC1 had been on loan for some time before finally being taken into stock. By now, vehicles were appearing in, or being repainted into, LBL red, although MC5 (H885 LOX) still carries the Roundabout name prominently. It was found in Orpington High Street on 27 December 1990, whilst on its way to Green Street Green.

Above: The contract to ferry staff between various DHSS London sites required the use of two minibuses, and London Forest acquired two Freight Rover Sherpas for the purpose. The first, SD1, was a former West Riding vehicle. SD2 (D212 GLJ) seen here in Baylis Road on 13 September 1991, bound no doubt for the offices on Waterloo Road, was new to Shamrock and Rambler but passed to London & Country following the Bournemouth operator's demise. Both SDs were returned off-lease in 1991 and were replaced, as will be seen, by Optare Metroriders.

Opposite above: The RW class were given, in my view, uncharacteristically ugly bodies by Wright's. Centrewest had ninety for the new E-Line network, and RW57 (HDZ 5457) had reached the Chiswick end of the E3 in Edensor Road when I found it, early on in its career. They were not destined to have long service lives in London; disposals took off once First Bus had gained control of Centrewest, and RW57 found itself transferred, along with fourteen others to Leicester CityBus where, I'm assured by a member of the garage staff, they had three more highly unpopular years prior to withdrawal.

Opposite below: Received in December 1990 though not actually entering service until 1991, the eight Iveco 49.10s FR1-8 were fitted with wheelchair lifts and were operated by London United for the Borough of Hounslow, whose distinctive livery is seen here on FR2 (H702 YUV). It may have been out of service at the time I saw it in Hounslow bus station, but its last duty seems to have been the H24 (Feltham-Hatton Cross), a new service introduced in September 1990 and operated by a mixture of MRs and, more occasionally, DRs, until these more specialised vehicles were ready.

1991

What's the worst that can happen when your network goes out to tender? Ask the managers of London Forest, which ceased to exist on 23 November. It was not a good year either for LBL, which might, under yet more Government proposals, have seen its role seriously reduced. Plans to privatise London Coaches were announced.

So far as the future intentions of the Government were concerned, there was yet another consultation paper. Published in March, 'A Bus Strategy for London' suggested that there would be a period of a year or so when LBL would operate in a deregulated environment before the privatisation process would start, and the earliest this might occur would be June 1994. Updating the fleet and selling off the garage estate separately from the operations were also mooted, but issues around Travelcards and all types of passes, currently an LRT responsibility, were skirted around. By July, the plan was to set up a London Bus Executive under Department of Transport control to oversee services. Needless to say, the LRT board was not amused,

Mention was made last year of the extraordinary vehicle constructed from the front section of DMS1515 (THM 515M), and mock-ups of part of a 1973 stock underground carriage and a Network South East Class 321, to be used to publicise Travelcards. The 'Supercar', as it was dubbed, began fulfilling those duties in 1991. In more recent times the 'train' became 321 434, matching a unit operating with Greater Anglia that has carried that number from new.

and the London Regional Passengers Committee remained implacably opposed to deregulation. On the other hand, Transit Holdings' Harry Blundred welcomed it with open arms. Nonetheless, his comment that it would lead to a 'great resurgence in bus service provision, resulting in a large increase in passengers and leading to a major contribution in the reduction of congestion on the streets of the capital' seems remarkably over-optimistic.

Compare that, however, with the admission by the Transport Secretary in the House of Commons that around 60 per cent of those who had bothered to comment on the consultation document were opposed to deregulation, and it was reported in *Buses* that the independent operators – those the government hoped to have on side with the proposals – were 'especially 'vitriolic' in their response. A manager from Grey-Green, one of the largest, called deregulation a 'redundant ideology'. Apart from an announcement from the Prime Minister in November that LRT would not become the new London Bus Authority/Executive, the whole sorry business was left to drag on for yet another year.

The forthcoming privatisation of London Coaches was announced in August, although the matter would not be decided until May 1992.

The end of London Forest was a serious affair in which none of the players emerged with any great credit. Having won the right to continue working eleven routes in the Walthamstow area in May, the harsh reality was that it was conditional upon a) an increase in working hours, b) a wage reduction of at least 25 per cent, and c) a cut in ancillary staff numbers. London Forest managers knew that to be successful, costs had to be reduced to achieve any kind of parity with the competition, but this exercise had already been carried out, just three years earlier, so asking the staff to go the extra mile once again was always going to be problematic. The unions were not happy, a number of one-day strikes took place, and Kentish Bus, Thamesway County Bus and Ensignbus all provided cover on strike-affected routes. With no progress being made in discussions with London Forest staff, the Tendered Bus Division awarded all eleven routes worked at Walthamstow to other operators:

- the 144, W15 and W16 to County Bus
- the W11 and W12 to Thamesway
- the 97, 97A, 123, 158, 212 and 215 to Ensignbus

...with contracts starting in November. Despite a return to something approaching normal working at the end of July, the resignation of London Forest's MD and an appraisal from the LBL Network Services Manager led to the announcement in September that London Forest operations would end on 23 November. On that date Walthamstow and Ash Grove garages would close; Leyton would move to East London and Hackney join Leaside, where it would get its old name of Clapton back. Ash Grove's routes were distributed to East London (30, D1, D6), East London/Metroline (6), London Central (35) and Leaside (106, 253). Five of London Forest's eleven routes changed hands before the November date for practical reasons, such as a shortage of drivers and the impracticability of recruiting when the company was due to close.

Also in November, Ensignbus adopted the name Capital Citybus, as well as a new livery of yellow with two red stripes, for its Walthamstow and Wood Green operations, which would henceforth use a new base at Northumberland Park.

Vehicle news – single deck fleet

The onward march of the Dennis Dart continued during 1991. A new class was established, and DR1-64 carried either Reeves Burgess or, after rationalisation by the parent company, Plaxton Pointer bodies. DR58-64 seated twenty-four passengers, as opposed to the more usual twenty-eight, and DRL1-16, being 9.8m in length as opposed to 8.5m, carried thirty-four. The first four of these, being bound for the P11, carried the names of characters from the TV sitcom *Only Fools and Horses*.

Further Darts were DT134-143 and 156-167 (Carlyle) and DW15-43, 52-99 and 101-112 (Wright). DW100 also officially joined the fleet, having been on loan for a year as DW00. Two Renault S56s stayed for several months and were given fleet numbers RB34/35.

Another loaned vehicle, a DAF SB220/Optare Delta demonstrator, was acquired in August, becoming DA10 and remaining with East London.

No fewer than sixty-four Optare Metroriders, MRL153-216, joined the fleet, along with a further ten Alexander bodied Mercedes Benz 811Ds, MA125-134.

New coaches appeared in the shape of DAF SB2305/Van Hool DV23/24/26-29/31, and two Leyland Tigers, TPL7 with the Plaxton Paramount 3200 body and TPL8 with the 3500 variant. TPL6 was another Leyland Tiger, ex Craig of Campbeltown, for East London. Westlink took fourteen-year old Volvo B58-61/Duple Dominant VT1 for use as a driver trainer.

Although technically the first fifty-two DR class Darts were said to be bodied by Reeves Burgess, in fact DR20-52 were Plaxton products, made under a sub-contract agreement. From DR53 onwards they were badged as Plaxton vehicles. DR32 (H532 XGK), with Streetline branding for the 156 (Wimbledon-Clapham Junction) does not appear to be going anywhere in the short term, but a second DR behind it will shortly set off on the route. The location is Victoria Crescent, Wimbledon, on 28 November 1991.

DA10 (G684 KNW) came to East London as a demonstrator in April 1990 and was bought by London Buses the following year. It can be said to have set the standard for the smart new silver grey livery, with red skirt and stripes, that was perpetuated on the next two batches, DA11-29 in 1992 and DA30-35 in 1993. East London was in fact the only company besides Westlink to operate the type. DA10 was on a 148 working to Leytonstone when photographed in Ilford.

Hastings & District supplied a Leyland National which became LSL2, which was converted to a mobility bus and transferred to Kentish Bus. Leyland Lynxes LX1/2 were taken into stock from the London Borough of Hillingdon.

Sales accounted for coaches AP2 and LP1, with DD91-93 returned off-lease. Ninety-seven Leyland Nationals also left the fleet, as did twelve Iveco 49.10s and nine Optare City Pacers (although one, OV2, was presented to the London Transport Museum). SD1/2 were returned to Carlyle.

Also in the news in 1990 were the two Freight Rover Sherpas used by London Forest for the DHSS shuttle contract. They were returned to Carlyle during 1991 and their place was taken by a pair of MCW Metroriders, MR104, and seen here in Waterloo Road on 14 November 1991, MR105 (F105 YVP), complete with 'The Shuttle' branding. Following the demise of London Forest later that month, the contract (and MR104, 105) moved to Clapton.

Vehicle news – double deck fleet

Twenty-three vehicles arrived during the year including the last of the Volvo B10M/Northern Counties, VC39. East London took Scania N113DRB/Alexander S10-31, which were used initially on three supplementary services introduced to support the DLR.

Leaside acquired an AEC Regent V/Park Royal, RV1, for special duties. It was new to East Kent in 1966.

An interesting second-hand acquisition was an Auwerter Neoplan N112/3 Skyliner from ILG, Ratby, which took fleet number SKY1 and entered service with London Northern in white livery.

Twenty-four RMs and three RMCs surrendered their registration numbers; Darts, Olympians and Volvo Citybuses were the recipients.

The temporary services introduced to support the Docklands Light Railway were revised in early December to operate as normal routes. East London had managed to acquire twenty Alexander bodied Scania N113s from dealer stock, and a number, including S19 (J819 HMC), carried Docklands Express branding for either the D1 or, as here in this photo at London Bridge, the D11. S19 spent under two years on DLR work before it was moved to Holloway for the X43 – more on that later. It was withdrawn in 2003 and has since worked for three Leicestershire independents.

RV1 (GJG 750D) was one of thirty AEC Regent Vs with Park Royal bodies new to East Kent in 1966. It passed through several hands, including those of Obsolete Fleet, before being acquired by Leaside for private hire and special duties. Being a London commuter, I reckoned that my only chance of seeing it would be at a rally, and so it proved, as it turned up at the North Weald event on 30 June 1991, not long after it had been refurbished in readiness for its new role. Next to it is West Riding 235, a Roe bodied Daimler Fleetline.

Sales activity was again dominated by the Fleetlines, with 180 leaving the fleet. Only around 250 were now left in stock. Routemaster numbers declined by thirty-seven, a figure that included a pair of RMAs, eight RMCs and solitary RMT2793. Eleven of the Volvo-Ailsas were sold, and fire victim T1069 was scrapped. Eleven Leyland Olympians and seventeen MCW Metrobuses from the Bexleybus and Harrow networks respectively were returned off-lease.

Service news

Early in the year, a pilot exercise began to speed up services between Old Street station and Highgate, which became known as a 'Red Route'. The parking and loading/unloading restrictions were stringently monitored.

An IRA mortar bomb attack on 7 February saw road closures put in place in the Westminster area for two days. As if that was not enough, a spell of extremely cold weather followed, and heavy snowfalls that night and early the next morning caused widespread disruption to services. It was a week before things returned to normal.

The Gold Arrow upgrade first saw RMs replaced by the MA class Mercedes 811Ds in April 1989. It's fair to say they were not well loved for a variety of reasons and within two years they were replaced, starting in February 1991, by Wright bodied Dennis Darts. DW93 (JDZ 2393) was new in September that year; it seated two less passengers than the MA, at twenty-six, but accommodated twenty standees, which was five more. It was photographed in Earls Court Road on 20 November 1991.

There was good news for London General when the results of the Wandsworth area tenders were announced; it won them all, thus saving the sort of embarrassment that the Bexleyheath retendering engendered. The only loss was part of the 37, which having been split into three sections, saw the western leg, renumbered H37, pass to London United. The revised Harrow network began on 11 January, and besides Metroline, involved vehicles from three other operators, Luton & District (which had taken over London Country North West the previous October), BTS Coaches and Sovereign Bus & Coach.

After less than two years in service the Gold Arrow MA class Mercedes 811Ds on the 31 were progressively replaced by Wright bodied Dennis Darts; the 28 would be similarly converted in 1992. New route 70 (Kensington High Street-East Acton, replacing that section of the 52A), also a Gold Arrow offering, was launched in March with the MAs.

Midibus route C1 (Waterloo Taxi Road-Kensington) was in the news when its withdrawal was announced. Only the section from Victoria to Waterloo would be saved, to be worked by a new Red Arrow service, the 511. London General thought differently, however, as did residents along the route of the C1, and from 28 September it was operated commercially, though with a 50p additional charge for Travelcard and pass holders. The 511 was still introduced, but was withdrawn in 1993, and the faith shown in the C1 was vindicated when it was readmitted to the LRT fold in February 1992.

Better known as a coach operator, Tellings Golden Miller of Byfleet joined the ranks of tendered operators when it won the 116 and 117 from Westlink. Acquired by Midland Fox – once the eastern part of Midland Red – in 1990, the company announced that it was seeking Leyland Nationals of 1979/80 vintage to work the routes, and come August, when the contract started, thirteen had been acquired, with R, S or T suffix registrations, all ex Midland Fox and still carrying their original fleet numbers.

Norbiton garage closed in September and its two remaining routes, the 57 and 71, transferred to Fulwell.

September also saw the end of the Hillingdon Local Service 128 after almost fourteen years. For those sections of route that fell within Greater London, alterations were made to the Uxbridge U-Line service U1 and a new U8 that replaced the former 128A. A Hertfordshire County Council route R1 based on Rickmansworth was operated by Centrewest.

A new Airbus A3 service between Stamford Brook garage and Stanstead Airport using Olympians from the Riverside Bus allocation began in July but was withdrawn after only two months due to lack of patronage.

The LT 'Original London Sightseeing Tour' turned 50, having begun in the year of the Festival of Britain. London Coaches introduced a new 'London Plus' hop-on/hop-off service in August, and six ERMs, and six RMAs gained the new livery – red up to the lower deck windows and cream above, with a red roof.

The introduction of one-person operation in November for cost-cutting purposes marked the end of RMCs on the X15, although they still worked the 15 and 15B. At the same time, three new services, the D9 (Bank-Crossharbour station), D10 (Liverpool Street-Canary Wharf/Leamouth) and D11 (London Bridge-Canary Wharf) were introduced, marking the end of the supplementary services referred to earlier. The honour of being the first route to reach Canary Wharf went to the 277 in July.

RMA65 (NMY 665E) was repainted into the new 'London Plus' livery in October 1991, and its closed-top configuration would have ensured plenty of work for it during the winter months. Unfortunately, there were not many takers on the day I found it at St Paul's Churchyard, 3 December 1991.

Right: Converted to open-top in 1989 after a roof accident, Centrewest made the most of the tourist potential RMC1510 (510 CLT) offered. It appeared on the 15 in the run-up to Christmas, allowing a better view of the decorations in Oxford Street and Regent Street, and would turn out in the summer when the weather was suitable on short workings of the 15. It was bound for St Pauls when I saw it in Duncannon Street on 9 August 1991. Its finest moment must however be that it was chosen to convey the Olympic Torch on Oxford Street in the run-up to the 2012 Games.

Below: So far as my working life and my interest in buses are concerned, I'd have to say that I've been fairly fortunate when it came to marrying the two. For ten years I had an office overlooking St Margaret's bus station in Leicester, and subsequently, for about a year, I enjoyed this view out onto the Strand, which enabled me to spot eastbound vehicles in plenty of time, and then hang out of the window to photograph them! My highlight was RMC1456 (456 CLT); demoted now so far as the X15 was concerned but still looking superbly turned out for its more mundane duties on the 15.

Other events

Smoking was banned on all double deckers with effect from 14 February. It had been prohibited on single deck vehicles for several years.

Upgrading the Metrobus and Titan fleets to the latest DiPTAC standards began. High visibility handrails in green, waist-level bell pushes, black and yellow 'shark's tooth' step markings and improved illuminated 'Bus Stopping' signs were all part of the scheme.

A by-product of the autonomy the operating companies now enjoyed was the creation of their own staff newsletters, which in turn spelled the end of LBL's own offering, 'Bus Talk', which had lasted for five years. Centrewest, Leaside, London Central, London Forest, London General and Metroline were among the first to avail themselves of this more personalised form of communication.

As usual, only Airbus A1 operated on Christmas Day, between 0730 and 1600. However, two free services which utilised privately owned Routemasters ran during the daytime as follows:

- 88A Holland Park-Pentonville South, with RM1571
- 113A Swiss Cottage-Euston, with RM2198

Once again, Foster's Lager sponsored New Year's Eve travel between 2345 and 0500 on New Year's Day. Given the way revellers liked to congregate in Trafalgar Square, the hub of operations was moved to Aldwych.

DIFFICULT CONDITIONS

Winter in England in 1990/91 saw some snowy days, none more so, particularly in London and the South East, than the night and morning of Friday 8 February 1991. Overnight falls deposited 20cm of snow at St James's Park, the most recorded since the big freeze of 1962/63. There were further showers in the east throughout the rest of the day and temperatures remained below freezing all day. Close examination of what can be seen of the blinds on RM2159 (CUV 159C) suggest that it is on its way to work the 36B (Grove Park-Victoria with peak journeys extended to Paddington). How long it will take to get there given the prevailing conditions is anybody's guess, but one pities the crew that will have to endure it. The 36B was converted to OPO a year later but was withdrawn in 1994. There appears not to have been any more snow after the Friday, but it took another ten days before conditions became more settled.

164 • LONDON'S BUSES, 1979–1994

Lewisham High Street on 8 February 1991, with two Titans caught up in the weather-related gridlock. The unidentified vehicle on the right is bound for New Cross Gate on the 21; a complete working would have taken it to Moorgate. T1076 (A76 THX) has come from Crystal Palace and will be hoping to reach Surrey Quays station, roughly four miles away. Introduced in 1960, the 108B would be withdrawn in November 1991.

FAREWELL TO LONDON FOREST

Opposite below: This was a lucky photo, as traffic in Trafalgar Square rarely slows enough to give such an uninterrupted view. RML2597 (JJD 597D) looked particularly smart; advertising for the 6 had been updated since that seen on RML2359 in 1988, and extra touches were a wider yellow band on which to display places of interest en route and the placing of the company name below the route and destination boxes. This was 9 August 1991; the decision to close London Forest had yet to be taken and would come during the following month. The 6 would be split between Metroline, which took the lion's share, and East London.

Below: London Forest were awarded the contract for the D1 Docklands Express which started in August 1990, running between Waterloo and Harbour Exchange Square on the Isle of Dogs. Ten Titans in this eye-catching livery were used, as shown on T840 (A840 SUL). It has parked up in Cornwall Road outside the Red Arrow Unit base on 14 November 1991, just nine days from the end. The D1 would be swapping garages from Ash Grove to West Ham as part of the transfer of the D1 to East London.

166 • LONDON'S BUSES, 1979–1994

It was said that towards the end, some London Forest vehicles displayed a changed logo, showing a felled oak tree. But so far as T143 (CUL 143V) is concerned, it still stood proudly, even though by 21 November there were only full two days of operations left. The 30 was for a time my route of choice between Aldwych, where this photo was taken, and King's Cross, and East London was again the beneficiary once London Forest ceased operations.

SUNDAY METROBUSES

All three photos were taken on Sunday 20 October 1991.

Opposite below: The 88 (Acton Green-Belmont) had a long and illustrious history but was increasingly a victim of congestion. In 1974 it was cut back to Mitcham, in 1987 to Tooting, and in 1990 to Clapham Common. In September 1990 it was split, becoming Marble Arch (Sundays) or Oxford Circus to Clapham Common, and a new route, the 94, took over between Trafalgar Square (Sundays) or Marble Arch and Acton Green. M1037 (A737 THV) was photographed at the Acton Green terminus on South Parade.

Below: With the 33 passing through Twickenham on its way back to Fulwell, the provision by London United of vehicles as 'Rugby Specials' seems like a particularly good idea. In fact, the company had six Metrobuses decked out in Rugby World Cup advertising, though not M836 (OJD 836Y), which was waiting for its next turn of duty at the Butterwick, Hammersmith.

Left: The 9, which began back at Mortlake, only went as far as Aldwych on Saturdays and Sundays, whereas in the week it ran through to Liverpool Street station. With the imposing arch of Barnes Bridge in the background, Hounslow's M1240 (B240 WUL) was about to leave the stop in The Terrace adjacent to the railway station.

1992

A General Election in April saw the Conservatives returned for a fourth term, and at first it seemed as though LBL was off the agenda. There was no sign or even the merest indication in the Queen's Speech of forthcoming enabling legislation. Wilfred Newton, LRT chairman, expressed disappointment in his introduction to the annual report that deregulation was not mentioned, claiming in a speech later that the delay was a 'powerful demotivating force' for managers. Perhaps he had meant 'uncertainty', not delay.

Worse still: with the UK still in the grip of a recession, the Chancellor of the Exchequer, Norman Lamont, included in his Autumn Statement cuts to capital spending of 30 per cent in 1993, with similar reductions in the next 2/3 years. But there came at last, on 4 December, an announcement from Steven Norris, Minister of Transport for London, which appeared to set a timetable for privatisation. Gone, you will note, was the indication in 1991's 'A Bus Strategy for London' that deregulation would take precedence. His statement to Parliament was as follows:

> My Rt Hon Friend [The Secretary of State for Transport, John MacGregor] has written to the Chairman of London Transport to inform him of the Government's agreement in principle to the early privatisation of London Buses Limited.
>
> Before the companies can be sold, the services they operate on behalf of London Transport must be put on a clear contractual basis. 40% of the LT network is already operated under contract by private firms or LBL companies and there will be a further round of competitive tendering next year to increase that proportion. The remaining routes operated by LBL subsidiaries will be put on a formal contractual basis from 1 April 1993, paving the way for the LBL companies to be offered for sale from late 1993 onwards.
>
> The Government remains firmly committed to deregulating the London bus market at the earliest opportunity. Early privatisation will help to ensure that competition in the deregulated market takes place on a free and fair basis.

Earlier in the year, London Coaches became the first to leave the LBL fold. It was not the easiest of processes; it was initially announced that Guide Friday Ltd, already an operator of sightseeing vehicles of some magnitude, was the preferred bidder. However, once the due diligence process had been completed, its initial bid of £750,000 was reduced by two-thirds. It was felt that this now undervalued the company, so alternatives were sought. On 19 May, a management buy-out was accepted, and thus was born Pullman Coaches Ltd trading as London Coaches. Probably the only outwardly visible sign of the change was a rebranding, with the word 'Transport' removed from the OLTST, making it simply the 'Original London Sightseeing Tour' (OLST).

One of London Coaches' DAF SB3000 coaches acquired in 1990, DV65 (G965 KJX) was part of the fleet in May 1992 when the management buy-out took place. It had taken a party to Cambridge, and was parked in St Andrew's Street, outside Emmanuel College, where presumably some sort of awards ceremony was taking place. Not the best place to offload, however; I grabbed this photo on one of the odd occasions when there was no traffic blocking the view. Otherwise, a steady stream of Cambus vehicles (usually Bristol VR3s), cars, trucks of varying sizes, not to mention cyclists in droves, were endeavouring to manoeuvre their way past.

Orders for new buses, at £14 million for around 200 vehicles, was the biggest investment by LBL for seven years. Roughly half were double deckers, which also bucked a trend that had prevailed since the mid-1980s. After some discussion, the decision was made that the Dennis Lance and Scania N113CRL should provide the chassis for London's first low floor saloons, for delivery in 1993.

Vehicle news – single deck fleet

The Dennis Dart continued to be the most sought after saloon. Plaxton Pointer bodied examples with twenty-four or twenty eight seats took fleet numbers DR65-153; new DRL17-73 seated thirty-four. Further Wright Handybus bodied examples were DW113-132. Smaller numbers of other types continued to appear; fifteen Optare Metroriders (MRL217-231) and a solitary Mercedes Benz 811D, MW17, also bodied by Wright. Larger saloons comprised nineteen Optare Deltas (DA11-29), which were painted in the red and silver colours East London had settled on for DA10, the former demonstrator, and sixteen Dennis Lance/Alexander, which became LA1-16. For them Selkent settled on a red livery with white window surrounds and black and white stripes atop a grey skirt, which also looked particularly smart. Ten DAFSB220LC/Ikarus (DK1-10) went to London Coaches for the 726, whose contract began in late February, as did DD35/36 (DAF SB2305/Plaxton 321).

In order to prolong the life of the Leyland National, East Lancs bodybuilders set up the Greenway project. This mid-life rebuild involved stripping the vehicle before new front and rear ends, windows, panels and interiors were fitted. They would also be re-engined. LBL sent LS466 for conversion, renumbering it GLS1 when it returned. At the end of the year, it was announced that forty-one of London General's Red Arrow Leyland National 2s would be rebuilt as Greenways, but whilst they would join the GLS class, they would retain their original LS numbers. Additionally, a former Crosville/North Western example that had undergone the process was acquired, becoming GLS2. It went to Centrewest for the 607.

One of two particularly interesting loans this year was that of South Yorkshire Transport Leyland DAB bendibus 2001 (C101 HDT), which was operated by Selkent during April and May.

Whilst Mercedes 811D/Reeves Burgess MTL3/4 were formally acquired, having been on long-term loan since 1990, MTL5 was returned to Mercedes Benz, and Renault S56/Plaxton RB34 also went back to the dealer. More CVE Omnis came from C & M Coaches of Aintree, taking fleet numbers CV5-7.

New arrivals in January, allocated to Selkent, were two DAF SB2305/Plaxton 321s, DD35/36. It also invested in a DAF MB230/Plaxton Paramount 3500 (DP1) and DAF MB230/Van Hool Alizee DV67. Metroline took a 1982 vintage Leyland Leopard/

Westlink operated services under contract for Kingston Polytechnic, for which former demonstrator MCW Metrorider MR134 received the establishment's colours. Further expansion came with three of the first fourteen 9m DWLs which had been acquired at the end of 1990 for the 371, starting with DWL1. By this time, the Polytechnic had become a University, and a sizeable number of students is waiting to board DWL2 (JDZ 2402) in Eden Street, Kingston.

While the people of Sheffield had been used to riding in bendibuses for some years, this was a first for London. South Yorkshire Transport loaned their Leyland-DAB 2001 (C101 HDT) for Selkent to try out on the 180 between Plumstead and Catford for a four-week trial. Thanks to Selkent News, we have a record of the vehicle leaving Plumstead on 6 April for an exhibition run prior to entering service. Bus company managers and directors, as well as a team from Greenwich Council Borough Engineers' Department, were there to evaluate the ride. Impressive though it appears to have been, it would be another twelve years before bendibuses took to the streets of London in any numbers.

As the new generation of small saloons continued its relentless march into all the London fleets, some stalwarts of the previous era were granted a makeover, thanks to changes in legislation relating to driver training. The twenty-five Bristol LH6Ls remaining in stock at the start of 1992 were shared between London United and Centrewest, whose BL81 (OJD 81R) was waiting for the next recruit in Eastbourne Terrace on 31 January.

Duple Dominant III (LD5), and TPL9, a Leyland Tiger/Plaxton Paramount 3200. LP5/6 moved from London United to Leaside, still for contract and private hire duties.

Disposals of Leyland Nationals reduced their numbers by forty-four. Forty of the fifty-two Optare City Pacers were sold, and the last three, the Carelink vehicles OV50-52, went on loan to F E Thorpe who now had the responsibility for the contract. Twelve Metroriders left the fleet, the first being MR15; they had reached five years' service, which was all that had been intended of them. Single examples of the Bristol LH (BL19) and Ford Transit (FS28) went for further service elsewhere.

Vehicle news – double deck fleet

The other interesting loan of the year was an Alexander bodied Leyland Olympian 'Megadekka' which Capital Citybus allowed Selkent to trial on the 180, just like the bendibus referred to earlier, In August. It would eventually find its way to Hong Kong to work in the parent company's fleet.

Selkent had something else with which to enthral both the passengers and the enthusiasts. Between 3 and 21 August this Leyland Olympian/Alexander 'Megadekka', which was on its way for service in Hong Kong, was loaned to Selkent by Capital Citybus, who had numbered it 331 (J248 WWK). The aim was to test the use of these leviathans in London conditions, and it operated mainly on a variant of the 180 (Abbey Wood-Catford garage), although it did also appear on the 123 and 248. It had been downseated from 102 to 96 (H51/45F) to satisfy the regulatory bodies, although one might observe that in 1992 Stagecoach was operating a 110-seater version, which had moved that year from East Midland to United Counties.

After the excitement generated by the appearances of the bendibus and the 'Megadekka', operations on the 180 returned to normal, with a mixed Olympian/Titan allocation from Plumstead. Representing the former, L111 (C111 CHM), en route to Abbey Wood, was crossing into King William Walk, under the watchful gaze of the 'Cutty Sark'.

Ninety-seven new double deckers were received during the year, comprising two different types. Of the twenty-four Optare Spectras on order, seventeen arrived in 1992; SP2 was the only dual-door example, which went to Metroline; SP1/3-17 were destined for London Central.

Alexander bodied Leyland Olympians L315-354 were delivered to Leaside between April and August. L351-354 had normal seating but were used on contract or private hire work, and if put out on service, would only appear on the 253. They were distinguished by large gold Leaside Buses lettering between decks.

Forty more Scania N113DRB/Northern Counties were taken into stock, becoming S32-71.

Perhaps with deregulation in mind, in which case a Routemaster would be a very handy vehicle to have at your disposal on central London routes, a programme began which would see 486 RMLs refurbished, following a successful trial with RML2360. This major upgrading included a complete rewiring, a new heating system and new fluorescent lighting, floor coverings and red, blue and grey moquette for seats and the lower deck side panels.

RM646 received a blue, red and yellow livery as the 'Brent EC Artbus', the first of the type to carry overall advertising since RM1237 (Wisdom toothbrushes) in 1979, the 1980s examples being RMLs.

The 26 was a new route introduced in July 1992 to replace that part of the 6 that ran between Aldwych and Hackney Wick, starting from Waterloo. East London's Scania N113DRB/Northern Counties were put to work on the route from new, and one of the later arrivals, S59 (K859 LMK) has emerged from the lay-over point and was pictured whilst at the first stop in Waterloo Road.

It was pretty nasty weather on this day early in 1992 when RM1528 (528 CLT) was bound for Liverpool Street station as it headed down Buckingham Palace Road. In the background, City of Oxford Leyland Tiger/Plaxton Paramount II 3500 Express 121 (B121 UUD) waits to make the turn into Ecclestone Bridge.

The Airbus fleet was treated to a make-over, one that had started in late 1991 and was completed during this year. Four early Metrobuses, M19/39/86/96 were converted as stand-by vehicles, which allowed M1178/87/88/90/91 to return to normal bus work.

Thirteen Fleetlines were given a red and yellow livery for use as driver trainers. They were reclassified DMT. Otherwise, their numbers declined significantly during the year with 188 leaving the fleet, leaving less than fifty in stock. Many were sold for further service elsewhere; for example, Midland Fox had twenty-nine for its Leicestershire operations, though they had all moved on by the end of 1994. There were forty-eight RMs, nine RMCs and three RMAs less by the year-end, while withdrawals also claimed two fire-damaged Metrobuses, including ex Tyne & Wear PTE 1485, and the experimental V3, which went ultimately to Black Prince of Morley, Leeds. Sales of Leyland Titans, almost all to other operators, accounted for the loss of sixty-eight vehicles, ranging from some of the earliest T41/47 to one of the latest (T1039), although that was an accident-damaged example. Merseybus took more than half of them.

Forty-five Routemasters of various types passed to the leasing company Hughes DAF upon the management buy-out of London Coaches, comprising eighteen RMs, eleven RCLs, ten ERMs and six RMAs. Also included were the three Dennis Dominators, H1-3.

Service news

Workings on the 9 were affected by the imposition of a weight limit on vehicles crossing Hammersmith Bridge. Crewed journeys on Monday-Saturday operated Hammersmith Broadway-Aldwych – the extension to Liverpool Street was withdrawn – with conversion to OPO in the evenings and to minibuses on Sundays, terminating at Mortlake. The Mortlake-Hammersmith section became the 9A, extended to Kensington (Palace Gate).

The Central London Route Review led to wholesale changes with effect from 18 July. Along with the revisions to the 9 detailed above, the following is a summary of the main changes:

- 1 extended from Aldwych to Holborn
- 6 withdrawn between Aldwych and Hackney Wick
- 15 withdrawn between Paddington and Westbourne Park
- 15B – a new route between East Ham and Mansion House/Aldwych
- 22B withdrawn between Tottenham Court Road and Piccadilly Circus
- 23 – a new route between Westbourne Park and Aldwych/Liverpool Street
- 25 withdrawn between Oxford Circus and Victoria
- 26 – a new route between Hackney Wick and Waterloo
- 55 extended from Tottenham Court Road to Oxford Circus
- 98 – a new route between Willesden garage and Bloomsbury
- 135 withdrawn peak hours between Marble Arch and Victoria
- 171 withdrawn between Holborn station and Islington
- Red Arrow 502, 513 withdrawn. Replaced by the 521 (Waterloo-London Bridge)

A significant revision to night bus services took place at the same time.

Ilford and Barking became the latest areas to have their services subjected to a thoroughgoing reorganisation. Notable among the results was the return of Transit Holdings with three routes. Other areas under scrutiny were Peckham, Camberwell and Newham.

Other events

Centrewest's 18 (Sudbury-King's Cross) was chosen for a trial of a system providing real-time service information. Dot matrix screens were fitted to 50 per cent of the bus stops along the line of route, while a combination of beacons fitted to lamp-posts and a wheel turn counter on the bus fed into a central computer allowed the estimated arrival time of the next three buses at any of the given stops to be calculated and displayed. A garage-based operator was also able to monitor performance.

The Red Route that had been set up along Archway Road now got its own dedicated 'Red Express', the X43, operated by London Northern and introduced on 3 August between North Finchley and London Bridge. Scanias were transferred from East London and received a red and white livery with route information prominently displayed.

Capital Citybus had owned RM429 (XMD 81A, *WLT 429*) since April 1991, having acquired it from Greater Manchester Buses. Painted initially in the company's yellow and silver livery, it was then treated to a makeover whose style was later replicated on the Megadekka. On 11 September 1992 it was seen at Heathrow Airport, making a guest appearance on the 111 on the occasion of Hounslow garage's open day. RM429 was sold again in 1998, and appeared in a number of films, not least *102 Dalmatians*, for which it was painted white with black spots.

London-wide bus maps were still being produced around this time, although perhaps not as regularly as they once were. This was perhaps unsurprising, given the scale of changes that contracting was bringing about. But with the current emphasis on reviews of services in a given area, a move towards a more localised offering was perhaps a sensible way forward. This 1992/93 edition is no. 27 in a series of 36; undated, although it refers to possible route changes in December 1992. With maps of the entire area as well as local centres (Stratford, East Ham, Bow, Leytonstone), information on routes and frequencies and other important information on available government and council services, shops and markets, it was a cut above previous offerings.

Hounslow garage's open day on 12 September drew not only the crowds but also some notable vehicles from the Routemaster family to work the 111. Included amongst them were Capital Citybus RM429 and Southend Transport's RM993, RM 994 and 1590 from London General, RMA8 and RMC 1485 from East London and ERM880 from London United. Open-top RM1515 and T512 worked a special circular tour numbered H99, and Blue Triangle RF401 took turns on the H23.

A trial of a new ticket machine known as the 'Clipper' was launched in the autumn on the 73. The plan was to replace all the ageing Gibson machines during 1993.

LEASIDE 'SPECIALS'

One of the last Mk 1 Metrobuses, M1437 (VLT 12, *C437 BUV*), joined the Leaside private hire fleet at the end of 1990, receiving the large gold logo and fleetnames, chrome wheel trims, and the registration from an early Routemaster, the conversion to single door configuration having taken place some years earlier. It was spotted in Northumberland Avenue on 18 March 1992, in company with another Metrobus, this one in London Northern ownership.

178 • LONDON'S BUSES, 1979–1994

When not on private hire duties, Leyland Olympian/Alexander RH L352 (J352 BSH) would appear on the 253, as in this November 1992 photo at Euston bus station shows.

AIRBUS METROBUSES

Opposite below: From the initial batch of Metrobuses, M433 (GYE 433W) was seen in the stygian gloom of Euston bus station in 1983 with a new route, the A3, which began in April that year. A daily operation, operating until the early afternoon, it ran via Russell Square, Oxford Street, Kensington, Hammersmith and the A4/M4, serving all three Heathrow terminals of the time. It may not have been as successful as hoped, however; after three years it was withdrawn and replaced by changes to the A2. M433 was reseated and transferred for normal service in 1984.

Below: The 1984 Metrobus order included replacements for the Airbus fleet. Appearing in April, M1006-29 had the same seating capacity as the originals. M1026 (A726 THV) was seen leaving Heathrow on its way back to Victoria early in its career.

Changes to the A2 in April 1986 saw it rerouted to Euston instead of Paddington. M1029 (A729 THV) was awaiting its next turn to Heathrow when photographed on 8 April 1988. That an MCW Metrobus is in the process of being passed by an MCW Metrocab (which type had first appeared the previous year) seems entirely appropriate.

October 1991 saw the start of the refurbishment of the twenty-four full-time members of the Airbus fleet, the work being carried out by Ensign Bus & Paint at Eastleigh. M1024 (A724 THV) returned to service by the end of 1991 after it had received attention, including new flooring, new heating, new seat moquette and stripes and branding in yellow, not white. Later upgrades featured a different, one-piece blind, with colour-coding for the A1 (green) and A2 (blue). Seen in Woburn Place on 29 January 1992, close to Russell Square, M1024 is already attracting some interest from potential customers. The type was displaced from Airbus duties by the arrival of nineteen Volvo Olympians with Alexander Royale bodywork, A112-30, in late 1995.

1993

The aim of the Conservative government to bring about change to the London bus scene, and the outcomes it expected to achieve, have so far been characterised by mixed messages and delay. But in 1993, at last, there was a definitive statement that laid out a proper timescale, so it is worth spending some time to consider how it finally came about.

Ever since the business of dismantling the National Bus Company and opening up the streets of the rest of Great Britain to competition had begun in the early 1980s, successive Secretaries of State had vacillated over what to do about the situation in the capital. As we have seen in earlier years, promises were made on an almost annual basis, only for them to fall by the wayside as more pressing issues arose. When, finally, a blueprint for the intended sale of the eleven operating companies was announced in December 1992, the incumbent at that time, John MacGregor, said he expected deregulation to follow after the sales were completed; the privatisation process would begin before the end of 1993, at which time a Bill would be put before parliament and that would pave the way for deregulation by the middle of 1995.

And things did at last begin to move in early summer with the appointment of investment bankers Barclays de Zoete Wedd to handle the sale of the ten subsidiaries (Westlink being marketed separately). They were, with their approximate fleet size:

- Centrewest (480)
- East London (580)
- Leaside (520)
- London United (450)
- London Central (500)
- London General (650)
- London Northern (340)
- Metroline (350)
- Selkent (450)
- South London (420)

Despite there being no reference to London's buses in the Queen's Speech, rumours began to circulate as the year wore on, that were given added credence by a report in the *Guardian* on 3 November 1993 which was confirmed by John MacGregor five days later. The press release in which the announcement appeared made the usual claims about the way these measures would deliver the best bus services for London – privatisation, a passengers' charter and the change from gross to net cost contracts. Only after this sugary pill came the statement that 'the Government no longer intends to bring forward legislation in this Parliament to deregulate London's bus services', although it added that deregulation 'remains the long term aim'. As it turned out, come 1 May 1997 and the next General Election, Labour achieved a landslide victory and deregulation was no longer an issue.

It has been speculated that as this announcement followed hard on the heels of a closely fought win on rail privatisation, and with local elections due and support in London falling, now was not the time for another root and branch reorganisation of transport services in the capital. What was not said, but was patently obvious, was that with the large groups, themselves the beneficiaries of Conservative privatisation legislation – Stagecoach, British Bus, Badgerline, Go-Ahead, GRT – waiting in the wings, each with fleets already measurable in thousands, any budding entrepreneurs would find it virtually impossible to gain even a toehold in the London market. Any battle to see them off, brief though it might be, would cause further chaos in London's already chronically congested streets.

So having removed the spectre of deregulation, it was time to consider how to effect the plan for privatisation. The competitive tendering process had been a pre-requisite, the aim being to give all purchasers a chance to operate in that environment before deregulation was introduced. Now the tendering regime would have to operate for a longer period than had been anticipated. By March 1993, LRT had put all the remaining untendered routes – approximately 60 per cent of the network – on a contractual basis. The Department of Transport required stated cost reduction targets and net cost contracts, where LRT paid (or received) a settlement representing the difference between the operator's projected costs and revenue. The operator kept all the revenue and a cut of other income such as Travelcard receipts. Under the gross cost contract system, used until now, LRT paid the contractor a fixed rate for operating the route and took all the revenue.

LRT was set four objectives relating to the sale of the ten operating units, namely:

- to manage the privatisation so as to promote sustained and fair competition in the provision of bus services in London
- to complete the privatisation process, if practicable, by 31 December 1994
- to provide an opportunity for the management and staff to take a stake in the privatised companies; and
- subject to the achievement of the first three objectives, to maximise as far as practicable the net proceeds of privatisation.

Conditions were also attached to prevent the creation of monopolies. No one purchaser was allowed to have more than 25 per cent of scheduled route mileage; the acquisition of adjacent companies would not generally be permitted, and regard would be had to existing operations immediately outside the London area – the Badgerline group's ownership of Thamesway would be an example.

It was reckoned that a two-month delay to the privatisation process had arisen because of the length of time it had taken to make a decision on deregulation. The various parties were nonetheless confident that this could be made up as it progressed. As a first step, on 3 December, the buses, garages, computer systems and other related items were vested in the subsidiaries, a move one correspondent likened to 'cutting them adrift'.

So what was the official explanation for this belated change of course? In November 1993 Stephen Norris was the Minister of Transport for London, and the editor of *Buses* magazine, Stephen Morris, was able to secure an interview with him which duly appeared in the January 1994 issue. I am grateful to Alan Millar, the editor when this chapter was written, for permission to use parts of it.

The first question that had to be answered was why deregulation had been kicked into the long grass? Norris 'did not believe in pursuing ideology for the sake of it and while deregulation was one tool for getting quality into bus services, others … which were available in London included privatisation and tendering. London had the most dense bus network in the UK … and privatisation and the change in emphasis in tendering would bring a better deal for the taxpayer and benefits to travellers.' He maintained it was 'far shrewder' to deliver the benefits in London without the 'downside' by which he almost certainly meant bus-induced traffic congestion.

As regards tendering, he was keen to see operators having 'an input to service specification', and 'to come in with their own initiatives via the road service licensing provisions', as had been done by Docklands Transit. As its eventual failure was down to it being 'frozen out' of the Travelcard and concessionary fares set-up, future entrants would be given full access to it. It was accepted that with the high proportion of Travelcard users in London, the complex method of dividing up the income between all the different operators based on passenger miles travelled would need to be sophisticated. He was 'confident that modern systems, notably Smartcard technology, can allow pretty accurate apportionment techniques.' He suggested that profitable routes might be auctioned, or that 'groups of routes, some profitable, some not, could be franchised out'. This would be a prime example of cross-subsidy, which the Government had come out firmly against not long before, but apparently now it 'made commercial sense if it was part of a franchise deal.'

On the issue of potential purchasers losing out should their investment go the same way as London Forest in 1991, he was quite sanguine. 'Some outside bidders had lost interest because deregulation would not be going ahead, though others would actually be attracted by the fact that regulation was here to stay. There had been a two-edged reaction', he said. 'Stagecoach for one told us that the announcement would not dissuade it from bidding for London Buses companies and in fact it welcomed the opportunity to buy into a regulated market. However, confirmation of details of the new contract arrangements would be needed.' Indeed, Stagecoach made mention of its desire to add LBL subsidiaries to its burgeoning portfolio in its stock market floatation prospectus.

The article also quoted John Card, Grey-Green's general manager, and it is interesting to contrast the views of the politician with the practitioner. Among the points Card mentioned were:

- deregulation would have led to over-provision on the main routes, with the inevitable congestion, at least in the absence of much greater bus priority
- the tendering system had been very successful and costs were still being driven down
- the problems in allocating Travelcard revenue.

However, an unnamed representative of Kentish Bus expressed disappointment that the company could not 'expand freely' in London.

In the midst of all this, it transpired that government funding was being cut from £768 million in 1992/93 to £540 million in 1993/94, and some of the subsidiaries were hit once again by industrial action. But it is worth mentioning, after more than eight years of the tender process, that the annual report for 1992/93 could point to 99 per cent of scheduled mileage being operated, London Buses subsidiaries retaining over 50 per cent of tendered routes (operating more than half of all tendered routes) and operating around 81 per cent of the network. With staff numbers of some 17,800 and a fleet of 5,254 vehicles, of which 3,649 were still double deckers, LBL had enabled 663 million passenger journeys, covering 1,434 million miles.

Vehicle news – single deck fleet

Six more DAF/Optare Deltas arrived for East London, DA30-35. Two new types were introduced to London, with Metroline taking thirty-one Dennis Lances with Northern Counties Paladin bodywork for the 113 and 302, LN1-31, while London General also went with Northern Counties to body thirteen Volvo B10Bs, VN1-13, introduced on the 88. A batch of ten Fiat Iveco Daily 49.10s with Marshall bodywork (a make last seen on AEC Swifts in the early 1970s) replaced most of the RHs in Roundabout service, receiving fleet numbers FM1-10.

The VN and LN classes both carried Northern Counties Paladin bodywork, so the essential difference between the London General and Metroline vehicles was in the livery application, with Metroline opting for a deeper skirt and a white band above window level. Although received early in the year, conversion of the 113 did not take place until the autumn, and I had to wait until 4 January 1994 – a particularly wet day – to get a photo of LN19 (K319 YJA) in Portman Street.

The livery carried by London General's Volvo B10Bs for the 88 was essentially the standard red and grey with the addition of a thin yellow stripe above the skirt. The unique selling point was the 'Clapham Omnibus' branding, well demonstrated by VN9 (K9 KLL), which was close to journey's end when I photographed it in Whitehall on 7 July, not long after it entered service.

More examples of existing mini- and midibus classes were taken into stock in 1993. New Dennis Darts were DRL74-158 (Plaxton Pointer), DW133-170 and DWL15-26 (Wright). Metroriders MRL232-241 and Mercedes Benz 811D/Wright MW18-37 completed the picture.

Selkent invested in four new coaches, DAF MB230/Van Hool Alizee DV36-39, whilst second-hand acquisitions were Duple bodied Leyland Tigers for Metroline, TDL1/2 and Volvo B10M/Plaxton Paramount 3200 VP1 for London Northern.

The thirty-eight much awaited 'Super Low Floor' Dennis Lances with Wright Pathfinder bodywork – the LLW class – were delayed in manufacture and did not make an appearance until 1994. They were destined for London United, Centrewest and Metroline. The same issues afflicted similar Scania N113CRLs, ordered by Leaside and East London.

London General National Greenway GLS493 (GUW 493W) had returned to service in October 1993, and on the 12th was about to take up duty on the 501 to London Bridge station. In the background stands the famous Old Vic theatre, which at that time was staging a revival of the musical *Hair* on the twenty-fifth anniversary of its first production.

From a total of around 140 Leyland Nationals at the start of the year, only forty-eight remained by the close, and all bar thirteen of these were Mark 2s. Twenty-eight Greenway conversions were completed, all retaining their original LS fleet number. Vehicles involved were GLS439/40/42/49/50/59/63/67-69/71/74/76/78/79/81/86/90-93/96/98/99, 501/02/05/06. A further thirteen were earmarked for attention in 1994, and these would become GLS438/43/46/48/52/55/60/73/77/80/83/87, 500.

Numbers of BLs declined by eight to sixteen, although it was notable that BL85 was returned to active service in Roundabout livery to cover while the FM class was introduced. The two newest members of the RB class, 34/35, were sold during the year, and Metroline returned its Leyland Tiger/Plaxton Paramount TPL9 off-lease.

Vehicle news – double deck fleet

The only new vehicles this year were Optare Spectras SP18-25, completing London Central's order. Conversion of the 3 (Crystal Palace-Oxford Circus), for which the class was intended, began in January.

With two crew-operated routes passing into the private sector, it was decided to lease Routemasters to the successful companies for the duration of the new contracts. Kentish Bus had twenty-four for the 19, and BTS a further twenty-two for the 13.

The ex Tyne and Wear PTE Metrobuses M1481-84 were sold, but the most significant decline in numbers was of Titans, with over 200 leaving the fleet. Some returned to London service, as London & Country took fifteen, ostensibly for the 188, London Coaches a further twenty-six, following its success in gaining the contract for the 52, and London Suburban Bus invested in thirty-two, having won the tenders for the 4, 41 and 271. But the bulk, as in 1992, went to Merseybus.

The first members of the SP class appeared in 1992 and were put to work on the 40 (Herne Hill-Poplar) until such time as enough were received to fully convert the 3, with an additional benefit in that they could be tested in service on a less demanding route. They finally took over the role for which they were intended in January. Most were treated to rear advertisements, which was a relatively new departure; and in more theatre-related news, a rear view of SP6 (K306 FYG), seen at Oxford Circus in October 1993, would have revealed that it was promoting *Buddy – the Musical*.

London & Country invested in fifteen Titans after winning the contract for the 188 (Euston-Greenwich), but in practice they could be found on the company's other routes, including the 176. Having just reached the spot where we saw the Greenway earlier, 912 (CUL 162V) was heading for Camberwell Green, also on 12 October. Heading in the opposite direction, a Titan from the London Suburban Bus fleet en route to Archway on the 4.

By the end of the year, there were fewer than 250 RMs still in service, although RML numbers had remained static for a couple of years at just over 500. The end was nigh for the remaining handful of Fleetlines; by the end of the year only the twelve DMTs at London General survived.

RT1530, last heard of here in 1985 when its Chiswick skid bus days were through, spent much of the next few years in store, moving finally to Hounslow Heath early in 1993. It was acquired for preservation by a group of Westlink drivers later in the year.

Service news

The 'Carelink' contract, won by F.E. Thorpe in 1992, was relaunched in January as 'Stationlink', when the two new Alexander bodied Mercedes Benz 709D were received. The three City Pacers, the former OV50-52, were retained by Thorpe. The service now

The City of London Corporation livery for its sponsorship of the 800 Waterloo & City Line replacement bus service sat particularly well on the Titans used by London Central. T1008 (A608 THV) arrives at Waterloo ready for an early service to Bank. Although the line was meant to reopen on the 19th, the service ran until the 23rd, on a reduced timetable, as cover in the event of any teething problems.

operated on a clockwise loop and took in new stops at Marylebone, Fenchurch Street, London Bridge and Victoria Coach Station.

The 88 was converted to one-person operation using VN1-13, which carried 'Clapham Omnibus' branding. It was said that their KLL registrations were an allusion to the London General MD's initials.

For the time it took to upgrade the Waterloo & City Line, the City of London Corporation sought tenders to run a bus replacement service. London Central won the contract, and used Titans drawn from Camberwell and New Cross, three of which, T894, 1008/53, received a special livery. The service was planned to run from 1 June to 9 July, but its operation was extended as the works were not completed on time.

Grand plans for a future guided busway in the Park Royal area got to the feasibility study stage. Its forerunner would be two Monday-Saturday midibus routes, the PR1 (Centrewest) and PR2 (Metroline), which began in November.

Service changes were implemented for the Newham network in September, with Peckham and Camberwell to come. Lewisham, Catford, Bromley, Brixton and Streatham were also in line for review, and routes that had already been tendered would potentially be affected.

Following the closure of Finchley garage on 4 December 1993, operation of the X43 moved to Potters Bar, allowing the 'Red Express' liveried Scanias the opportunity to visit pastures new. S11 (J811 HMC) displays its special branding to good effect at the St Albans rail station terminus of the 84, some twenty-two miles from central London.

The five garage closures in 1993 were Seven Kings and Hanwell in March, Chalk Farm and Victoria in June and Finchley in December. Continuing the trend towards smaller bases for midibus fleets, new sites were opened by London General at Battersea Bridge and Centrewest at Greenford. Cricklewood and Edgware swapped roles, with the latter now becoming the outstation of the former.

Other events

There were two birthdays to celebrate; London Transport was 60 on 1 July and the capital's first bus lane, on the eastern side of Park Lane, turned twenty-five.

Westlink was put up for sale, but no announcement regarding the successful bidder had been made by the end of the year.

Centrewest abandoned the 'U-Line' branding and replaced it with 'Uxbridge Buses'. Big buses at Westbourne Park were inducted into the 'Gold Arrow' fleet. Out also went the 'E-Line', which became Ealing Buses on all routes out of Greenford and Acton, plus the 195 and 282.

Left: Heathrow Airport is the location for this 1993 photo of Mercedes Benz 811D MA68 (F668 XMS), which has now received the 'Uxbridge Buses' branding in place of the earlier 'U-Line' version. In five years' time it will be one of over twenty transferred to First Western National in Cornwall when its London days are done. Behind it, relief Airbus M187 (BYX 187V) in the revised livery, received in mid-1993, is bound for Russell Square on the A2.

Below left: London General M435 (GYE 435W) received this rather splendid blue/white livery for a special service linking the two venues taking part in the 'American Art in the 20th Century' exhibition, the Royal Academy of Arts in Piccadilly and the Saatchi Museum in NW8. It was doing good business when I spotted it in Regent Street, rather fortuitously when there was a gap in southbound traffic.

Westbourne Park became the last garage to replace its Gibson ticket machines with Clippers.

Right: Once again, the London Bus Map underwent a makeover, and became, perhaps more properly, the 'All London Bus Guide', thus complementing the local editions of which there were still thirty-five. The map measures 970x630mm, which makes it 112 per cent bigger than the London Transport equivalent of 1979. It was produced in association with Royal Mail International, who advertised on three of the sixty available panels.

1994

At the start of the year, figures in the vicinity of £75-100 million were being suggested as the likely outcome of the sale of the LBL subsidiaries. When the maths was done after South London became the final disposal, the proceeds actually turned out to be more than £230 million; 'a triumph', according to Steven Norris, though some might conclude that the original forecasts left a lot to be desired.

Privatisation finally launched on 24 March, when all ten subsidiaries sent a vehicle to show off at Hyde Park Corner. Despite what he had said only four months earlier, Steven Norris was still banging the deregulation drum, claiming that what was happening that day was just the first stage in the process. It was announced that purchasers of the ten subsidiaries had to retain the traditional red livery for all services in central London (although independent operators with a presence in Zones 1 and 2, which is how 'central' was generally interpreted, would be allowed to keep their existing schemes).

The deadline for bids was 12 May, and it was reported that there was a considerable level of interest, at home and overseas. As to the actual mechanics of the process, proposed management and employee buy-outs would be given preferred bidder status if they were within 5 per cent of another potential buyer, and measures to guard against asset-stripping – which had occurred when the National Bus Company was sold off – were set at a ten-year period.

The bids were evaluated and a shortlist drawn up by 14 July, after which greater examination of the subsidiaries was permitted so that bids might, if thought necessary, be adjusted. Preferred bidders were selected by the end of August, and everyone waited for the news that had been the best part of sixteen years in the making. Rather like the tender process had been, the results were mixed.

Centrewest was the first company to be sold, on 2 September, to an in-house team led by MD Peter Hendy, for a figure of £25 million. The garages at Acton, Alperton and Westbourne Park, Greenford and Uxbridge were included, the latter two being leased from Ealing Council and LRT respectively, with a fleet size of 507.

Four days later on 6 September the Stagecoach group bagged both East London and Selkent in a deal worth £42 million. Brian Cox became chairman at East London, with garages at Barking, Bow (with its Stratford outstation), Leyton, Romford and Upton Park; Barry Hinkley filled the same role at Selkent, which was responsible for Bromley, Catford and Orpington, as well as the leased Plumstead. East London's fleet totalled 590, that of Selkent 414.

The fourth sale also went to the private sector, with a £23.8 million bid for London Central being accepted from the Go-Ahead group on 22 September, although it was not ratified until the day after a shareholders' meeting on 17 October. Douglas Adie

Centrewest became the first of the London Buses subsidiaries to be privatised when it was sold to its management team on 2 September. A few months earlier, M319 (EYE 319V) displays the old order as it crawls along Greenford Road in queueing traffic with a 105 to Heathrow Airport.

remained as MD. Bexleyheath, Camberwell, New Cross and Peckham garages were included, the last-named being leased premises, along with 498 buses.

The Cowie group, owners of Grey-Green, were successful in their bid for Leaside on 29 September of £29.5 million. Steve Clayton became MD, and six garages, Clapton, Enfield, Palmers Green, Stamford Hill, Tottenham and Wood Green, were involved. It was stated that Leaside and Grey-Green would continue to operate independently of each other post-sale. Leaside had 520 buses (Grey-Green had around 185 at this point).

Metroline was the sixth privatisation on 7 October, raising £20 million. The successful management/employee buy-out was led by MD Declan O'Farrell, and 383 vehicles and garages at Cricklewood, Harlesden, Harrow Weald (with its outstations at Edgware and North Wembley) and Willesden passed to the new owners. The Atlas Bus & Coach operations were then acquired from the Pullmans group on 28 November.

MTL Holdings was formed when Merseybus Transport Ltd was sold to its management and staff at the start of 1993. On 26 October it expanded into the capital with the acquisition of London Northern for £20.55 million. Dominic Brady became the new MD. The company had only two garages, at Holloway and Potters Bar, which housed 340 buses.

Management buy-outs were not successful in every case. Indeed, London Northern as the seventh sale, was also the fourth, following East London and Selkent (to Stagecoach), London Central (the Go-Ahead group) and Leaside (the Cowie group) to fall to outside interests, in this case MTL Trust Holdings of Liverpool. It took effect from 26 October 1994, and RML2699 (SMK 699F), on layover at the Archway end of the 10, displays the style of branding applied to the fleet.

London General became the eighth company to leave the fold, passing to a management and employee buy-out, on 2 November. Volvo Citybus/Northern Counties VC11 (WLT 311, *G111 NGN*) demonstrates that there has been minimal change to the livery post-privatisation as it makes its way to Wandsworth on the 77A in this view at Charing Cross.

London General under MD Keith Ludeman succeeded with a management and employee bid of £28 million, the result finally becoming known on 2 November. Garages at Battersea, Merton, Putney, Stockwell, Sutton and Waterloo were included. London General was the biggest of the subsidiaries, operating 639 buses.

The penultimate sale followed three days later on 5 November, when a similar management/employee bid for London United to the tune of £25 million was accepted. MD David Humphrey presided over an estate comprising the garages at Fulwell, Hounslow, Shepherds Bush (whose premises at Wood Lane would shortly close) and Stamford Brook, with its outstation at Heathrow, and a fleet of 464 vehicles.

This just left South London, whose situation was somewhat precarious. Its management had been summoned to appear before the Traffic Commissioners on 3 & 4 November to discuss maintenance issues; there had been vehicle prohibitions following depot inspections. As a result, the expiry date for the all-important Operator Licence period was cut to 30 April 1995, and more spot-checks were promised if the company was to seek a renewal. But a sale took place on 8 December with the Cowie group assuming responsibility for Brixton, Croydon, Norwood and Thornton Heath garages and 440 buses under the leadership of the Leaside MD. The price, £16.3 million, was a reflection of the difficulties the company had been facing in the short-term. It was not formally completed until 10 January 1995.

South London was the problem child of the privatisation process, having been before the Traffic Commissioners in early November. However, in happier times, having won the tender for the 159 from 29 January, the company set about revitalising some of its RMs, which involved a cream band and roof and route details between decks. RM1801 (801 DYE), which emerged from the paint shop in March, and complete with pole-hanging conductor, was making the turn from Regent Street to Oxford Street on 14 July 1994.

Meanwhile a repaint involving a wide cream band between decks indicated that the vehicle could be used for private hire work, although when seen in Croydon on this occasion, L169 (D169 FYM) was on its way to Wallington on the 407, a contract that South London would lose to London & Country later in the year.

So at last the deed was done, and for the first time since 1933, the operation, if not the oversight, of London's buses was back in the private sector. It is interesting to note that the four management buy-outs were to last less than six years:

- London General joined London Central in the Go-Ahead group in May 1996
- Centrewest was acquired by FirstBus in March 1997
- in August 1997 London United was sold to the French company Transdev, and
- in March 2000 Metroline, which eighteen months earlier had completed the purchase of MTL London Northern, fell to DelGro, an investment company based in Singapore.

Also in the news in 1994 was Westlink. Its long, drawn-out sale was finally concluded on 19 January in the shape of a management buy-out which raised around £2 million. 118 buses were included but the two garages, Kingston and Hounslow Heath, being leased, were not. There was controversy when it was reported that Go-Ahead Northern, whose bid was around £2.5 million, pulled out when deregulation was dropped, but the remaining two bidders, Midland Red South and Stevensons, were not permitted to continue. Then, lo and behold, it was sold again, twelve weeks later, to West Midlands Travel, for between £2-2.5 million for a 90 per cent stake. Concern over the company's future with privatisation and the big groups that were waiting in the wings was said to be behind the decision.

Jumping ahead just a little, it should be noted that Westlink was sold for a third time in September 1995, to London United.

Another issue arising from privatisation was that a new set-up would be required to replace the centralised functions that had been provided by LBL. London Transport Buses (LTB) was the answer, with effect from 1 April. Responsibilities included setting fare levels, marketing, oversight and maintenance of bus stops and terminals, bus stations, and the Tendered Bus Unit. And, in the light of the pronouncements about the colour of buses, approval of proposed liveries.

Vehicle news – single deck fleet

Two new classes of low-floor saloons made their debuts in 1994. Dennis Lance SLF/Wright Pathfinder LLW1-10 went to London United, LLW11-24 to Centrewest and LLW25-38 to Metroline. The SLW, which sported the same bodywork but on

After some delay, London United finally received its ten Dennis Lance SLFs with Wright Pathfinder bodywork and put them onto the 120 (Hounslow-Northolt) early in 1994. The branding to show off the vehicle's low floor credentials is anything but subtle, but maybe that wasn't such a bad thing. I failed to see the type in service that year, but LLW10 (ODZ 8910) made an appearance at Showbus, which had to suffice.

the Scania N113CRL, went to Leaside (SLW1-14) and East London (SLW15-30). A further newcomer was the Dennis Lance/Plaxton Verde, with Selkent taking eleven (LV1-11).

The first vehicles for a newly privatised company were the nine Plaxton Pointer bodied Dennis Darts for Metroline, EDR1-9. Other new classes that appeared earlier in the year were East Lancs bodied Darts for London Central, DEL1-11, and London Northern's DNL101-10/12-20, with the attractive Northern Counties bodywork.

The last two DRLs, 170/171, were received and despatched to London United.

The Greenway programme was completed with a total of forty-three vehicles upgraded. Numbers of Mark 1 Nationals declined to the point that the only three Mark 1s remaining were mobility buses on loan at East London. After privatisation, Selkent borrowed Iveco 49.10/Robin Hood 58-61 from United Counties for the rest of the year and into 1995. They were used on the Bromley Park & Ride.

The major disposals were the RB class, with numbers reduced from thirty-three to six. They were said to have been troublesome throughout their short career with East

New in 1994 were nineteen Northern Counties bodied Dennis Darts, most of which received Camden Link branding for the C2, as shown on DNL103 (L103 HHV), picking up in Albany Street on its way to Parliament Hill Fields. London Northern would shortly be acquired by MTL Holdings before passing to Metroline in 1998. The entire DNL fleet of nineteen vehicles was sold to Ensignbus between August and October 2003.

The more usual Plaxton Pointer bodywork adorns South London's DRL153 (L153 WAG), which just managed to predate the last two vehicles illustrated by entering service in December 1993. It was put to work on the 322 (Crystal Palace-Elephant and Castle), for which it received stylised 'Connexions' branding. The 322 was a new route, started in October 1992 to partially replace a section of the 2. It was initially worked by Optare Star Riders.

London. CVE/Omni CV4 left the fleet, the remaining six in the class staying with Westlink. The Metrorider (MR) fleet reduced by eighteen, Darlington Transport being the principal purchaser.

The solitary Dodge minibus, A1, was sold in December.

Stagecoach decided to concentrate coaching work at East London, as a result of which all eight of Selkent's coaches – DD35/36, DP1, DV36-39/67 – moved to Bluebird Northern in Aberdeen. Volvo B10M/Plaxton 3200 VP2 for East London and similar VP3 for Metroline were second-hand additions during the year.

Vehicle news – double deck fleet

There were no new vehicles to report under this heading in 1994, and nothing particularly out of the ordinary so far as disposals were concerned. Numbers of RMs declined by around half to just over 110, but the RML fleet remained intact and only two RMCs were withdrawn. Around fifty Titans were sold.

By the time the privatisations started, very few Fleetlines were left. Leaside and Selkent had three open-tops, DMS2291 at Stamford Hill and DM948, 1102 at Plumstead – both of those soon being despatched to Stagecoach Cumberland at Whitehaven. Leaside also retained two ordinary examples, DMS681, 1868. London General had twelve of the DMT class and DMS2347, 2445, all trainers. London Northern's two were DMS2168, for 'special purposes' use, and DM2556, another open-top example.

London Northern's SKY1 was returned off lease.

Service news

Life went on at the sharp end while the privatisation juggernaut ran its course, but aside from the changes brought about by the tendering process, most of what happened this year, and there were still plenty, was of a more routine nature; routes extended, truncated or diverted, change of vehicle type, etc.

No sooner had the Spectras taken up duty on the 3 than problems arose with street furniture in West Dulwich. Titans took over until these were rectified.

September saw the introduction of a raft of changes to services in the Lewisham, Woolwich, Erith and Thamesmead areas, involving fifteen routes and operators London Central, Selkent and Kentish Bus. Changes in October involved routes in the Uxbridge and Northwood area.

Although it seems to have been with us for ever, Sunday trading was only permissible on today's scale after the Sunday Trading Act came into force on 26 August. Brent Cross Shopping Centre was able to throw open its doors on a Sunday from 30 October, and ten services which visited on weekdays and Saturdays operated there at Bank Holiday frequencies: Metroline 16A, 143, 182, 186, 266; Leaside 102; Luton & District 142; Grey-Green 210, London Northern 326 and R & I Buses C11.

Christmas Day saw the usual A1 Airbus operation until mid-afternoon, but Routemaster Travel operated its 715 service, as it had in 1993, and Selkent provided T1118/22 on a circular route between the hospitals at Bromley, Queen Mary's, Orpington and Farnborough, numbered 700. New Year's Eve arrangements followed the same pattern as in 1993, but this year sponsorship came from Barrs, makers of Irn-Bru.

Improvements for route 54 starting 8th October 1994

* More buses during shopping hours - now every 15 minutes

* More through buses during Monday to Friday "peak" hours

* Earlier buses to Croydon and from Croydon to Elmers End and Beckenham

* More reliable service

* Timetable slightly revised on Saturdays and Sundays

New timetable inside

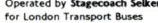

Although the changes to the 54 (West Croydon-Woolwich Arsenal) were agreed prior to the take-over, no time was wasted in getting the Stagecoach logo onto the publicity material. Having said that, however, it was an excellent production; headline information on page 1 of the folded A5 publication; timetables on pages 2 and 3, and places to visit in each of the six larger centres visited by the 54 on page 4.

Other events

A trial using Smartcard technology began in Harrow in February. The first roll-out saw the replacement of passes and Travelcards of more than seven days duration, but a future phase would be to allow passengers to store monetary value on them so that they could be used in place of cash (the Oyster card of the future). An additional benefit to LTB would be the enhanced data that would be provided.

A Bill was passed allowing the construction of the Croydon Tramlink. It would be officially opened six year hence, in May 2000.

Capital Citybus exhibited a red liveried ex British Airways Leyland-DAB/Roe bendibus at the North Weald rally, RLN 233W. The company wanted to use the type, of which it had purchased five, on the Red Arrow network, which was soon to be retendered. In the event, the contracts remained with London General, who would introduce bendibuses of their own, Mercedes Benz Citaros, in 2002.

Countdown, the system which provided real-time information to intending passengers as to how long their next bus will be, was to be extended to Haringey, Islington and Camden. It was already in use in Harrow, along the Uxbridge Road, and on the Wandsworth-Harlesden 220 line of route.

A return to larger advertisements on buses began around this time, most notably on the Optare Spectras, although other types were similarly decorated, with the rear being the preferred location, at least for the time being. London General's M1436 (VLT 136, *C436 BUV*), employed on the 74 and seen in Allsop Place on 14 July 1994, carries a design to the order of Saab car dealers. Interestingly, the vehicle in front, M1315 (C109 NGH, *VLT 15, C315 BUV*) is on its third registration.

ONE LAST TIME ON THE SIGHTSEERS

London Coaches was arguably still the market leader as 1994 drew to a close, although London Pride had the bigger fleet. In full red and cream OLST livery, RCL2240 (CUV 240C) was waiting outside Baker Street station on Marylebone Road on 14 July 1994, while one of its sisters to the rear was having what seems to have been a maintenance inspection.

DMS2391 (OJD 391R) passed to Blue Triangle in 1992, a company active in the central London sightseeing market since 1988. Whilst the Fleetline was the most numerous type in the fleet, four RTs, an RCL, the prototype Titan and the first Swift (SM1) could also be found. In this August 1993 photo DMS2391 was approaching Hyde Park Corner, having overtaken the East London Titan on the 38.

Might it have been that the 'pride' of the London Pride fleet was 182 (UJF 182), a Daimler CSG6/MCW, one of six new to Leicester City Transport in 1958? They were not popular with their first owner; I recall that they were particularly slow, and were withdrawn in 1971, four years earlier than their contemporaries. 182 found its way to Cityrama as a driver trainer in 1986, and superbly presented, it was in use on the new 'Docklands Diversion' sightseeing service, along with RT3232, in early April 1994.

London Sightseeing Tours was the trading name for Maybury's, although this was not connected with The Big Bus Company, another Maybury family enterprise. The fleet of twenty was exclusively Fleetline based, several of which operated in advertising livery. Somewhat incongruously, the former DMS868 (TGX 868M), seen in Victoria Street in 1992, was promoting Tetley tea bags.

ONE LAST TIME WITH THE ROUTEMASTERS

Right: The second production Routemaster, RM6 (VLT6) entered service at West Ham in November 1959. Here it was, twenty-seven years later on 2 January 1987 working out of Stamford Brook on the 237 in Chiswick High Road. It was one of the RMs given the South London red and cream 159 livery in 1994, and eight years after that, gold for the Queen's Jubilee.

Below: RM567 (WLT 567) makes its way along Kensington High Street on its way to Chelsea (World's End) in 1987, at which point conversion of the route to minibus operation was still two years away. Westbourne Park was the twelfth and final depot from which it worked during a twenty-nine year career.

Left: RML885 (WLT 885), photographed at The George in Farnborough. Its last run of the night will be to Ash Grove, which had the responsibility for the 47 from April 1981, when Dalston garage closed, to September 1982, when the terminus was cut back from Farnborough to Bromley. That was also when RML885 went in for overhaul and was subsequently reassigned to Bow. So is this the last night of operation to Farnborough? It might be noted that the lower deck has been decorated with balloons, indicating some sort of celebration.

Below: Once a stalwart of the Green Line network, RCL2221 (CUV 221C) was acquired again by LT in March 1978 and converted the following January to an exhibition and cinema bus, a role it continued to perform, latterly for LUL Distribution Services, until 2008. It was then acquired by Timebus Travel, where it remains. My photograph was taken at Shepherds Bush Green on 20 March 1989.

APPENDICES
LONDON BUSES FLEET LIST 1979–1994

The aim here has been to list all the vehicles operated during the period 1979-1994 with their type codes. Apart from the Merlins, RFs, RTs and the first four RMs, the entire class is listed in all cases.

(1) DOUBLE DECK FLEET

B15 – Prototype Leyland Titan
004 (NHG 732P), **005** (BCK 706R)

C – Volvo B10M Citybus/Alexander
1 (C101 CUL)

THE FLEETLINE FAMILY

DMS – Daimler Fleetline (CRG6/CRL6) or Leyland Fleetline (FE30AGR/FE30ALR)/ Park Royal (1-1217, 2058-2246, 2347-2646) or Metro-Cammell (1218-2057, 2247-2346). The **DMS** was one-person operated and incorporated a standee area while the **DM** was the crew-operated version. A later variation was the **D, a** modified DM for one-person operation.
1-136 (EGP1-136J), **137-414** (JGF137-414K), **415-695** (MLK 415-695L), **696-900** (TGX 696-900M), **901-947** (SMU 901-47N), **948-1124** (GHV 948-999, 500, 1-124N), **1125-1247** (KUC 125-247P), **1248-1297** (JGU 248-297K), **1298-1499** (MLH298-499L), **1500-1720** (THM 500-720M), **1721-1739** (SMU 721-739N), **1740-1897** (GHM 740-897N), **1898-1999** (KUC 898-999P), **2000-2024** (KJD 500, 1-24P), **2025-2057** (OUC 25-57R), **2058-2122** (KJD 58-122P), **2123-2267** (OJD 123-267R), **2268-2346** (THX 268-346S), **2347-2472** (OJD 347-472R), **2473-2646** (THX 473-646S)

DMO – Daimler Fleetline/Weymann (convertible open-top, ex Bournemouth)
1-7 (CRU 182-187, 189C)

DMT – DMSs reclassified for driver training work
2257, 2281, 2283, 2290, 2304, 2347, 2351, 2367, 2384, 2397, 2413, 2476, 2489

H – Hestair-Dennis Dominator/Northern Counties
1-3 (B101-103 WUW)

L – Leyland Olympian/ECW (1-263), Northern Counties (264-291), Leyland (292-314) or Alexander RH (315-354). L264-291 carried Bexleybus fleet numbers 1-28
1-3 (A101-103 SYE), **4-20** (C804-820 BYY), **21-122** (C21-122 CHM), **123-260** (D123-260 FYM), **261-263** (D261-263 FUL), **264-291** (E901-928 KYR), **292-314** (G292-314 UYK), **315-354** (J315-354 BSH)

LC – Leyland Olympian/East Lancs
1, 2 (C201-202 DYE)

LE – Leyland PD2/East Lancs
Ex private owner, new to Warrington
1 (AED 26B)

LF – Daimler Fleetline/Park Royal
Leased by LBL for Harrow Buses in 1987/88, new to Greater Manchester PTE
55, 307, 309, 311-322, 326, 328-330, 332, 333, 335, 336, 339, 340, 352, 370 (WWH 55L, YNA 307M etc)

M – MCW Metrobus/MCW or Alexander (1448, 1449); originally MT
1441/42 – Mark 2 Metrobuses; 1443-47 ex Greater Manchester Travel; 1448-51 ex Yorkshire Rider; 1452-80 Harrow Buses; 1481-85 ex Busways Travel
1-5 (THX 101-105S), **6-95** (WYW 6-95T), **96-315** (BYX 96-315V), **316-345** (EYE 316-345V), **346-605** (GYE 346-605W), **606-631** (KYO 606-631X), **632-805** (KYV 632-805X), **806-891** (OJD 806-891Y), **892-955** (A892-955 SUL), **956-999** (A956-999 SYF), **1000-1055** (A700-755 THV), **1056-1305** (B56-305 WUL), **1306-1440** (C306-440 BUV), **1441, 1442** (A441-442 UUV), **1443-47** (GBU 1, 4, 5, 8 ,9V), **1448, 1449** (UWW 518, 519X), **1450, 1451** (CUB 539, 540Y), **1452-1478** (E452-478 SON), **1479, 1480** (E479, 480 UOF), **1481-1485** (VRG 415-419T)

MD – Metro-Scania BR111DH (Metropolitan)/Metro-Cammell
1-83 (KJD 201-83P), **84-164** (OUC 84-164R)

OM – Midland Red (BMMO) D9/Carlyle hired from Obsolete Fleet
Ex Midland Red. The OMs were open-top vehicles. Closed top examples were coded BM
OM1-7 (903 KHA, 6301, 2959, 3043, 3016, 3035 HA, 917 KHA). **BM8-10** (6341, 6360, 6314 HA)

THE ROUTEMASTER FAMILY

RM – AEC Routemaster/Park Royal. Includes **RMF1254** (see below), **RMC (1453-1520)** Routemaster Coach, originally for Green Line work; **RCL (2218-2260)** Routemaster Coach Lengthened, **RML (880-903, 2261-2760)** Routemaster Lengthened, seating 72 as opposed to 64
5-300 (VLT 5-300), **301-999** (WLT 301-999), **1000** (100 BXL), **1001-1600** (1-600 CLT), **1601-1865** (601-865 DYE), **1866-2000** (ALD 866-999, ALM 200B), **2001-2105** (ALM 1-105B), **2106-2363** (CUV 106-363C), **2364-2598** (JJD 364-598D), **2599-2657** (NML 599-657E), **2658-2760** (SMK 658-760F)

ERM – London Coaches' RMs extended by the addition of a fifth bay, seating 76 as opposed to 64
80, 84, 90, 94, 143, 163, 235, 237, 242, 281

FRM – front entrance, rear-engined version of the RM
1 (KGY 4D)

RMA – front entrance, built initially for BEA services to Heathrow
1 (KGJ 621D), **2-13** (NMY 626, 627, 629, 635, 638-640, 646-648, 652, 656E), **14-19** (KGJ 602, 611, 614, 617, 618, 622D), **20-27** (NMY 633, 642, 645, 649, 650, 653, 660, 661E), **28-45** (KGJ 601, 603-10, 612, 613, 615, 616, 619, 620, 623-625D), **46-65** (NMY 628, 630-632, 634, 636, 637, 641, 643, 644, 651, 654, 655, 657-659, 662-665E)

RMF – front entrance RML. 1254 was built for LT, later sold to Northern General; 2761-2769 were new to Northern General
1254 (254 CLT); **2761-2772** (FPT 582, 584, 585, 601, 602, 604C, EUP 404B, RCN 687, 696, FPT 600C, RCN 701, 697)

RMT – Routemaster Tour Bus, acquired from a private owner, new to Northern General
2793 (EUP 406B)

RT – AEC Regent III/Park Royal (1654, 1790, 2345, 2541, 2671, 3697, 4347, 4548) or Weymann (remainder)
The following RTs were still extant at 1 January 1979, although only ten were scheduled for service, out of 173 in stock. Many others had however found further use as driver trainers
624 (JXC 432), **851** (JXN 229), **1301** (KLB 550), **1654** (KXW 276), **1790, 1798** (KYY 628, 653), **1989, 2061** (LUC 90, 324), **2240, 2345** (KGU 169, 374), **2541** (LYF 190), **2671** (LYR 655), **3016** (NLE 906), **3251, 3254** (LLU 610, 613), **3697** (NLE 804), **4118** (LUC 467), **4347** (NLP 512), **4548** (OLD 768), **4627, 4633** (NXP 880, 886)

RV – AEC Regent V/Park Royal
Ex Wealden, Kent; new to East Kent
1 (GJG 750D)

S – Scania N112DRB/Alexander (1-29) or Northern Counties Palatine (30-71)
1-9 (F421-429 GWG), **10-29** (J810-829 HMC), **30, 31** (J230, 231 XKY), **32-45** (J132-145 HMT), **46-71** (K846-871 LMK)

SP – DAF DB250/Optare Spectra
1-25 (K301-325 FYG)

T – Leyland Titan/Leyland or Park Royal (1-250); originally TN
T1126-30 ex West Midlands PTE, T1131 was the B15 prototype (see above)
1, 2 (THX 401, 402S), **3-67** (WYV 3-67T), **68-225** (CUL 68-225V), **226-250** (EYE 226-250V), **251-281** (GYE 251-281W), **282-310** (KYN 282-310X), **311-550** (KYV 311-550X), **551-675** (NUW 551-675Y), **676-815** (OHV 676-815Y), **816-822** (RYK 816-822Y), **823-885** (A823-885 SUL), **886-999** (A886-999 SYE), **1000-1055** (A600–655 THV), **1056-1078** (A56-78 THX), **1079-1125** (B79-125 WUV), **1126-30** (WDA 1-5T), **1131** (BCK 706R)

V – Volvo-Ailsa B55/1 Mk III/Alexander (1-3), Van Hool McArdle (4-15) or Alexander (16-65)
4-15 ex South Yorkshire PTE, 16-65 ex West Midlands Travel
1-3 (A101-103 SUU), **4-15** (LWB 389, 408, 409, 375, 394P, NAK 412, 413, 416, 420R, LWB 369, 377, 387P), **16-65** (JOV 766-787, 738-765P)

VC – Volvo B10M Citybus/Northern Counties
1-27 (G101-127 NGN), **28-39** (G127-138 PGK, J139 DGF)

(2) SINGLE DECK FLEET

BL – Bristol LH6L/ECW
1-40 (KJD 401-440P), **41-95** (OJD 41-95R)

BS – Bristol LHS6L/ECW
1-6 (GHV 501-506N), **7-17** (OJD 7-17R)

DA – DAF SB220/Optare Delta
1 (F54 CWY), **2** (F551 SHX), **3-9** (G931-937 MYG), **10** (G684 KNW), **11-29** (J711-729 CYG), **30-35** (K630-635 HWX)

THE DENNIS DART FAMILY

DEL – Dennis Dart/East Lancs
1-11 (L901-911 JRN)

DNL – Dennis Dart/Northern Counties
101-110, 112-120 (L101-110, 112-120 HHV)

DR – Dennis Dart/Reeves Burgess (1-19) or Plaxton (20-153)
1-31 (H101-110 THE, H611 TKU, H112-120 THE, H621 TKU, H122-131 THE), **32-52** (H532-552 XGK), **53-61** (J653-655 XHL, J156-161 GAT), **62-98** (J362-398 GKH), **99-141** (J599, 610, 101-141 DUV), **142-148** (K242-248 PAG), **149-153** (K149-153 LGO)

DRL – Dennis Dart/Reeves Burgess
1-16 (J601-616 XHL), **17-28** (K817-828 NKH), **29-37** (K429-437 OKH), **38-52** (K538-552 ORH), **53-73** (K853-873 LGN), **74-95** (K574-595 MGT), **96-108** (K96-98, 199, 210, 101-108 SAG), **109-135** (K109, 110, 211, 112-135 SRH), **136-146** (L136-146 VRH), **147-158** (L247, 148-158 WAG), **159-171** (L159-164 XRH, L165-169 YAT, L170-171 CKH)

DT – Dennis Dart/Duple (1-27, 168) or Carlyle (remainder)
1-27 (G501-527 VYE), **28-57** (G28-57 TGW), **58-70** (H458-470 UGO), **71-90** (H71-74 MOB, H575 MOC, H76 MOB, H577 MOC, H78, 79 MOB, H880 LOX, H81-87 MOB, H588 MOC, H89 MOB, H890 LOX), **91-168** (H91-98 MOB, H899 LOX, H620 MOM, H101-110 MOB, H611 MOM, H112-156 MOB, **157-168** (H157-168 NON)

DW – Dennis Dart/Wright
1-65 (JDZ 2301-2365), **66-70** (H366-370 XGC), **71-100** (JDZ 2371-2399, 2300), **101-112** (KDZ 5101-5112), **113-126** (LDZ 9113-9126), **127-132** (K127-132 LGO), **133-170** (NDZ 3133-3170)

DWL – Dennis Dart/Wright
1-14 (JDZ 2401-2414), **15-26** (NDZ 3015-3026)

EDR – Dennis Dart/Plaxton Pointer
1-9 (M101-109 BLE)

DK – DAF SB220LC/Ikarus
1-10 (J801-810 KHD)

DMB – Dennis Domino/Northern Counties
On loan from Greater Manchester PTE in 1985/86
1 (C760 YBA)

LA – Dennis Lance/Alexander
1-16 (J101-110, 411, 112-116 WSC)

LLW – Dennis Lance/Wright Pathfinder
1-24 (ODZ 8901-8924), **25-38** (L25-38 WLH)

LN – Dennis Lance/Northern Counties Paladin
1-31 (K301-331 YJA)

THE LEYLAND NATIONAL FAMILY

LS – Leyland National/Leyland LS438-506 - Leyland National 2
1-6 (TGY 101-106M), **7-57** (KJD 507-557P), **58-107** (OJD 858-907R), **108-267** (THX 108-267S), **268-297** (YYE 268-297T), **298-354** (AYR 298-354T), **355-437** (BYW 355-437V), **438-506** (GUW 438-506W)

GLS – Leyland National 2/East Lancs Greenway conversion
GLS2 ex Crosville
1 (GUW 466W), **2** (FCA 9X)
Forty-two vehicles on the Red Arrow network were rebuilt by East Lancs to Greenway specification between 1992-94. They formed a new class and apart from LS466, which became GLS1, retained their old fleet numbers.
   They were the former **438-440, 442, 443, 446, 448-50, 452, 455, 459, 460, 463, 466-469, 471, 473, 474, 476-481, 483, 486, 487, 490-493, 496, 498-502, 505, 506**

LSL – Leyland National 'Long' Owned by the LRT Disability Unit and converted for use as Mobility Buses
   1 ex Southdown 65; 2 ex Hastings & District, new as Southdown 42
1 (WYJ 165S), **2** (RUF 42R)

LV – Dennis Lance/Plaxton Verde
1-12 (L201-212 YAG)

LX – Leyland Lynx/Leyland
LX9-11 ex Merthyr Tydfil
1, 2 (F101, 102 GRM), **3-8** (G73-78 UYV), **9-11** (D105, 106, 111 NDW)

MB – AEC Swift 4MP2R/Metro-Cammell
The **MB** was the basic bus, known as a Merlin. There were two sub-classes: **MBA** Arrow – used on Red Arrow services, and **MBS,** which incorporated a standee area
Sixty-nine MBAs were held in stock at 1 January 1979. As they play a relatively small part in this history, they are listed by year of registration only, viz:
27 of those registered VLW ***G
42 of those registered AML ***H

MS – Scania CR111MH (Metro-Scania)/Metro-Cammell
Originally six in total, only one remained, in withdrawn condition at Chiswick, at 1 January 1979
2 (PGC 202L)

RF – AEC Regal IV/Metro-Cammell
The following RFs were still extant on 1 January 1979, with nineteen scheduled for service out of twenty-four in stock
314 (MLL 951), **369, 381, 428, 437, 441, 452, 471, 481, 486, 492, 495, 502, 504, 505, 507, 510-512** (MXX 11, 23, 405, 414, 418, 429, 448, 458, 463, 469, 472, 479, 481, 482, 484, 487-489), **516, 520, 522** (MLL 934, 938, 940), **536, 537** (NLE 536, 537)

RN – Renault PR100/2/Northern Counties
1 (G276 VML)

SA – Scania N113CRB/Alexander
1 (F113 OMJ)

SLW – Scania N113CRL/Wright Pathfinder
1-14 (RDZ 1701-1714), **15-30** (RDZ 6115-6130)

SM – AEC Swift 4MP2R/Metro-Cammell
The SM was the 'short Merlin" and was otherwise known as a Swift. There were two sub-classes: a single door conversion of the SMS, the **SMD**, and the **SMS**, which incorporated a standee area
269 SMs, SMDs and SMSs were held in stock (excluding withdrawals and driver trainers) on 1 January 1979. As they play a relatively small part in this history, they are listed by year of registration only, viz:
42 of those registered AML **H
173 of those registered EGN ***J
54 of those registered JGF ***K

VN – Volvo B10B-58/Northern Counties
1-13 (K100, 2-6, 70, 8-13 KLL)

(3) MIDIBUS AND MINIBUS FLEET

A – Dodge 50 S56C/Rootes
1, 2 (NYN 1, 2Y)

CV – OMNI-CVE/City Vehicle Engineering
1-3 owned by the London Borough of Hounslow, 5-7 ex C & M, Aintree, owned by the London Borough of Richmond
1-4 (F265-268 WDC), **5-7** (A2-4 LBR, *G195-197 CHN*)

FM – Iveco Daily 49.10/Marshall
1-10 (K521-530 EFL)

FR – Iveco Daily 49.10/Reeves Burgess (with tail-lift)
1-8 (H701-708 YUV)

FS – Ford Transit/Strachans (1-20), Dormobile (21-26) or Carlyle (27-29)
1-12, 15-20 (MLK 701-712, 715-720L), **21** (GHM 721N), **22-26** (CYT 22-26V), **27-29** (C502, 503, 501 HOE)

THE MERCEDES BENZ FAMILY

MA – Mercedes Benz 811D/Alexander
1-107 (F601-645 XMS, 946-955 BMS, 656-707 XMS), **108-124** (G108-124 PGT), **125-134** (H425-434 XGK)

MC – Mercedes Benz 811D/Carlyle
1-5 (F430 BOP, H882-885 LOX)

MT – Mercedes Benz 709D/Reeves Burgess
MT6 was later renumbered MTL6
1-5 (F391-395 DHL), **7, 8** (G537, 538 GBD)

MTL – Mercedes Benz 709D/Reeves Burges
1-6 (G621 XLO, G222 KWE, H189, 191, 192 RWF, F396 DHL)

MW – Mercedes Benz 811D/Wright
1-16 (HDZ 2601-2616), **17** (LDZ 9017), **18-36** (NDZ 7918-7936), **37** (K476 FYN)

SR – Mercedes Benz 811D/Optare Star Rider
1-4 (E711-714 LYU), **5-28** (F905-928 YWY), **29-53** (F29-53 CWY), **54-81** (F154-181 FWY), **82-121** (G82-121 KUB), **122, 123** (G122, 123 SMV)

MR/MRL – MCW Metrorider/MCW (1-134) or Optare (remainder)
MR93-98 originally carried fleet numbers SG1-6
1-22 (D461-482 PON), **23-52** (E123-152 KYW), **53, 54** (E929, 930 KYR), **55-74** (E631-650 KYW), **75, 76** (E705, 706 LYU), **77-92** (F197, 182-196 YDA), **93, 94** (E873, 874 NJD), **95-98** (F895-898 OYR), **99-133** (F99-133 YVP), **134** (D482 NOX), **135** (H135 TGO),

136-159 (H136-159 UUA), **160-176** (H160-163 WWT, H564 WWR, H165-176 WWT), **177-190** (H677-690 YGO), **191-209** (J691-699, 710, 701-709 CGK), **210-221** (J210-221 BWU), **222-241** (K422 HWY, K223 MGT, K424-441 HWY)

OV – Volkswagen LT55/Optare City Pacer
1-4 (C525 DYM, C526-528 DYT), **5** (D529 FYL), **6-49** (D338-381 JUM), **50-52** (E998, 999 TWU, E638 TWW)

RB – Renault 50/Reeves Burgess
1-25 (G871-895 WML), **26-33** (H126-33 AML), **34, 35** (J134 HME, J235 LLK)

RH – Iveco Daily 49.10/Robin Hood
1-24 (C501-512 DYM, D513, 514 FYL, C515-518 DYM, D519, 520 FYL, C521 DYM, D522 FYL, C523 DYM, D524 FYL)

RW – Renault 50/Wright
1-90 (HDZ 5401-5490)

SC – Freight Rover Sherpa/Carlyle
1 (D585 OOV), **2** (D974 PJW)

SD - Freight Rover Sherpa/Dormobile
SD1 was new to West Riding, SD2 to Shamrock & Rambler
SD1 (D811 KWT, 2 (D212 GLJ)

(4) COACHES

The London Coaches fleet is recorded for the period up to May 1992, when it was privatised. Also included are coaches owned by districts that were incorporated into the same numbering system.

AD – AEC Reliance/Duple Dominant II
1 (AHE 996T)

AP – AEC Reliance/Plaxton Supreme
2 (RPH 622R)

BP – Bedford YNT/Plaxton Supreme V
1 (TRA 52X)
Loaned for a short time during 1987

DB – DAF MB200/Berkhof Esprite
DB1 was originally numbered TC1
DB2 – London Northern
1 (B593 XNO), **2** (C708 HWC)

DD – DAF MB200DKFL or MB200DKVL/Duple Caribbean 2 Executive
The original DD1-3 were returned off lease in 1990 but were reacquired later that year when they became DD91-93

DD35, 36 - Selkent
Short term leases in 1988 were DD54, DD60 (E654, 660 KCX)
1-4 (G901-904 MCX), **5** (C645 LVH), **7-9** (C27-29 MCX), **35, 36** (J35, 36 GCX), **42** (E342 EVH), **91-93** (D291-293 XCX), **97** (D297 XCX)

DP – DAF MB230/Plaxton Paramount 3500
With Selkent
1 (F637 OHD)
Short term leases were of DP60 (D360 PJA) in 1988 and DP86 (D286 XCX) in 1991

DS – Volvo B10M/Duple Laser (2 Plaxton Paramount 2)
Ex Digby Stewart College, Roehampton
1, 2 (RMU 967Y, B127 PEL), **3** (KJF 300V)

DV – DAF MB2300DKFL/Van Hool Alizee
67 with Selkent
1-3 (D133 ACX, E312, 313 EVH), **4-7** (E604-607 LVH), **8-22** (F608-622 HGO), **23, 24, 26-29, 31** (H523, 524, 526-529, 531 YCX), **51-60** (F251-260 RJX), **62-66** (G962-966 KJX), **67** (E648 KCX)
A short term lease in 1988 was DV19 (D619 YCX)

LC – Leyland Olympian/East Lancs
1, 2 (C201, 202 DYE)

LD – Leyland Leopard/Duple Dominant
Ex Crosville Wales; with Selkent
3, 4 (OMA 508, 504V)

LD – Leyland Tiger/Duple Caribbean 2
5 with Metroline
1, 2 (C766, 767 DYO), **5** (WGV 867X)

LM – Leyland PD2/MCW Orion
2 (MCO 669)

LP – Leyland Leopard/Plaxton Supreme
5, 6 ex Cambus; with London United, then Leaside
1 (GFV 183S), **2** (KAD 348V), **3** (PWK 12W), **5, 6** (JVF 815, 816V)

ML – MCW Metroliner/Metro-Cammell Weymann
1-4 (C101-104 DYE)

RT – AEC Regent III/Weymann
Unlicensed
1530 (KGU290)

SKY – Auwerter/Neoplan Skyliner
Ex ILG, Ratby, Leicestershire; with London Northern
1 (E469 YWJ)

TDL – Leyland Tiger/Duple
With Metroline
1, 2 (F789, 791 GNA)

TP – Leyland Tiger/Plaxton Paramount
Ex London Country TP14, 31. TP1 with London Forest, TP2 with London Central
1, 2 (A114, 131 EPA)

TPL - Leyland Tiger/Plaxton Paramount except TPL6 (Duple 340)
1 and 2 with Leaside; 3, 5, 7 and 8 with London Forest, then East London (3, 5, 7) or Leaside (8); 9 with Metroline
1-4 (G661, 662 WMD, G100 VMM, G608 SGU), **5-8** (G601 XMD, E771 WSB, H642, 643 GRO), **9** (D602 MVR)

VP – Volvo B10M/Plaxton Paramount 3200
1 with London Northern, 2 with East London, 3 with Metroline
1 (G91 RGG), **2** (F24 HGG), **3** (H637 UWR)

VT – Volvo B58-61/Duple
With (Stanwell Buses (Westlink)
1 (YTA 612S)

LRT TENDERING RESULTS 1985–1994

In this section the tendering and retendering results for every year between 1985 and 1994 are recorded, using the following format:

- route number and outer termini
- operator gaining the route
- subsequent changes of operator, route number etc.
- any other relevant information

The lists do not include successful retenders where there is no change of operator unless there is a subsidiary reason for doing so.

1985

81	Hounslow-Slough (London Buslines)
84A	Turnpike Lane-Barnet (LBL/London Northern)
146	Bromley North-Downe (Crystals of Orpington)
	1991 – won by Metrobus
152	Surbiton-Mitcham (LBL/London General)
	1988 – to Suttonbus (now Kingston-Mitcham)
193	Hornchurch-Romford (Eastern National/Thamesway)
215	Kingston-upon-Thames-Esher/Lower Green (LBL)
	1987 – renumbered K3
228	Eltham-Sidcup & Chislehurst (LBL/Selkent)
	1988 – withdrawn, replaced by 228A and 228C
258	Watford Junction-South Harrow (LBL/Harrow Buses)
	1991 – won by Luton & District
313	Chingford-Potters Bar, (London Country/London Country North East)
	1988 – contract reassigned to Grey-Green after an 11- day strike at London Country North East
H2	Golders Green-Hampstead Garden Suburb circular) (LBL/London Northern)
	1989 – won by R & I Coaches
P4	Brixton-Lewisham (London Country/London & Country)
	1991 – won by Selkent
W9	Muswell Hill-Enfield Town (Eastern National/Thamesway)

SUCCESSES IN 1985

The H2 began life in 1976 following the 'Hampstead Dial-a-Ride' experiment started two years previously. It has always been a route for the smaller vehicle, and Ford Transits displaying the craft of three different body builders had by this time appeared on it. The Strachans and Dormobile examples were replaced by Carlyle bodied FS27-29 in November 1985, three months after a new contract for the H2 began, and the first of these, FS27 (C502 HOE), was photographed at Golders Green bus station in early 1987. All three were put into store when the H2 passed to R&I Coaches in 1989 but did subsequently find work elsewhere in the network.

London Country took the 313 in the first round of tendering, just over a year before the company was split into four units in preparation for privatisation. The 313 went to the North East division, and LR39 (A139 DPE), a Roe bodied Leyland Olympian, was seen at Potters Bar in early 1987. At this stage the only outward sign of change is the addition of the 'North East' to the fleetname which, along with the band between decks, was rendered in pale green, although by now a new livery was starting to appear. The NBC 'double N' symbol is also conspicuous by its absence, although London Country North East still had a year to go before it became the seventy-second and last member of the NBC to be privatised.

Len Wright Travel Ltd started life in 1977 as a coaching operation, but like so many companies in the 1980s, it was alive to the opportunities that the tender process could bring. So London Buslines opened for business on 13 July 1985, using ex LBL Fleetlines in a yellow and brown livery on the 81. The 195 followed in 1986, when a further batch was acquired, taking the total to fifteen. The first new vehicles were six Leyland Lynxes in 1987, and it is one of these, 52 (D752 DLO), that was photographed in central Slough whilst on its way back to Hounslow.

1986

London Country was split into four separate companies on 7 September 1986 as a prelude to their eventual privatisation. These were, with the LRT contracts operated at that time, London Country North East (298, 313), London Country North West (142, 268), London Country South East (51, 493, P4) and London Country South West (127, 127A, 197, 197A, 197B, 293, 403).

20	Walthamstow-Debden (Eastern National/Thamesway)
	1992 – won by Grey-Green
51	Woolwich-Orpington/Green Street Green (London Country South East/Kentish Bus)
	1992 – won by London Central
61	Bromley North-Chislehurst (Metrobus)
61B	Chislehurst-Eltham (LBL/Selkent)
79A	Edgware-Alperton (LBL)
	1987 – won by London Buslines, renumbered 79
84	New Barnet-St Albans (LBL/London Northern (Hertfordshire CC contract)

107	New Barnet-Queensbury (LBL/London Northern)
	1989 – won by Pan Atlas Coaches trading as Atlas Bus)
	1994 – won by Metroline
116	Hounslow-Bedfont-Staines (Westlink)
	1991 – won by Tellings Golden Miller
	1992 – contract reassigned to London & Country
117	Brentford-Staines (Westlink)
	1991 – won by Tellings Golden Miller
	1992 – contract reassigned to London & Country
125	North Finchley-Enfield (LBL)
	1987 – won by Grey-Green
127	Selsdon-Tooting, to London Country/London Country South West/London & Country
127A	Selsdon-Streatham Hill, to London Country/London Country South West
	1989 – withdrawn (merged with 127)
142	Watford Junction-Brent Cross, to London Country/London Country North West
145	Redbridge-Dagenham/Ford Works, to Ensignbus
	1991 – won by East London
145A	Chingford-Goodmayes (Eastern National) ex 145, school journeys, later renumbered **345**
	345 1989 – won by London Forest
	345 1991 – transferred from London Forest to East London
	345 1993 – won by Capital Citybus
167	Ilford-Loughton (Eastern National/Thamesway)
	1992 – won by Grey-Green
179	Barking-Chingford (LBL)
	1987 – won by Grey-Green
179A	Chingford-Yardley Lane Estate (LBL)
	1987 – won by Grey-Green, renumbered **379**
	379 1990 – won by Eastern National/Thamesway
195	Charville Lane (Hayes)-Ealing Hospital (London Buslines)
	1991 – won by Centrewest
197	Croydon-Norwood Junction (London Country/London Country South West/London & Country)
	1989 – won by South London
197A	West Croydon-Caterham Valley (London Country/London Country South West/London & Country)
	1989 – won by South London; extended to Wallington in 1991 and renumbered **407**
	407 1994 – won by **London & Country**
197B	Caterham Valley-Norwood Junction (London Country/London Country South West/London & Country)
	1989 – won by South London
	1991 – withdrawn (replaced by the 197 and part 407)
200	Streatham Hill-Raynes Park (Cityrama)
	1988 – surrendered by Cityrama, to London United on a temporary basis
	1989 – reassigned to London General
201	Buckhurst Hill-Ongar (West's Coaches) (Essex CC contract)
203	Brentford-Staines (Westlink)

		1991 – won by London Buslines
	206	Walthamstow-Chigwell (Eastern National)
		1989 – withdrawn, replaced by W14
	208	Orpington-Lewisham (LBL/Selkent)
	217B	Enfield-Upshire (Sampsons)
		1987 – won again by Sampsons after retendering by Essex CC, renumbered **317**
	317	**1988** – surrendered by Sampsons, reassigned to Leaside
	317	**1994** – won by London Northern (Enfield-Waltham Cross)
	229	Erith-Sidcup (LBL/Bexleybus)
		1990 – won by London Central
	242	Potters Bar-Waltham Abbey (LBL/London Northern) (Herts CC contract)
		1992 – Mondays-Saturdays commercial operation, London Northern, Sundays Thamesway
	250	South Woodford-Waltham Cross (Sampsons)
		1987 – won again by Sampsons after retendering by Essex CC
		1988 – surrendered by Sampsons; reassigned to Frontrunner South East
	251	Waltham Cross-Upshire (ex 250A) (Sampsons)
		1987 – won again by Sampsons after retendering by Essex CC
		1988 – surrendered by Sampsons; reassigned to Frontrunner South East
	252	Chingford-Waltham Cross (ex 242 school journeys) (Eastern National) (Essex CC contract)
	261	Bromley Common-Lewisham (LBL)
		1987 – won by Metrobus
	263	Archway-Potters Bar (LBL/London Northern)
	268	Golders Green-Finchley Road (London Country/London Country North West)
		1989 – won by R & I Coaches (MTL London 1994)
	275	Walthamstow-Barkingside (Eastern National/Thamesway)
		1992 – won by Grey-Green
	283	East Acton-West Brompton (Scancoaches)
		1989 – won by London United (Riverside Bus fleetname from 1990)
	293	Hackbridge-Epsom (London Country/London Country South West/London & Country)
		1990 – Epsom-Morden section retained by London & Country on a commercial (non-LRT) basis
	298	South Mimms-Turnpike Lane (London Country/London Country North East)
		1988 – contract reassigned to Grey-Green after an 11- day strike at London Country North East
		1992 – won by Capital Citybus
	307	New Barnet-Brimsdown (Eastern National/Thamesway) (ex 107)
	359	Hammond Street-Manor House (new route, ex 259, operated by London Country North East for the first three months, then Eastern National/Thamesway)
		1992 – withdrawn
	361	Bromley Common-Green Street Green (Metrobus)
		1992 – withdrawn
	403	Cheam Village/Wallington-Warlingham Park Hospital (London Country route brought into LRT tendering process, retained, London Country South West/London & Country)

LRT TENDERING RESULTS 1985–1994 • 221

	1989 – won by South London
	1994 – won by London & Country
493	Orpington-Ramsden Estate (London Country route brought into LRT tendering process, retained, Kentish Bus)
	1991 – won by London & Country
PB1	Potters Bar circular (North Mymms Coaches, taken out of LRT tendering process)
R1-R6	Orpington network (LBL/Roundabout). Originally L1-L6, the R2 was formerly the 858, operated by Crystals of Orpington
	1993 – R5 & R6 won by Kentish Bus

SUCCESSES IN 1986

Ensignbus moved into commuter work early in 1986 as a precursor to operation of the 145 on 21 June of that year. It acquired RT3232 (KYY 961) from LT in 1979 and which by this time was sporting the attractive light blue and silver-grey livery of the sightseeing fleet. It would make occasional appearances on LRT routes, and in Dagenham in 1986, it was working the 145, keeping company with a pair of Titans from North Street that were engaged on the 175.

By the end of 1986 Eastern National were operating ten routes on behalf of LRT, and vehicles allocated to those services were given the stylised 'CityBus' logo and the legend 'Running in London for London Regional Transport'. The 20 changed hands on 24 May 1986; on 2 December that year 1825 (VAR 902S) was preparing for the trip to Debden at Walthamstow Central bus station. A decent crowd is waiting to board; normally they would be accommodated aboard a double decker, usually a VR3, as the press release for the change of operator indicated that saloons would only appear on the 167 and 206, two other services won by Eastern National in the same tranche.

The attractive blue and yellow livery of Metrobus was becoming more regularly seen on the streets of south east London. The 61 was a particularly good win for the company, which required no fewer than thirteen former DMSs in 1986, including KUC 922P, an MCW bodied example. It was seen on lay-over at the rear of Bromley North railway station.

1987

London Country South East was renamed Kentish Bus on 27 April.

Two major awards based on areas were implemented in 1987. The Kingston-upon-Thames scheme involved routes 65, 71, 85, 131, 213, and K1/K2 (originally L1/L2). The Harrow scheme involved routes H11-H15, 114, 136, 140, 183, 209 and 340. A third scheme for the Bexleyheath area was not implemented until January 1988.

4	Archway-Waterloo (LBL/London Northern)
42	Aldgate-Camberwell Green (London Country South East/Kentish Bus)
51A	Woolwich-Swanley (Kentish Bus)
	1992 – route withdrawn
62	Barking-Gants Hill, (Ensignbus)
	1991 – won by East London

62A	Barking-Little Heath (new route, Ensignbus)
	1991 – withdrawn
65	Ealing-Kingston (Kingston Bus)
71	Richmond-Chessington Zoo (Kingston Bus)
	1990 – Kingston-Chessington World of Adventure section retained by London United after retendering
85	Putney Bridge-Kingston (Kingston Bus)
	1990 – won by London & Country
110	Twickenham-Cranford (London Country South West/London & Country)
	1990 – won by Westlink
114	Ruislip/Mill Hill Broadway/Mill Hill East (Harrow Buses)
	1991 – won by BTS Coaches, later Sovereign Bus & Coach
131	West Molesey-Wimbledon/Clapham Common (London Country South West/London & Country)
	1990 – won by Westlink
136	Harrow-Northwick Park (Mondays-Fridays, peaks only) (Harrow Buses)
	1991 – withdrawn
140	Harrow Weald-Heathrow Terminal 4-Harrow Weald (Harrow Buses)
	1990 – won by London United
153	Archway-Angel Islington section only (London Country North West)
	1988 – contract surrendered, transferred to London General (permanent 2-year contract from 1989)
	1992 – won by Capital Citybus
173	Stratford-Becontree Heath (Grey-Green)
183	Golders Green-Pinner/Northwood Hills (Harrow Buses/Metroline)
196	Norwood Junction-Kennington Oval/Islington (London Country South East but reassigned to Cityrama)
	1989 – temporarily contracted to London & Country
	1990 – won by London General
209	South Harrow-Stanmore Broadway (school journeys) (Harrow Buses/Metroline)
	1992 – withdrawn
213	Kingston-Sutton/St Helier/West Croydon (Kingston Bus)
	1990 – won by London General
289	Elmers End Green-Purley (London Country South East but reassigned to London Country South West/London & Country)
292	Borehamwood-Edgware/Colindale (London Country North East)
	1988 – contract reassigned to BTS Coaches after 11- day strike at London Country North East
	1993 – won by Metroline
297	Willesden-Ealing Broadway/Wembley Trading Estate (LBL/Metroline)
	1990 – won by Centrewest (journeys to Wembley Trading Estate withdrawn)
340	Edgware-Harrow/South Harrow (Harrow Buses/Metroline)
	1991 – won by Luton & District
398	Ruislip-Northolt, operated by Scorpio Coaches within the LRT network
500	Harlow-Romford (LBL/London Forest) (Sundays, Essex CC contract)
	1988 – won by Blue Triangle
508	Sutton-Epsom (LBL/London General) (Sundays, Surrey CC contract)
	1990 – transferred to Epsom Buses

224 • LONDON'S BUSES, 1979–1994

520	Sutton-Walton-on-the-Hill (LBL/London General) (Surrey CC contract)
522	Sutton-Redhill/Earlswood (LBL/London General) (Surrey CC contract)
C2	Oxford Circus-Parliament Hill Fields (ex 53) (London Country North West)
	1988 – contract surrendered, transferred to London General (permanent contract from 1989)
	1993 – won by London Northern
H11	Northwood station-Harrow bus station (LBL-Harrow Buses)
	1990 – won by Sovereign Bus & Coach; extended to Northwick Park Hospital)
H12	South Harrow station-Harrow Weald (Harrow Buses/Metroline)
H13	Pinner Green-Ruislip Lido (Harrow Buses)
	1990 – won by Sovereign Bus & Coach
H14	Northwick Park Hospital-Hatch End (LBL-Harrow Buses/Metroline)
H15	Northwick Park Hospital-Harrow Weald (LBL-Harrow Buses/Metroline)
K1	New Malden-Surbiton (LBL-Westlink)
K2	Hook-Kingston (LBL-Westlink)
K3	Kingston-Belmont/St Helier/Sutton/Croydon (LBL-Westlink)
R11	Queen Mary's Hospital Sidcup-Green Street Green (LBL-Roundabout)

SUCCESSES IN 1987

London Country South East took over the 42 in February, some ten weeks before the company name change to Kentish Bus. Picking up in Minories on its way to Camberwell Green on 3 June 1987, SNB483 (BPL 483T) will soon be plain 483. Nothing plain about the livery, however; an NBC green and National London dual-purpose hybrid.

Left: These were still the early days of mass minibus operation in London, and when awarding the contract for the new C2 route to London Country North West, introduced on 24 March 1987 between Oxford Circus and Parliament Hill Fields, LRT provided the vehicles from its recently acquired batch of Optare City Pacers. Hence MBV49 (D379 JUM) carries red livery rather than that of LCNW, and branded as the Camden Hoppa, with route information provided above the windows, it was seen in New Burlington Street on 13 April.

Below: The contract for the 4 (Waterloo-Archway) began on 7 February 1987 and six weeks later, on 19 March, Holloway's M1076 (B76 WUL) was standing in the Cornwall Street parking area before the next northbound journey. To all intents and purposes, nothing has changed; there is no indication that this is now an LRT tendered route. Alongside was sister vehicle M1248 (B248 WUL), displaying what must have been a very recently acquired Leaside black skirt.

1988

The results of several schemes were implemented in 1988. Locations and routes involved were:

- Bexleyheath (Selkent); the 96, 99, 132, 178, 228A/C, 229, 233, 244, 269, 272, 291, 401, 422, 469, 472, 492 and B11-15
- Hornchurch (East London); the 165, 246, 248, 252, 256, 346 and 446
- Sutton (London General) took the trading name Suttonbus; the 80, 93, 151, 152, 154, 157, 163, 164 and 352

Smaller minibus networks were also set up in Peckham and Walthamstow.

The privatisation of the four London Country companies was completed in 1988. London Country North West was the subject of a management buy-out on 5 January. London Country South West was sold to the Drawlane Group on 19 February. Kentish Bus was acquired by the Proudmutual group, owners of Northumbria, on 15 March. London Country North East was sold to the AJS Group on 22 April.

Frontrunner Buses South East, a subsidiary of East Midlands Motor Services, was created as a means of managing the expanding London operations. The 250/251 were operated from Wyatts Green, and the 248/252 from a new base at Rainham.

24	Pimlico-Hampstead Heath (Grey-Green)
80	Morden-Belmont/Banstead (Suttonbus)
93	Putney Bridge-North Cheam (Suttonbus)
96	Dartford-Woolwich (Bexleybus)
	1991 – won by Kentish Bus
99	Woolwich-Erith (Bexleybus)
	1990 – won by London Central
112	Ealing Broadway-Palmers Green (Pan Atlas Coaches trading as Atlas Bus)
	1994 – won by R & I Buses (Ealing Broadway-Brent Cross). One schools journey Ealing Broadway-East Finchley to Centrewest later renumbered 612
132	Eltham circular (Boro'line Maidstone)
	1992 – reassigned to Kentish Bus
151	Wallington-Sutton/Lower Morden (Suttonbus)
154	West Croydon-Sutton/Morden (Suttonbus)
157	Crystal Palace-Morden (Suttonbus)
163	Morden-Wimbledon (Suttonbus)
164	Belmont-Wimbledon (Suttonbus)
165	Havering Park-Rainham (Ensignbus)
178	Lewisham-Thamesmead (Bexleybus)
	1990 – won by London Central
188	Greenwich (Cutty Sark)-Euston (Boro'line Maidstone)
	1990 – won by Selkent
	1993 – won by London & Country
189	Tooting Broadway-Brixton (school journeys) (South London)
	1991 – won by London General
	1993 – won by London & Country
228A	Eltham-Sidcup circular, to Boro'line Maidstone, renumbered **328**
	328 1992 – reassigned to Kentish Bus

228C	Eltham-Sidcup circular, to Boro'line Maidstone, renumbered **228**
	228 1992 – reassigned to Kentish Bus
233	Eltham-Swanley (Boro'line Maidstone)
	1992 – reassigned to Kentish Bus
244	Woolwich-Broadwaters (Bexleybus)
	1990 – won by London Central
246	Harold Hill-Corbets Tey (Ensignbus)
248	Romford-Cranham (Frontrunner South East)
252	Collier Row-Gidea Park (Frontrunner South East)
256	Hornchurch-Harold Hill/Noak Hill (East London)
	1990 – won by County Bus
269	Bexleyheath-Bromley North (Bexleybus)
	1991 – won by Kentish Bus
271	Moorgate-Highgate Village/Hendon Central (London Northern)
	1993 – won by London Suburban Bus
272	Woolwich-Thamesmead circular (Bexleybus)
	1990 – won by Boro'line Maidstone
	1992 – reassigned to Kentish Bus
291	Woolwich-Plumstead (Bexleybus)
	1990 – won by London Central
317	Enfield-Waltham Cross-Upshire (temporary contract to Leaside, ex Sampsons; permanent contract awarded 1989)
	1994 – won by London Northern
346	Upminster Park Estate-Upminster station (East London)
	1990 – won by County Bus
352	Eastfields-Merton/Wimbledon (Suttonbus)
365	Havering Park-Mardyke Estate (Ensignbus)
389	Thornton Heath-West Croydon (school journeys) (South London)
	1990 – worked by London & Country for the final four weeks of operation
401	Bexleyheath-Thamesmead (part ex Kentish Bus 401) (Bexleybus)
	1990 – won by London Central
422	Woolwich-Bexleyheath (part ex 122) (Bexleybus)
	1988 – transferred to Boro'line Maidstone
	1992 – reassigned to Kentish Bus
446	Cranham-Corbets Tey (ex 246A) (Ensignbus)
469	Woolwich-Bexleyheath (part ex 269) (Bexleybus)
	1990 – won by London Central
472	Thamesmead-Woolwich (Saturday shopping hours) (Bexleybus)
	1990 – won by Boro'line Maidstone
	1992 – reassigned to Kentish Bus
492	Sidcup-Dartford (part ex Kentish Bus) (Bexleybus)
	1988 – transferred to Boro'line Maidstone
	1992 – reassigned to Kentish Bus
550	Gidea Park-Cranham (school journeys) (Frontrunner South East)
576	Brettgrave-Epsom/Langley Vale (Suttonbus) (ex Epsom Buses, Surrey CC contract)
	1991 – withdrawn
B11	Bexleyheath-Lodge Hill (Bexleybus)
	1991 – won by Kentish Bus

B12	Bexleyheath-Erith (Bexleybus)
	1990 – won by London Central
B13	Bexleyheath-Avery Hill Road (Bexleybus)
	1990 – won by London Central
B14	Bexleyheath-Erith (Bexleybus)
	1988 – withdrawn (replaced by revised B13)
B15	Bexleyheath-Joydens Wood Estate (Bexleybus)
	1991 – won by TransCity (Kentish Bus 1993)
H16	Hatch End-Pinner (school journeys) (Metroline)
P11	Peckham-Waterloo (London Central)
P12	Peckham circular (London Central)
P13	Peckham-Pepys Estate (London Central)
P14	Surrey Docks-Isle of Dogs (Kentish Bus)
	1992 – won by East London
	1993 – won by London Central
W11	Walthamstow (Crooked Billet)-Walthamstow Central (London Forest)
	1991 – won by London Forest, reassigned to Thamesway
W12	Walthamstow (South Grove)-Wanstead (London Forest)
	1991 – won by London Forest, reassigned to Thamesway
W15	Walthamstow Central-Hackney Central (new route, London Forest)
	1991 – won by London Forest, reassigned to County Bus

SUCCESSES IN 1988/89

Atlas Bus acquired eight new Leyland Lynxes with which to work the 112, numbering them AB51-58. This is AB57 (E965 PME), picking up at Brent Cross shopping centre on its way to Palmers Green.

New vehicles were on order for Boro'line Maidstone's 132 and 188 but they had not yet appeared when contracts began, on 16 January and 14 November respectively. So second-hand stock was drafted in, which in the case of the 132, started to be displaced by new Leyland Olympians from February onwards. Fourteen former Kingston-Upon-Hull Leyland Atlanteans with Roe bodywork were supplied in total, and 375 (WAG 375X), carrying Hull's colours and crest, was still working the 132 when found in Bexleyheath on 5 March. New Volvo Citybuses for the 188 started to arrive four months into the contract, and in the meantime, Fleetlines from Nottingham and Atlanteans from Ipswich were hired in but were not a great advertisement for either the operator or the process. I was late getting to the office on 23 November, ten days in, having watched several of these venerable specimens before catching this one, Nottingham 196 (PAU 196R), for my journey to Aldwych. The name 'Mr Fred', on an Ipswich-style scroll, was added after its arrival in London.

Above: The London Country North East strike led to the contracts for the 292, 298 and 313 being reassigned. Grey-Green were awarded the latter two, and this is their MCW Metrobus 457 (EWF 457V), one of ten received from South Yorkshire Transport that year. The orange, brown and white livery had been adopted after the first tender, for the 173, had been won in 1986 and allocated to their Dix Travel subsidiary. Soon, however, with the award of the 24, illustrated in the chapter dealing with 1988, vehicles would appear in a new grey and green scheme with an orange stripe. In the meantime though, 457 was speeding through Chingford on 20 June 1988, en route to Potters Bar.

Opposite above: Having used a mixture of Atlanteans and Olympians on the 51 and 51A, Kentish Bus introduced five new Alexander bodied Scania N112s starting in July 1988, which may have been a factor in the company successfully retaining the route in 1989. The last of the five, 705 (F705 JCN), was discovered in Greens End, Woolwich on its way to Green Street Green when less than a month old.

Opposite below: R&I acquired a fleet of eleven Iveco 49.10s with Robin Hood bodywork seating either nineteen or twenty-three passengers, all new in 1989. This is 206 (F206 HGN), preparing to leave Golders Green bus station with an H2 working for the Garden Suburb on 28 September 1989.

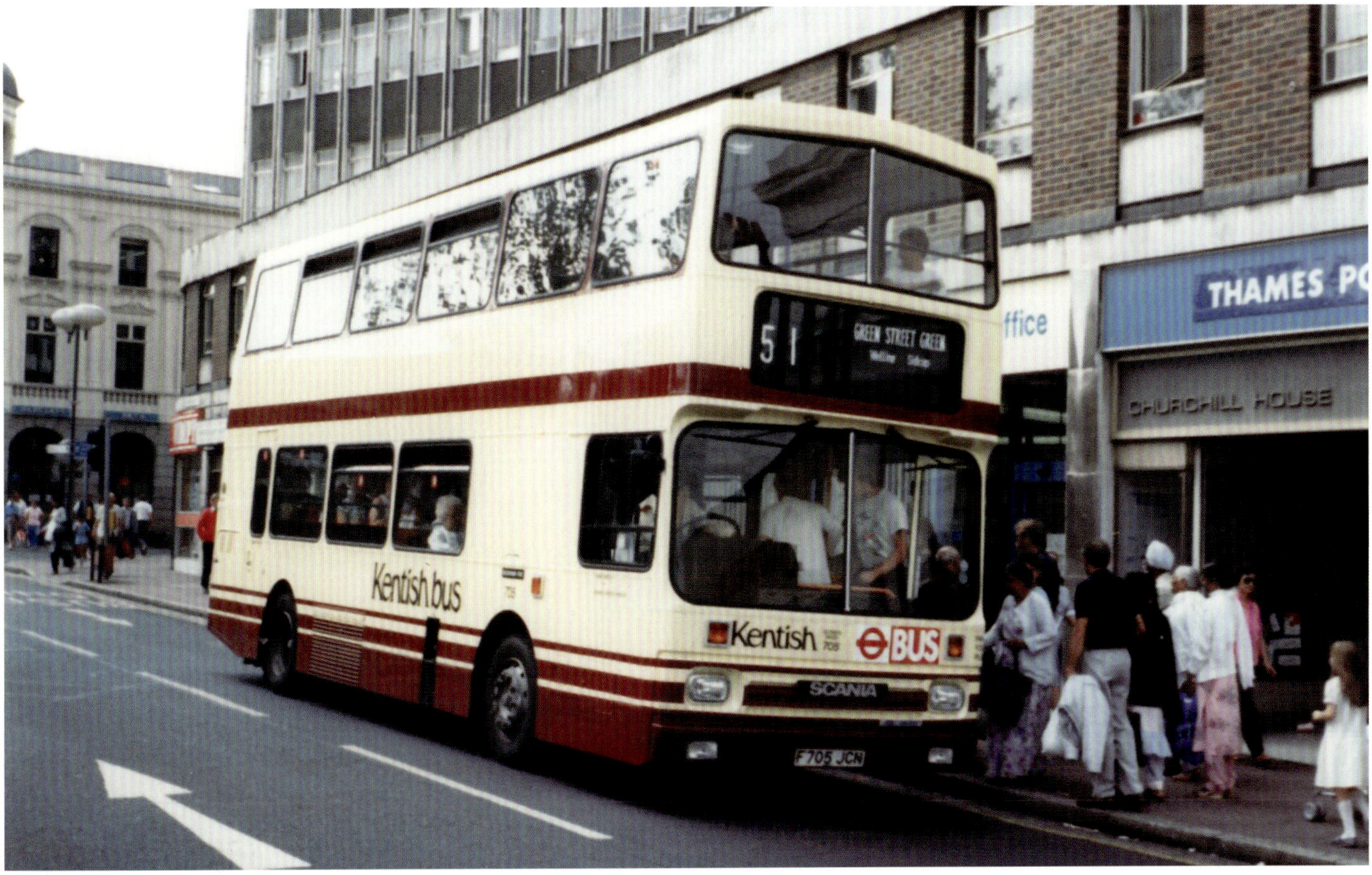
51
GREEN STREET GREEN
THAMES PO
CHURCHILL HOUSE
Kentish bus
Kentish
BUS
SCANIA
F705 JCN

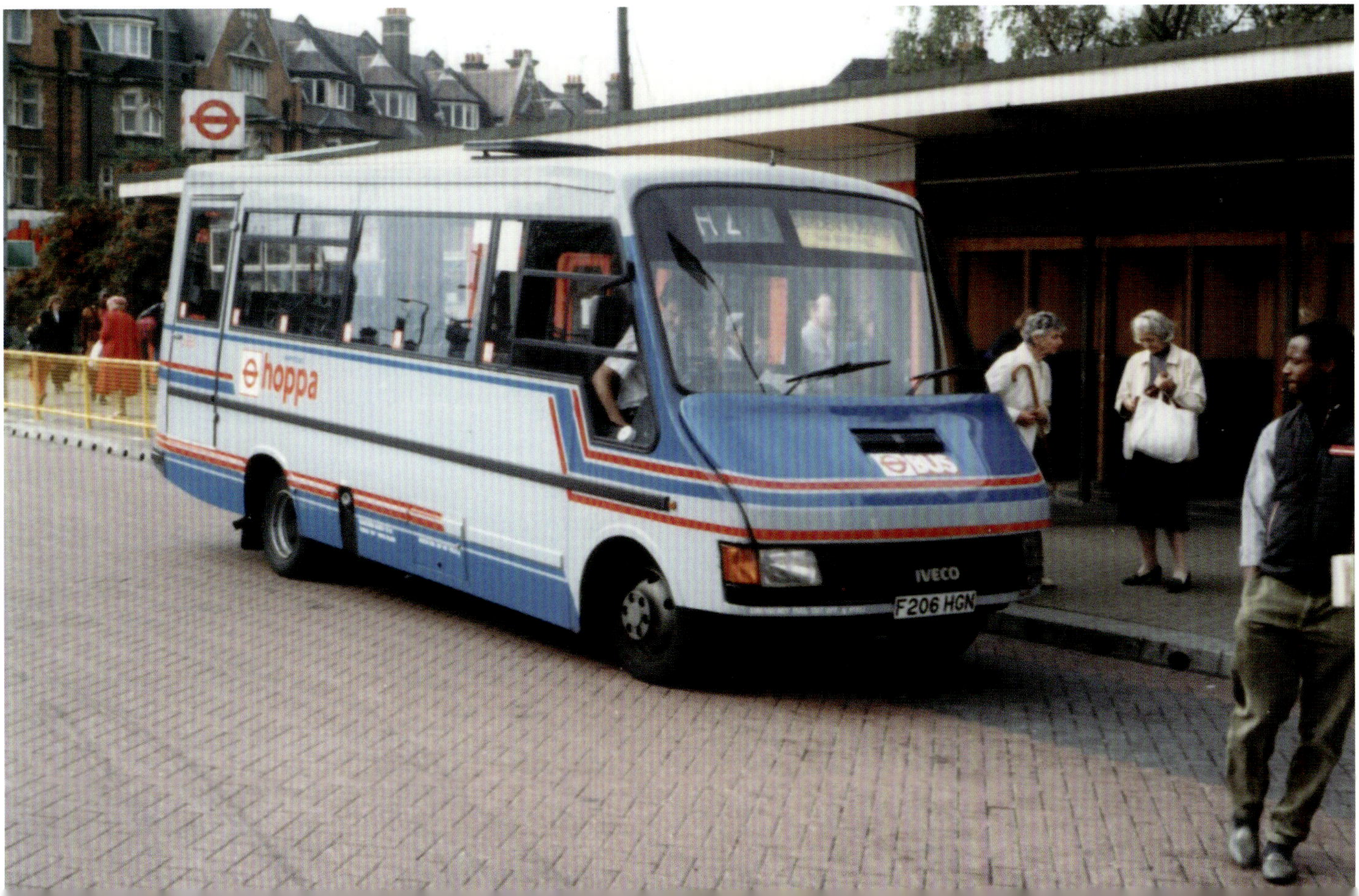
hoppa
BUS
IVECO
F206 HGN

1989

London Country North East was split in January: the western part became Sovereign Bus & Coach, the eastern side County Bus & Coach. London Country South West was renamed London & Country on 27 April.

In April East Midland was acquired by the Stagecoach group, a move that included Frontrunner South East operations. But at the end of June, this was sold to Ensignbus, a move that added the 248 and 252 to their portfolio. The 550 was retained after retendering.

57	Streatham Hill-Kingston (London United)
	1992 – won by London & Country
90B	Kew Gardens-Yeading (renumbered **90**, London Buslines)
108	Wanstead-Lewisham (Boro'line Maidstone, after three months temporary operation by LBL-East London)
	1992 – reassigned to Kentish Bus
211	Waltham Cross-Breach Barns, from Sampsons, won by London Forest (Essex CC contract)
	1991 – transferred to Leaside
213	Waltham Cross-Upshire, from Sampsons, won by London Forest (Essex CC contract)
	1991 – transferred to Leaside
235	Leytonstone-Woodford Wells, school journeys only; remainder to W13 (Eastern National/Thamesway)
	1992 – won by Grey-Green
286	Greenwich-Eltham 'Greenwich Hoppa' (London Central)
	1992 – won by Transcity (Kentish Bus 1993)
347	Brentwood-Romford, from County Bus (commercial operation) to Ensignbus (LRT contract)
393	Hackbridge-Morden/Merton, ex 293 (London & Country)
	1991 – won by London General
471	Orpington-Green Street Green, from Selkent, won by Kentish Bus
699	Romford-Upminster 'Parks Rider' (East London) (Essex CC contract)
842	Potters Bar-St Albans school journeys from Sovereign Bus & Coach, won by London Northern (Hertfordshire CC contract)
	1991 – operated commercially by Sovereign Bus & Coach
C4	Putney Pier (or Putney Bridge at very high tides)-Chelsea Harbour (London Buslines)
H17	Harrow-Sudbury (R & I Coaches)
	1991 – won by Sovereign Bus & Coach
W13	Leytonstone-Woodford Wells, ex 235 for all but school journeys (Eastern National/Thamesway)
W14	Leytonstone-Claybury, ex 206 (Eastern National/Thamesway)
	1991 – won by County Bus
W16	Chingford Mount-Leytonstone (London Forest)
	1991 – won by London Forest, reassigned to County Bus

1990

Westlink took over the 600 (Hanworth-Bedfont Green) and 602 (Feltham-Shepperton) after the collapse of Fountain Coaches.

Following its acquisition by the Badgerline group in April, Eastern National was split in two, with all LRT contracts operated by Thamesway, a new company formed to take over the southern area. It was responsible for the 20, 167, 193, 235, 275, 307, 359, 379, W9, W13 and W14.

Routes 62, 62A, 145, 165, 246, 248, 252, 347, 365, 446, 550, N99 and some commercial routes were transferred from Ensignbus to Frontrunner (South East) in July.

London Country North West was taken over by Luton & District in October, the 142 becoming one of its routes.

Bexleybus was consigned to history when the results of the network retendering were known. Routes 99, 178, 229, 244, 291, 401, 469, B12 and B13 passed to London Central, which also took over Bexleyheath garage on 24 November, earlier than the planned date in January 1991. The 188, 272 and 472 changed hands at the same time. Boro'line Maidstone retained the 132, 228, 233, 422 and 492, whilst also gaining the 272 and 472; it lost the 188 to Selkent. The 96 and B11 went to Kentish Bus and the B15 to Transcity.

In December, Ensignbus was acquired by the Hong Kong based CNT group.

22A	London Bridge-Clapton Park Estate (Kentish Bus)
22B	Homerton Hospital-Piccadilly Circus (Kentish Bus)
48	London Bridge-Walthamstow Central (London Forest)
50	Streatham-Old Coulsdon (South London)
55	Clapton Pond-Tottenham Court Road (Kentish Bus)
56	Whipps Cross-Barts Hospital (London Forest)
60	Clapham Common-South Croydon (South London)
63	King's Cross-Crystal Palace (London Central)
64	Thornton Heath-New Addington (South London)
65	Ealing Broadway-Kingston (Armchair Passenger Transport – but worked by London & Country on a temporary contract until January 1991)
66	Romford-Leytonstone (County Bus)
78	Shoreditch-Forest Hill (London & Country)
85	Kingston-Putney Bridge (London & Country)
92	Ealing Hospital-Neasden (London Buslines)
100	Liverpool Street-Wapping circular (new route in 1989 with Leaside, contract won by East London in 1990
103	Romford-North Rainham (County Bus) **1991** – contract transferred to Grey-Green
133	Liverpool Street-Tooting Broadway (London General)
168	Hampstead Heath-Waterloo (Grey-Green)
176	Oxford Circus-Penge (London & Country)
182	Harrow Weald-Brent Cross (Metroline)
187	South Harrow-West Kilburn (Metroline)
210	Finsbury Park-Golders Green/Brent Cross (Grey-Green)
217	Turnpike Lane-Waltham Cross (London Northern)
231	Turnpike Lane-Carterhatch (London Northern)
237	Shepherds Bush Green-Sunbury Village (London United-Riverside Bus)
250	Brixton-Croydon (South London)

260	North Finchley-Shepherds Bush (Armchair Passenger Transport)
264	Tooting Broadway-South Croydon (South London)
276	Stoke Newington-North Woolwich (East London)
277	Highbury & Islington-Poplar Baths (East London)
281	Hounslow-Tolworth Broadway (London United)
282	Mount Vernon Hospital-Hanwell Broadway (Centrewest)
312	Peckham-South Croydon (South London)
320	Bromley North-Biggin Hill-Westerham, replacing London & Country 410/Kentish Bus 20, retained by London & Country. Sunday service provided by Kentish Bus as the 320
362	Chadwell Heath-Barkingside (Thamesway)
371	Richmond-Kingston-upon-Thames, ex 71 (Westlink)
384	Cockfosters-Barnet (London Northern)
412	West Croydon-Purley, ex 12A (South London)
413	Belmont-Sutton, ex 213 (London General)
572	Stoneleigh Broadway-Langley Vale (London General) (Surrey CC contract)
C11	Archway-North Cricklewood/Brent Cross (R & I Tours, together with new C12, the King's Cross-West Hampstead section)
D1	Docklands Express: Waterloo-Isle of Dogs (London Forest)
H24	Feltham-Hatton Cross (London United) **1993** – withdrawn
H25	Hanworth (Butts Farm)-Feltham (London United)
S2	Lea Valley Ice Centre-Clapton/Stratford (East London)
X71	Ham-Chessington (London United) **1991** – withdrawn

SUCCESSES IN 1990/91

M293 (BYX 293V) speeds along Hook Road with a return journey from the BAC Works in Ham, around the time the X71 was introduced. Overall, the route lasted just under three years – ironically, the length of the contract awarded in 1990 – until June 1991.

Above: The 131 passed to Westlink in September 1990, with a requirement for ten double deckers. Titans were preferred, and were sourced from around the districts. T965 (A965 SYE) came from Camberwell and was repainted into Westlink livery before entering service. It was waiting in Victoria Crescent, Wimbledon in November 1991 when I saw it; it lasted another eighteen months before being repainted into red livery and moving to East London.

Below: County Bus took over on the 66 in August, and eight Leyland Lynxes were acquired to run it. This is LX254 (H254 GEV), making its way to Romford station.

Above: Armchair Passenger Transport won its first contract in June 1990, for the 260 (North Finchley-Shepherds Bush). Twelve Alexander bodied Leyland Olympians were acquired, of which this is the last numerically, G372 YUR, on Finchley Road; fleet numbers were not carried. There seems to have been problems with the blinds, not least of which is the rather unfortunate misspelling of the destination as 'Sheperds Bush'. Armchair would go on to win the 65 later in the year, although delays in receiving new vehicles led to London & Country stepping in on a temporary basis.

Opposite above: The Wandsworth area scheme implemented on 25 May 1991 saw the lengthy and delay-prone 37 split into three sections. The eastern end between Peckham and Putney, retained the number 37, while the middle section from Clapham Junction to Richmond became the 337. Both of these were worked by London General from Stockwell garage. To the west, Richmond to Hounslow became a London United 'Harrier' operation, taking route number H37. London General M250 (BYX 250V) was on its way to Clapham when spotted in Upper Richmond Road.

Opposite below: Midland Fox subsidiary Tellings Golden Miller, trading as TGM Buses, won both the 116 and 117 from Westlink with effect from 10 August 1991. Six months later, and as a result of poor performance – hardly surprising with a fleet consisting entirely of ageing Leyland Nationals – the contracts were reassigned to London & Country. Nonetheless, the TGM livery of blue and white would continue to be seen for some time. Fleet numbering followed the Midland Fox system, so this is 3551 (ERP 551T) on a 116 working to Brentford; new to United Counties (551), Midland Fox obtained it from Luton & District and operated it in Leicester for just one day before despatching it down south. It was one of those selected by London & Country in 1994 to receive the East Lancs Greenway conversion.

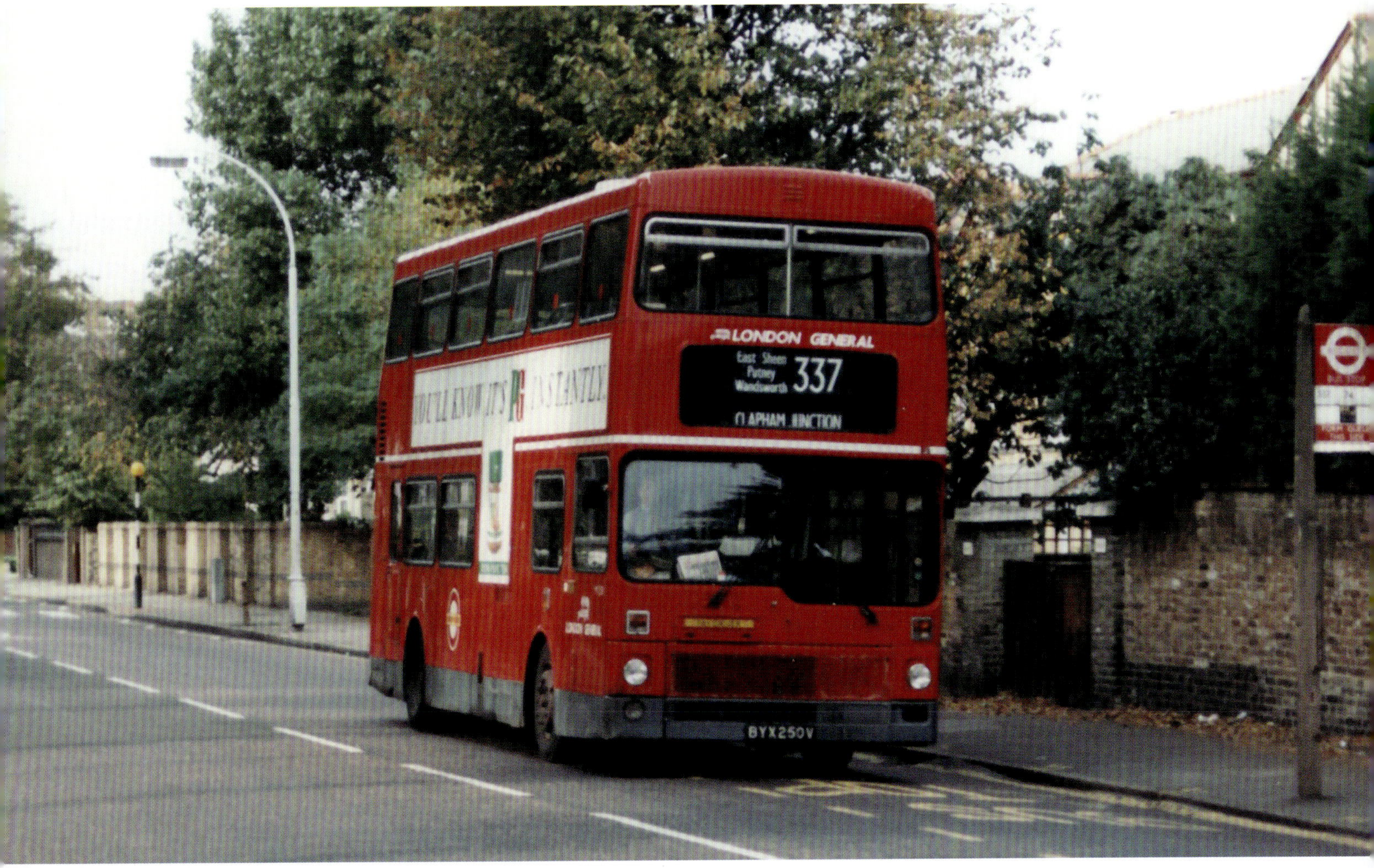
LONDON GENERAL
East Sheen
Putney
Wandsworth
337
CLAPHAM JUNCTION
BYX250V

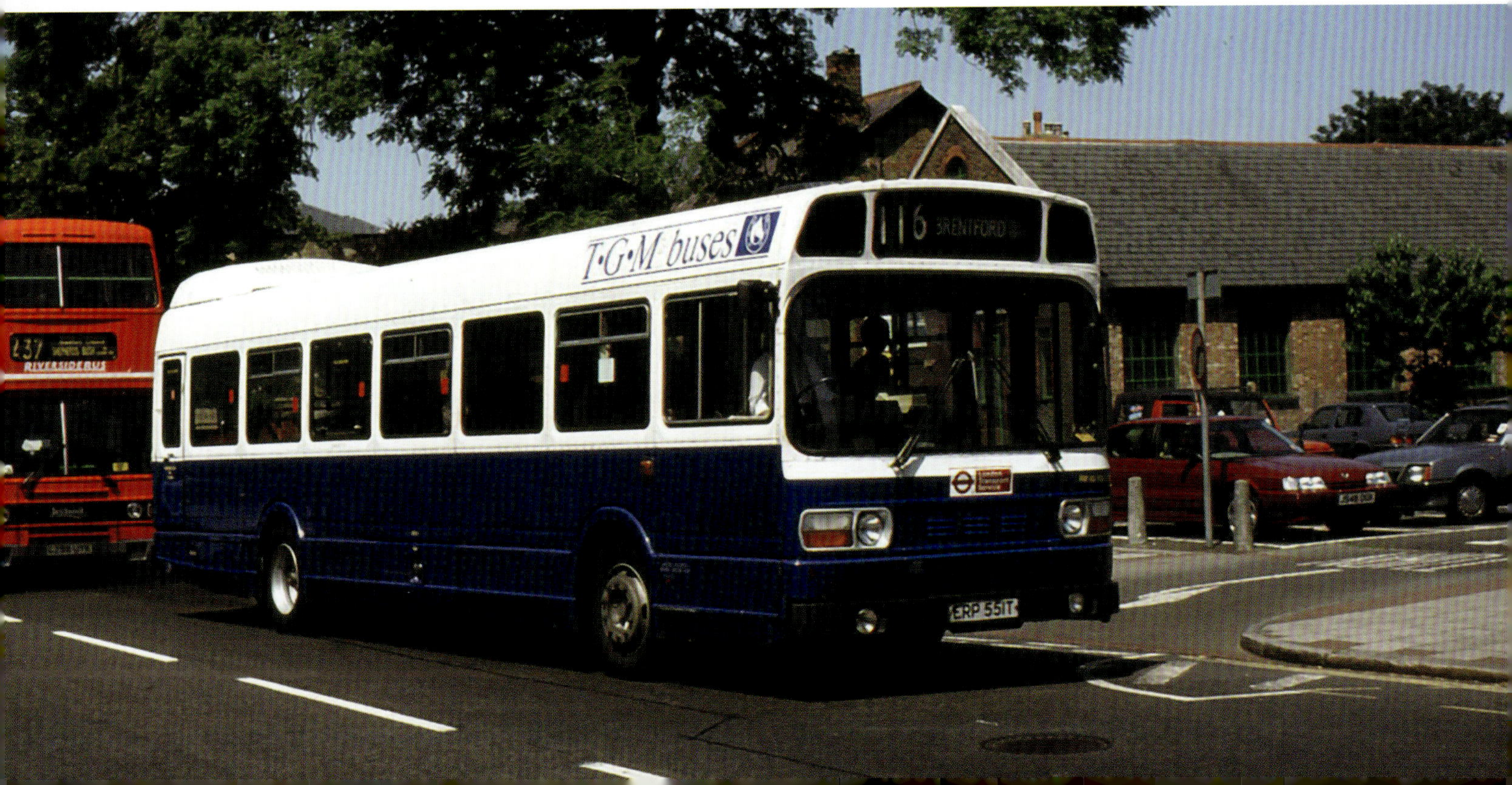
T·G·M buses
116 BRENTFORD
RIVERSIDEBUS
ERP 551T

1991

County Bus and Sovereign Bus & Coach changed hands. County was bought by its director using a new holding company, Lynton Travel. Sovereign's directors formed the Blazefield Group.

17A	East Finchley-Holloway, temporary contract 2 February-25 May (London Northern)
27	Camden Town-Turnham Green (London United)
37	Peckham-Putney (London General)
44	Vauxhall-Tooting (London General)
49	Shepherds Bush-Clapham Junction (London General)
77	Waterloo-Tooting (London General)
77A	Aldwych-Wandsworth (London General)
77C	Clapham Junction-Tibbetts Corner, school journeys (London General)
97	Chingford-Leyton, won by London Forest, reassigned to Capital Citybus
97A	Chingford-Walthamstow Central, won by London Forest, reassigned to Ensign/Capital Citybus
123	Wood Green-Ilford, won by London Forest, reassigned to Ensign/Capital Citybus
135	Archway-Marble Arch/Victoria (London Northern)
144	Muswell Hill/Turnpike Lane-Chingford, won by London Forest, reassigned to County Bus, renumbered **444**
158	Stratford-Chingford Mount, won by London Forest, reassigned to Ensign/Capital Citybus
174	Noaks Hill-Dagenham (East London)
175	North Romford (Hillrise Estate)-Dagenham (Fords) (East London)
201	Hounslow-Staines, new route (London Buslines)
212	Chingford-Walthamstow Central, won by London Forest, reassigned to Capital Citybus
215	Walthamstow Central-Lee Valley Camp Site, won by London Forest, reassigned to Capital Citybus
219	Sloane Square-Colliers Wood (London General)
257	Stratford-Walthamstow Central (Capital Citybus)
270	Putney Bridge-Mitcham (London General)
337	Richmond-Clapham Junction (London General)
351	Penge-Bromley (Metrobus)
391	Hammersmith-Richmond (Sundays) (R & I Coaches)
476	Swanley-Dartford (London Central) (Kent CC contract)
726	Dartford-Heathrow Airport Central, brought into LRT network, temporary contract to Luton & District/Kentish Bus **1992** – won by London Coaches
C10	Victoria-Elephant & Castle, new route partly replacing Red Arrow 510 (London General-Central Minibus Unit)
D8	Stratford-Crossharbour station (East London) **1992** – won by Thamesway (Monday-Friday daytime). Other times remained with East London for two months, then won by Kentish Bus
D9	Bank-Crossharbour station (East London) 1992–won by Grey-Green (Saturday daytime) and Kentish Bus (Monday-Saturday evenings and all day Sunday)

H10	Harrow circular, ex 201 (Sovereign Bus & Coach)
H18	Harrow circular, ex part 136 (Metroline)
H37	Richmond-Hounslow (London United)
R1	Rickmansworth circular, replacement for the 128 (Centrewest) (Hertfordshire CC contract)
W4	Wood Green-Tottenham Hale (London Northern)

SUCCESSES IN 1991/92

By now, the LBL subsidiaries were becoming more adept at not only winning contracts but also hanging onto them when they came up for renewal. This was the case with the P13 (Peckham-Pepys Estate), a new route in 1988 which went to London Central and which was retained in 1991, when it was cut back to Surrey Quays. This is where I saw Optare Star Rider SR19 (F919 YWY) on a grey March day in 1992, being followed by a Selkent Titan on the 47 bound for Catford garage.

Above: The W7 Finsbury Park-Muswell Hill Broadway) was put out to tender for the first time in 1992. It was awarded to London Northern, which was the incumbent operator, and the only change of any note was that the previous allocation of Metrobuses and Titans was changed; from 15 August onwards, the Titans were withdrawn. Photographed before the change, T746 (OHV 746Y) keeps company with M558 (GYE 558W) at the Muswell Hill terminus.

Opposite above: When LRT decided to bring the 726 (Dartford-Heathrow Airport Central) into its network, the existing arrangement of a joint service operated by Luton & District and Kentish Bus was perpetuated by way of a temporary contract. When put out to tender in 1992, it was won by London Coaches, which used ten new DAF SB220s with Ikarus bodywork and dual-purpose seating, all carrying dedicated livery. Here, DK2 (J802 KHD) was seen departing from the bus station at Heathrow for the journey of around fifty miles to Dartford.

Opposite below: The portfolio of routes operated by Capital Citybus for LRT continued to grow in 1992. The year started particularly well with six routes being won, including the D6 (Hackney Central-Isle of Dogs), which had begun life in 1988 with London Forest, passing to East London in 1991. Four of the Metrobuses used on the Harrow network were acquired (amongst many other new and second-hand purchases), including the former M1478, now Capital Citybus 178 (E478 SON). It had recently arrived at the Isle of Dogs Asda soon after the start of the contract on 9 May.

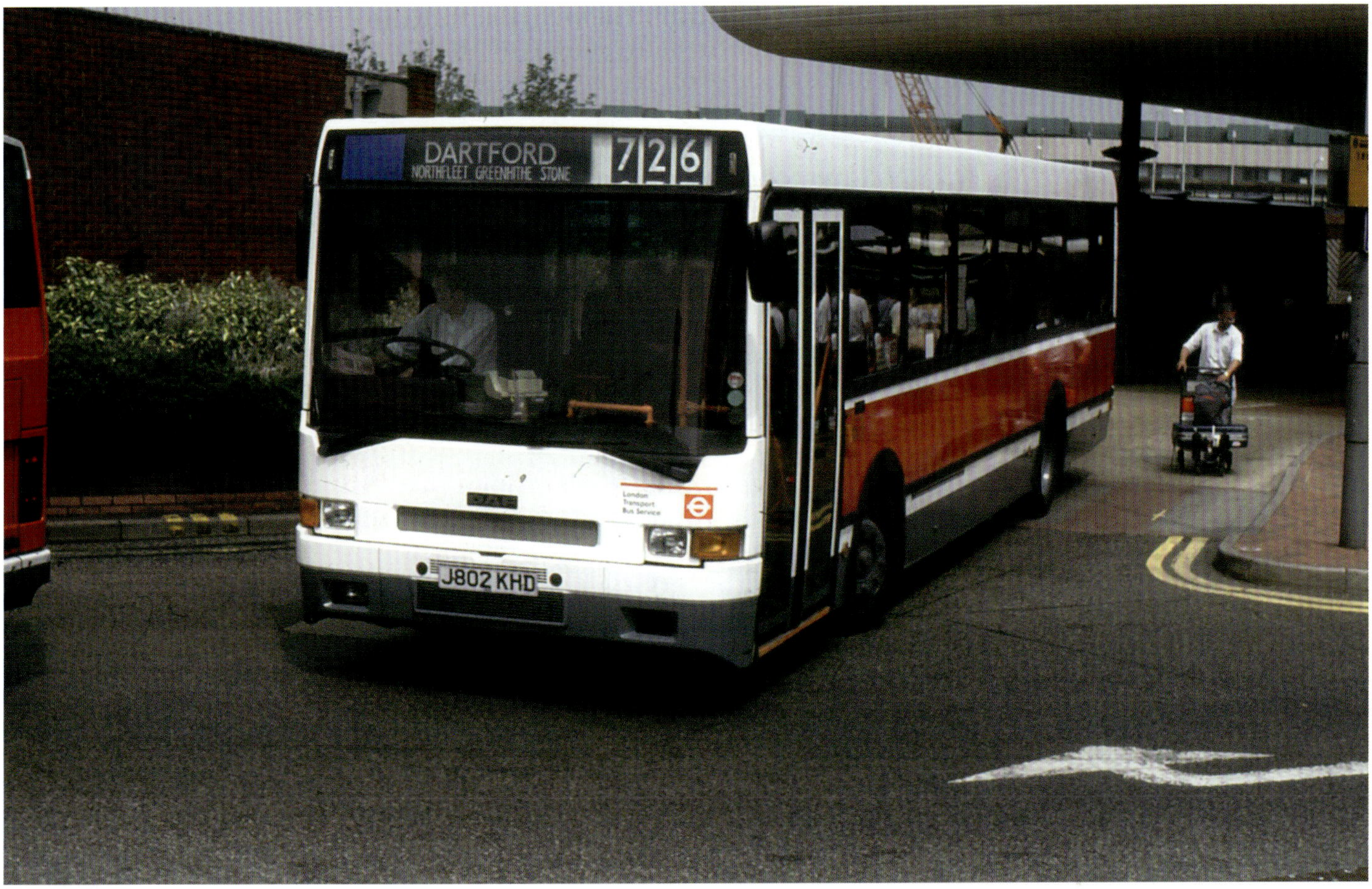
DARTFORD
NORTHFLEET GREENHITHE STONE
726
J802 KHD

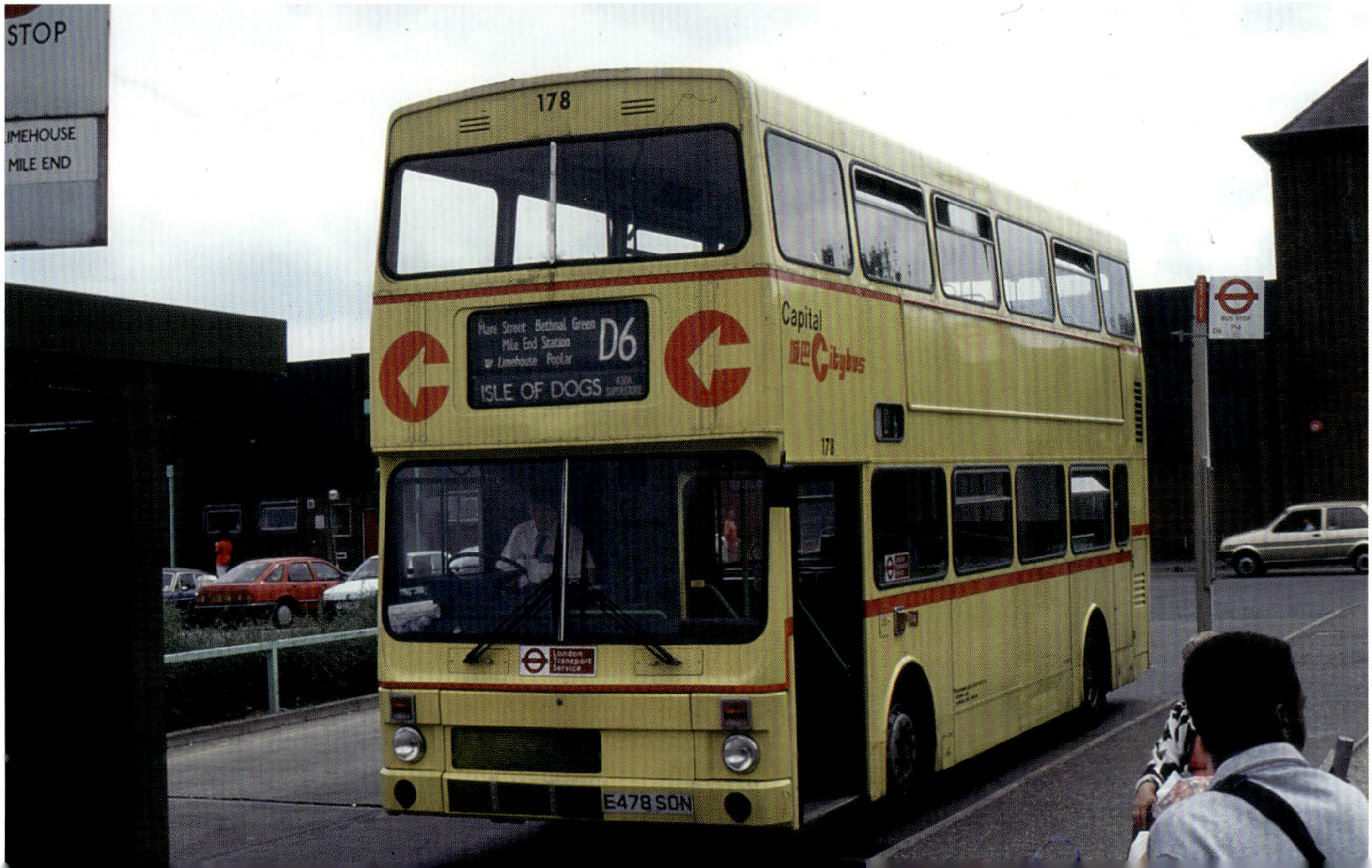
STOP
MILE END
178
Mare Street Bethnal Green
Mile End Station
Limehouse Poplar
D6
ISLE OF DOGS
Capital
Citybus
London Transport Service
E478 SON

1992

Drawlane, owners of London & Country, underwent a reorganisation and in November its bus interests were renamed British Bus.

3B	Herne Hill-Holborn (London General)
	1994 – route withdrawn
29	Trafalgar Square-Palmers Green (Leaside)
119	Bromley North-West Croydon (Selkent)
141	Wood Green-Moorgate/Liverpool Street (Grey-Green)
166	Chipstead Valley-Shirley (Selkent)
194	Forest Hill-Croydon Airport (Selkent)
198	Thornton Heath-Shrublands Estate (Selkent)
214	Liverpool Street-Parliament Hill Fields (Thamesway)
227	Crystal Palace-Bromley North (Kentish Bus)
236	Finsbury Park-Hackney Wick (Capital Citybus)
240	Edgware-Golders Green (Metroline)
266	Hammersmith-Brent Cross/Cricklewood garage (Metroline)
295	Ladbroke Grove-Clapham Junction (London United)
296	Ilford-Harold Wood (Capital Citybus)
299	Cockfosters-Muswell Hill Broadway (Capital Citybus)
329	Turnpike Lane-Enfield (Leaside)
449	County Park Estate-Romford (East London)
545	Rainham circular (County Bus-Thameside)
552	Rainham-Upminster, school journeys (Capital Citybus)
666	Stanwell Moor-Matthew Arnold School (school journeys) (Westlink)
D4	Mile End-Poplar (Capital Citybus)
D6	Hackney central-Isle of Dogs (Asda) (Capital Citybus)
L2	New Cross-Deptford (London Central)
R7	Petts Wood-St Mary Cray (Kentish Bus)
R8	Chelsfield-St Mary Cray (Selkent)
R61	Richmond-Queen Mary's Hospital (Westlink)
R62	Teddington-West Middlesex Hospital (Westlink)
W5	Archway-Harringay (Sainsbury's) (London Northern)
W6	Southgate-Lower Edmonton (Capital Citybus)
W7	Finsbury Park-Muswell Hill Broadway (London Northern)
W10	Enfield-Crews Hill (Capital Citybus)

1993

From April, LBL subsidiaries had to bid for continued support for those routes which had been operated under the block grant system. However, some of the bids were deemed to be too high, so the Tendered Bus Division put twenty-four of them out to tender, in four phases, all of which would begin in 1994.

The routes and vehicles of Transcity were acquired by Kentish Bus on 29 October.

Routemasters for the 13 and 19 were leased to BTS Coaches and Kentish Bus respectively (note that at contract's end they were reassigned to what had become the privatised LBL companies. The vehicles involved were:

BTS Coaches: RML 2265, 2322/41, 2404/43/87, 2527/38/63/69/82/98, 2627/33/59/63/68/74/86/94, 2719/56

Kentish Bus: 2266, 2301/43/47/82/83/87, 2410/52, 2505/12/14/23/24/31/33/36/48/74/77/86/91, 2619, 2715

4	Archway-Waterloo) (London Suburban Bus)
13	Golders Green-Aldwych (BTS Coaches)
19	Finsbury Park-Battersea Bridge (Kentish Bus)
46	Kensal Rise-King's Cross/Farringdon Street (London Northern)
52	Victoria-Willesden (London Coaches/Atlas Bus & Coach/Metroline)
87	Barking-Romford (East London)
118	Morden-Brixton (South London)
138	Catford Bridge-Coney Hall (Kentish Bus)
169	Clayhall-Barking (East London)
287	Rainham-Barking (Docklands Transit)
304	Park Royal-Wembley Arena/Queensbury Station, new Sunday service (London Buslines)
366	Barking-Leytonstone (Docklands Transit)
368	Chadwell Heath-Barking (Docklands Transit)
387	Little Heath-Creekmouth (East London)
399	Barnet General Hospital-Barnet circular (Sovereign – Welwyn & Hatfield Line)
511	Hainault-Romford (County Bus), experimental six-month contract
1994 – retendered, won by Capital Citybus starting in 1995
555	Walton-on-Thames/Chertsey– Heathrow Central (London United, Surrey CC contract)
556	Walton-on-Thames-Heathrow Central (London United, Surrey CC contract)
557	Walton-on-Thames– Heathrow Central, evenings (London United, Surrey CC contract)
575	Chertsey-Sunbury (London United, Surrey CC contract)
D5	Mile End-Isle of Dogs Asda (Capital Citybus)
H26	Sparrow Farm Estate-Hatton Cross (Capital Coaches)
K50	Chessington World of Adventure-Kingston, Saturday Xmas shopping Park & Ride (Javelin Coaches)
1994 – reinstated for the Christmas period
S1	Sutton-Beddington Corner (London & Country)

SUCCESSES IN 1993/94

These are the first tendered routes to involve Routemasters. Kentish Bus RML2382 (JJD 382D) was seen on the 19 in Shaftesbury Avenue on 7 July 1993, chased by East London's 'proper' red RML2328 (CUV 328C) on the 38. Meanwhile BTS Coaches RML 2322 (CUV 322C) was pictured in an otherwise strangely deserted Oxford Street with a 13 working to Aldwych on 4 January 1994.

Winner of the contracts for the 4 and 271 in 1993 and the 41 in 1994, Gemsam Holdings was a Merseyside company associated with Liverbus, whose vehicles were periodically seen filling in on London services. Certainly that was the case on 12 October 1993, when 61 (C376 CAS), an Alexander RL bodied Leyland Olympian new to Highland Scottish as its F376, was awaiting its next turn of duty on the 4 in Waterloo Road. With prominent Liverbus branding to possibly confuse the punters, at least management remembered to place a small LT contract notice in the front window.

London Coaches took on the 52/N52 in December 1993 and the Titans it acquired from LBL were decked out in a revised livery with a much greater area of white and route details on each side between decks. There then followed four Bristol VR3s from East Kent with the less common Willowbrook bodywork, and while the intention was that they should be used on sightseeing duties, that did not stop occasional appearances on the 52, such as that made by BW91 (TFN 991T), seen in Grosvenor Gardens on 11 May 1994.

The 484 might be described as a composite route, introduced in March 1994 between Lewisham and Camberwell Green, thus replacing sections of the L1, P2 and 124. London Central utilised its new East Lancs bodied Dennis Darts on the service, of which DEL11 (L911 JRN) was the last of the bunch. It was seen in Lewisham bus station.

1994

Westlink was sold to its management in January, who then sold it to West Midlands Travel in April. WMT also acquired County Bus & Coach in October.

In July, both Kentish Bus, through its parent company Proudmutual, and Luton & District, were sold to the British Bus group.

Blazefield Holdings, owners of Sovereign Buses, acquired BTS Coaches in August.

The Atlas Bus contract operations were subsumed by London Coaches, now part of the Pullmans Group, in July. The 112 passed to R&I Buses (with some Centrewest involvement) on 6 August; a new company, Atlas Bus & Coach Ltd was set up and took over the responsibility for the Titans London Coaches had been using on the 52/N52. On 29 November, Metroline took over Atlas Bus & Coach Ltd.

Although it falls outside the scope of this history by one day, it should be noted that London & Country operations from the garages at Croydon, Walworth and Dunton Green passed to a new company, Londonlinks Buses Ltd, with effect from 1 January 1995.

41	Archway-Tottenham Hale (London Suburban Buses)
126	Bromley South-Eltham (Kentish Bus)
159	Baker Street-Streatham (South London)
161	Woolwich-Chislehurst (Kentish Bus)
162	Beckenham Junction-Chislehurst/Petts Wood (Kentish Bus)
172	Liverpool Street-Grove Park/Bromley North (London Central)
181	Lewisham-Downham (Kentish Bus)
225	Lewisham-Bermondsey (Kentish Bus)
232	Wood Green-St Raphael's Estate, ex part 112 (London Northern)
284	Lewisham-Grove Park (Kentish Bus)
335	Slough-Chalfont Common/Bucks College Centrewest) (Bucks CC contract)
367	West Croydon-Bromley North (London & Country)
400	Wallington-Caterham (London & Country)
424	Avery Hill-Crown Woods School-Grove Park (Selkent), school journeys, replacing 124S & 160S, renumbered **624**
484	Lewisham-Camberwell Green (London Central)
833	Carpenter's Park-Garston (St Michael's School), school journeys (Metroline) (Herts CC contract)

An unnumbered Bromley Park & Ride service was operated on contract to LRT by Stagecoach Selkent, starting on 1 October. A similar service between Ewell and Epsom for Surrey CC was worked by London General from 19 November.

In May LRT announced six separate phases of routes that were to be put out for tender in 1994/95. The winners from phases 1 & 2 were announced before the end of 1994, viz:

115	Shaftesbury Estate-Tulse Hill/Dulwich College – from South London to London & Country
200	Raynes Park-Streatham Hill – retained by London General
322	Crystal Palace-Elephant & Castle – retained by South London
C4	Putney Pier-Hurlingham – from London Buslines to F E Thorpe
D1	County Hall-Harbour Exchange – from East London to London Central
D11	London Bridge-Leamouth – incorporated into the revised D1
G1	Clapham Junction-Norwood Grange – retained by South London
H28	(new) Hounslow-Osterley – won by London & Country
P5	Elephant & Castle-Brixton/Clapham North – retained by London Central
P14	Surrey Docks-West India Pier – from London Central to Stagecoach East London
R61	Richmond-Roehampton – from Westlink to London & Country
R62	West Middlesex Hospital-Teddington – from Westlink to London & Country
X15	Trafalgar Square-East Beckton – incorporated into the revised D1

Also agreed towards the end of 1994 were:
201	Mitcham-Tulse Hill, to London General
S3	Sutton-Worcester Park, new, sponsored by the London Borough of Sutton, to Tellings Golden Miller

All these contracts would begin in the first half of 1995.

900 SERIES MOBILITY ROUTES

Starting from 27 November 1984 in Forest district with one converted Leyland National 2, the services run by the LRT Mobility Unit grew substantially in number over the next ten years. It was not until 1990 that operators were asked to tender for the work, and Centrewest, East London, Leaside and London Forest amongst the LBL subsidiaries, and Capital Citybus, Javelin Coaches, Kentish Bus and London Buslines from the independent sector, became major players over the next four years. Mention should also be made of the Carelink service, for which London General won the initial contract in 1988. In 1992, this passed to F E Thorpe after retendering, with effect from 24 October.

From its humble beginnings with Leyland National 2 LS454, the Mobility Unit quickly got hold of several older Leyland Nationals, which were purchased by LRT and leased back to LBL; twelve in total, namely LS105/39/56/92, 202/56/90/93, 308/20/56/96. To these were subsequently added further examples, new to Southdown, which became the LSL class. In later years, new wheelchair accessible mini– and midibuses would become a feature of contractors' fleets.

Opposite: The conversion of LS454 (GUW 454W) as a 'Mobility Bus' was touched upon in the chapter on 1984. But the original 925 was a circular route based on Enfield that ran on Thursdays only from 28 October 1985 to December 1986. The number was reused on 18 January 1989 for a Wednesday-only service between Leyton Green and Victoria bus station. As the timetable allowed ninety minutes or more for whatever passengers wanted to do, and given the restrictions on space at Victoria, LS454 had made its way to the layover area at Marble Arch to wait time before the return journey.

Below: From their first entry into the mobility bus market in 1992, when eight contracts were won in the Kingston and Richmond area, Javelin Coaches had gained three more routes by the end of 1994, all being operated with a fleet of seven Mercedes Benz 709Ds with Wadham Stringer sixteen or twenty seat bodies, augmented by a single Talbot/Freeway. This is one of the original 709Ds, J520 WTW, returning to Kingston after working the Monday only 939 from Worcester Park station.

LONDON TRANSPORT GARAGES 1979–1994

CODE	GARAGE	DISTRICT	1988 OPERATING UNIT	1994 PRIVATISED TO...	OTHER INFORMATION
A	SUTTON	Wandle	London General	London General	
AA	COLLIERS WOOD				London General outstation of Sutton opened 3/6/1989; outstation of Merton from 23/2/91; closed by 1992
AC	WILLESDEN	Watling	Metroline	Metroline	To Cardinal district (1984)
AD	PALMERS GREEN	Leaside	Leaside	Leaside	
AE	HENDON	Watling			To Leaside district (1984). Closed 6/6/1987
AF	PUTNEY	Abbey	London General	London General	To Wandle district (1987)
AG	ASH GROVE	Abbey (1981)	London Forest		New, opened 25/4/1981; Forest district (1987). Closed 23/11/1991
AK	STREATHAM	Wandle	South London		Closed for rebuilding 27/10/1984; reopened 7/2/1987; closed 13/3/1992
AL	MERTON	Wandle	London General	London General	
AM	PLUMSTEAD	Selkent			Closed 30/10/1981; replaced by PD
AP	SEVEN KINGS	Forest	East London		Closed 20/3/1993
AR	TOTTENHAM	Leaside	Leaside	Leaside	
AT	ACTON			Centrewest	Former tram depot Reopened by Centrewest on 16/5/1990
AV	HOUNSLOW	Cardinal	London United	London United	
AW	ABBEY WOOD	Selkent			Closed 30/10/1981; replaced by PD

CODE	GARAGE	DISTRICT	1988 OPERATING UNIT	1994 PRIVATISED TO...	OTHER INFORMATION
B	BATTERSEA	Abbey			Closed 2/11/1985; used operationally by the Commercial Operations Unit January 1986 to 16/4/1988, and for storage until 1990
B	WOOD LANE			London United	London United midibus outstation opened 18/7/1992; would be closed in April 1995
BB	BATTERSEA BRIDGE			London General	London General outstation opened 12/6/1993
BK	BARKING	Forest	East London	Stagecoach East London	
BN	BRIXTON	Wandle	South London	South London	
BW	BOW	Tower	East London	Stagecoach East London	To Forest district (1984)
BX	BEXLEYHEATH	Selkent	Selkent	London Central	Closed 15/8/1986. Reopened 16/1/1988 for Bexleybus operations. Passed to London Central November 1990
CA	CLAPHAM	Wandle (1981)			Reopened 25/4/1981 during Norwood rebuilding (to 26/10/1984) and Streatham rebuilding (from 27/10/1984), for which garage code AK was used; closed 6/2/1987
CF	CHALK FARM	Abbey	London Northern		To Leaside district (1987). Closed 30/6/1993
CT	CLAPTON (HACKNEY)	Tower		Leaside	Abbey district (1984). Closed 15/8/1987; reopened by London Forest from 27/5/1989 and renamed Hackney; transferred to Leaside 23/11/1991 following closure of London Forest, reverted to old name
D	DALSTON	Tower			Closed 24/4/1981; replaced by AG
E	ENFIELD	Leaside	Leaside	Leaside	
ED	ELMERS END	Wandle			Closed 25/10/1986
EM	EDMONTON	Leaside			Closed 1/2/1986

CODE	GARAGE	DISTRICT	1988 OPERATING UNIT	1994 PRIVATISED TO...	OTHER INFORMATION
EW	EDGWARE	Watling	Metroline	Metroline	Leaside district (1984); new premises officially opened 13/10/1984. Outstation of Cricklewood from 6/3/1993
FW	FULWELL	Cardinal	London United	London United	
FY	FINCHLEY	Leaside	London Northern		Closed 4/12/1993
G	GREENFORD			Centrewest	Centrewest midibus base opened 27/3/1993
GB	VICTORIA BASEMENT	Abbey	London General		Central Minibus Unit 25/10/1986; to Wandle district (1987); closed 29/1/1994
GM	VICTORIA	Abbey	London General		To Wandle district (1987); closed 19/6/1993
H	HACKNEY	Tower			Closed 24/4/1981; replaced by AG
HD	HARROW WEALD	Watling	Metroline	Metroline	To Leaside district (1984)
HL	HANWELL	Cardinal	Centrewest		Closed 27/3/1993
HR	HARLESDEN				Acquired by Metroline with the business of Atlas Bus 28/11/1994
HT	HOLLOWAY	Abbey	London Northern	MTL London Northern	To Leaside district (1987)
HW	SOUTHALL	Cardinal			Closed 8/8/1986
K	KINGSTON	Cardinal	Westlink	Westlink	Closed 13/1/1984; reopened for Westlink
L	LOUGHTON	Forest			Closed 24/5/1986
M	MORTLAKE	Cardinal			Closed 24/6/1983
MH	MUSWELL HILL	Leaside	London Northern		Closed 20/7/1990
N	NORWOOD	Wandle	South London	South London	Closed for complete rebuilding 24/4/1981; reopened 27/10/1984
NB	NORBITON	Cardinal	London United		Closed 6/9/1991
NS	NORTH STREET	Forest	East London	Stagecoach East London	

LONDON TRANSPORT GARAGES 1979–1994 • 253

CODE	GARAGE	DISTRICT	1988 OPERATING UNIT	1994 PRIVATISED TO...	OTHER INFORMATION
NW	NORTH WEMBLEY	Leaside (1987)	Metroline	Metroline	Harrow Buses outstation from 14/11/1987
NX	NEW CROSS	Selkent	London Central	London Central	
OB	ORPINGTON	Selkent (1986)	Selkent	Stagecoach Selkent	New base for Roundabout services from 16/8/1986
ON	ALPERTON	Watling	Centrewest	Centrewest	To Cardinal district (1984)
PB	POTTERS BAR	Leaside	London Northern	MTL London Northern	
PD	PLUMSTEAD	Selkent (1981)	Selkent	Stagecoach Selkent	New, opened 31/10/1981
PM	*PECKHAM*	*Selkent*	*London Central*		*Peckham High Street site closed 29/1/1994*
PM	PECKHAM			London Central	New site on Copeland Road opened 30/1/1994
PR	*POPLAR*	*Tower*			*To Forest district (1984). Closed 2/11/1985*
Q	CAMBERWELL	Tower	London Central	London Central	To Selkent district (1984)
R	*RIVERSIDE*	*Abbey*			*Closed 24/6/1983*
RA	*WALWORTH*	*Wandle (1987)*	*London General*		*Reopened 15/8/1987 for the Red Arrow fleet; closed 28/10/1990*
RA	WATERLOO RED ARROW			London General	London General; operational with effect from 30/10/1990
RD	*HORNCHURCH*	*Forest*	*East London*		*Closed 23/9/1988*
S	SHEPHERDS BUSH	Abbey	London United	London United	To Cardinal district (1987)
SD	STRATFORD			Stagecoach East London	East London midibus outstation opened 26/9/1992
SE	*STONEBRIDGE*	*Watling*			*Closed 14/8/1981; replaced by Westbourne Park*
SF	STAMFORD HILL	Leaside	Leaside	Leaside	Scheduled for closure in May 1995
SP	*SIDCUP*	*Selkent*	*Selkent*		*Closed 16/1/1988*
SW	STOCKWELL	Abbey	London General	London General	To Wandle district (1984)

CODE	GARAGE	DISTRICT	1988 OPERATING UNIT	1994 PRIVATISED TO...	OTHER INFORMATION
T	LEYTON	Forest	London Forest	Stagecoach East London	Transferred to East London 23/11/1991 following closure of London Forest
TB	BROMLEY	Selkent	Selkent	Stagecoach Selkent	
TC	CROYDON	Wandle	South London	South London	
TH	THORNTON HEATH	Wandle	South London	South London	
TL	CATFORD	Selkent	Selkent	Stagecoach Selkent	
U	UPTON PARK	Forest	East London	Stagecoach East London	
UX	UXBRIDGE	Cardinal	Centrewest	Centrewest	New Denham garage closed and new premises at Bakers Road opened 3/12/1983
V	*TURNHAM GREEN*	*Cardinal*			*Closed 9/5/1980; replaced by Stamford Brook*
V	STAMFORD BROOK	Cardinal	London United	London United	Former Chiswick tram depot. Opened after reconstruction 9/5/1980
W	CRICKLEWOOD	Watling	Metroline	Metroline	To Cardinal district (1984). Outstation of Edgware between 19/1/1991 and 6/3/1993
WD	*WANDSWORTH*	*Abbey*	*London Coaches*		*Closed 11/7/1987; to the Commercial Operations Unit by 16/4/1988. See notes on London Coaches below*
WH	*WEST HAM*	*Tower*	*East London*		*To Forest district (1984). Closed 9/10/1992*
WK	HOUNSLOW	Westlink (1986)	Westlink	Westlink	New base for Stanwell Buses trading as Westlink from 9/8/1986. Renamed Hounslow Heath
WL	*WALWORTH*	*Tower*			*To Selkent district (1984). Closed 2/11/1985; reopened 15/8/1987 (see RA)*
WN	WOOD GREEN	Leaside	Leaside	Leaside	

CODE	GARAGE	DISTRICT	1988 OPERATING UNIT	1994 PRIVATISED TO...	OTHER INFORMATION
WW	*WALTHAMSTOW*	*Forest*	*London Forest*		*Closed 23/11/1991*
X	*MIDDLE ROW*	*Abbey*			*Closed 14/8/1981; replaced by Westbourne Park*
X	WESTBOURNE PARK	Abbey (1981)	Centrewest	Centrewest	New, opened 15/8/1981; to Cardinal district (1987)

London Coaches – besides Wandsworth, outstations were established as follows:
- Dartford (Kentish Bus garage) from 5/4/1988 until the spring of 1989
- Northfleet (Horlock's garage) from the spring of 1989 until 15/12/90
- Borough Green (Maidstone & District garage) from 19/3/1990 until 15/12/1990
- Northfleet (Lower Road) from 15/12/1990

Total LBL garages at 1 January 1979 – 67
Total at 31 December 1994 (excluding outstations) – 46